SCOTS
IN GEORGIA
AND
THE DEEP SOUTH,
1735–1845

SCOTS
IN GEORGIA
AND
THE DEEP SOUTH,
1735–1845

David Dobson

Copyright © 2000
Genealogical Publishing Co., Inc.
Baltimore, Maryland

Library of Congress Catalogue Card Number 99-76674
International Standard Book Number 0-8063-1629-2
Made in the United States of America

INTRODUCTION

The area of North America to become known as Georgia, was, during the late seventeenth and early eighteenth centuries, a frontier zone between British-governed South Carolina and Spanish-governed Florida. The existing international rivalry intensified when the French arrived in the Mississippi delta.

During this period there is no evidence of a Scottish presence, although earlier Thomas Blake, a Scots merchant in Mexico, had participated in Coronado's march through what is now the American Southwest. Other than the occasional Indian trader, no Scots ventured into the Southeast. In 1681 the Scots Privy Council had considered the possibility of settling a colony in northern Florida, and Thomas Nairn, the Indian agent based in Charleston, proposed settling the delta of the Mississippi in 1708. There were also those such as George Bell in 1712 or Sir Robert Montgomery of Skelmorlie in 1717, who promoted the settlement of Georgia and surrounding territories. In the same year Montgomery published his fancifully named *Discourse Concerning the Designed Establishment of a New Colony to the South of Carolina in the Most Delightful Country of the Universe,* but his ambitious plans did not materialize. Another Scot who promoted settlement in the south was John Law, but this was for the settlement of French immigrants in the Mississippi delta.

Settlement of the region by the British did not take place until the founding of the colony of Georgia in 1732, when power and authority to establish a colony were vested in the hands of twenty-one, later twenty-four, trustees, one of whom was James Edward Oglethorpe from England, a philanthropist who wished to provide a refuge for the English urban poor and discharged prisoners.

Scottish immigration to Georgia in the 1730s can be divided into two distinct categories of immigrants: Lowlanders and Highlanders. The Lowlanders went for purely economic reasons, as farmers and later as merchants, and the

Highlanders were recruited for strategic purposes, basically to guard the southern frontier from Spanish incursions.

The agreements negotiated at the end of the French and Indian War in 1763 led to the withdrawal of the Spanish from Florida and the French from their settlements east of the Mississippi. The removal of the Spanish threat and the acquisition of new lands by the British led to an influx of settlers, including Scots, into Florida, as far west as Mobile. Many former soldiers and landed gentry in Great Britain, such as the Grants of Monymusk, were allocated land in Florida on the condition they developed it and settled immigrants within a few years. After the American Revolution, however, Florida was returned to Spanish jurisdiction, and British settlers and Loyalists who had taken refuge there during the war left.

The Louisiana Purchase, when Napoleon sold French Louisiana to the United States for $15,000,000 in 1803, pushed the American frontier west beyond the Mississippi and encouraged significant migration west. Direct emigration to the Deep South from Scotland was small-scale after the original settlers of the 1730s, 1740s, and 1770s. Other than these times, most Scots arrived as individuals or part of family groups, often as two-stage migrants from elsewhere in the United States, especially the Carolinas.

Research for this book has been carried out in Scotland, England and the United States with emphasis on primary sources. These include probate records, court records, family papers, contemporary newspapers and journals, naturalization papers, church registers, gravestone inscriptions, government documents and census returns.

David Dobson
St Andrews, Scotland
1999

Acknowledgements

I should like to express my gratitude for the assistance given during the research for this book to Scott Buie in Texas, Jim McDonald in Savannah (Clan Donald USA Genealogist), Ken Tilley (State Reference Archivist of Alabama), and the Mississippi Department of Archives and History.

REFERENCES

ARCHIVES

BM	=	British Museum, London
DRTL	=	Daughters of the Republic of Texas Library
DU	=	Duke University, North Carolina
GHS	=	Georgia Historical Society
NAS	=	National Archives of Scotland, Edinburgh
NCSA	=	North Carolina State Archives, Raleigh
NLS	=	National Library of Scotland, Edinburgh
PCC	=	Prerogative Court of Canterbury, London
PRO	=	Public Record Office, London
SPCK	=	Society for the Propagation of Christian Knowledge, London
UGA	=	University of Georgia, Athens
UNC	=	University of North Carolina, Raleigh
USNA	=	United States National Archives, Washington DC

PUBLICATIONS

AC	=	Augusta Chronicle, series
AGA	=	Account of Georgia in America [London, 1741]
AH	=	Augusta Herald, series
AJ	=	Aberdeen Journal, series
ANY	=	Bio. Register of the St Andrews Society of New York
BaGaz	=	Bahamas Gazette, series
BM	=	Book of Mackay, Angus Mackay [Edinburgh, 1906]
C	=	US Census, 1850
Car.	=	Caribbeana, series
CC	=	Columbia Centinel, series
CaM	=	Caledonian Mercury, series
CG	=	Camden Gazette, series
CM	=	Colonial Museum & Savannah Advertiser, series
DarG	=	Darien Gazette, series
DG	=	Daily Georgian, series
DPCA	=	Dundee, Perth and Cupar Advertiser, series

EA	=	Edinburgh Advertiser, series
EEC	=	Edinburgh Evening Courant, series
EFR	=	East Fife Record, series
ESG	=	List of the Early Settlers of Georgia, Coulter and Saye [Baltimore, 1983]
F	=	Fasti Ecclesiae Scoticanae, J. Scott [Edinburgh, 1915]
FH	=	Fife Herald, series
FHR	=	Florida Historical Review, series
FJ	=	Fife Journal, series
FPA	=	Fulham Papers in the Lambeth Palace Library W.Manross, [Oxford, 1965]
GaCoRec	=	Georgia Council Records, series
GaGaz	=	Georgia Gazette, series
GC	=	Georgia Courier, series
GE	=	Georgia Express, series
GFC	=	Georgia for the Country, series
GHR	=	Georgia Historical Review, series
GJ	=	Georgia Journal, series
GM	=	Gentleman's Magazine, series
GR	=	Georgia Republican, series
GSG	=	Georgia State Gazette, series
GSP	=	Glasgow Saturday Post, series
IT	=	Indian Traders of the Southeastern Spanish Borderlands, Coker & Watson [Pensacola, 1986]
JCTP	=	Journal of Commissioners for Trade and the Plantations
LGS	=	Louisiana Genealogical Society Journal, series
MAGU	=	Matriculation Albums of Glasgow University 1727-1858, W.I.Addison [Glasgow, 1913]
MOT	=	Mirror of the Times, series
Mowat	=	East Florida as a British Province, 1763-1784, C.L.Mowat [California, 1943]
MT	=	Macon Telegraph, series
NWI	=	New World Immigrants, M.Tepper [Baltimore, 1980]
PA	=	Perthshire Advertiser, series
PCCol	=	Acts of the Privy Council, Colonial, series
PHGA	=	Pennsylvania Herald & General Advertiser, series
RGS	=	Register of the Great Seal of Scotland, series
S	=	Scotsman, series
SavC	=	Savannah Courier, series

SCGaz	=	South Carolina Gazette, series
SGen	=	Scottish Genealogist, series
SG	=	Scottish Guardian, series
SGC	=	Georgia for the Country, Savannah, series
SHCG	=	Scottish Highlanders in Colonial Georgia, A.W.Parker [1998]
SM	=	Scots Magazine, series
SP	=	Statesman Patriot, series
SPC	=	Calendar of State Papers, Colonial, series
SPAWI	=	State Papers, America and the West Indies, series
SR	=	Savannah Republican, series
SSS	=	History of the St Andrew's Society, Savannah, J.F.MacGowan [Savannah, 1972]
T	=	Telescope, series
W	=	Witness, series
WS	=	History of the Society of Writers to HM Signet
1812	=	British Aliens in the USA in 1812, K.Scott [Baltimore, 1979]

Also

"English Crown Grants in St John's Parish, Georgia 1755-1775",
    M.R.Hemperley [Atlanta, 1972]
"English Crown Grants in Christ Church parish, Georgia, 1755-1775",
    M.R.Hemperley [Atlanta, 1973]

SCOTS IN GEORGIA
AND THE DEEP SOUTH
1735-1845

ADAMS, JOHN A., born in Scotland during 1815, a merchant, wife Mary born in Ireland in 1818, children Robert, Thomas, William, and Mary, (all born in Ireland), settled in Mobile, Alabama. [C]

ADAMSON, HENRY, born in Scotland during 1815, a physician in Tattnell County, Georgia. [C]

AFFLICK, HANS, born in Scotland during 1812, wife Ann M. born in 1817, children J. A. born in 1843 and J. Dunbar born in 1845, all born in Mississippi, settled in Adams County, Mississippi. [C]

AIKMAN, GEORGE, a planter in Florida, died by 1781. [NAS.NRAS#0174]

AIKMAN, JOSEPH, a merchant in Mobile 1767. [NLS#MS119]

AIR, JOHN, born in 1752, a gentleman from Georgia, returning home via London to Georgia on the Beaufort in September 1775. [PRO.T47.9/11]

AIRD, JAMES, from Ayr, a carpenter on Orangefield Plantation, Pensacola, West Florida, in 1778. [PRO.CO55.613.536]

AKINS, WILLIAM, born in 1755, an overseer, died on 5 August 1810. [Savannah Death Register]

ALBIN, THOMAS, born in Scotland during 1800, Elizabeth Albin born in Georgia in 1829, settled in Walton County, Florida. [C]

ALEXANDER, ADAM, a physician and surgeon, emigrated from Inverness to Georgia before 1810. [American Ancestry#4/92]

ALEXANDER, FRANCIS, born in Toull on 20 November 1806, baptised in Buittle parish, Kirkcudbrightshire, on 27 November 1806, son of William Alexander and Violet Kirk, died in Tuscaloosa, Alabama, on 20 August 1856. [Buittle g/s][Buittle OPR]

ALEXANDER, GEORGE, died on 30 September 1806. [Colonial Museum and Savannah Advertiser: 1 October 1806]

ALEXANDER, JAMES, born in 1749, a music professor, died on 11 September 1805. [Savannah Death Register]; ? grant of 200 acres in Christchurch parish, Georgia, on 5 September 1769. [Grant book G, #403]

ALEXANDER, JANET, born in 1751, {possibly daughter of James Alexander and Jean Aitken, baptised on 14 November 1750 in parish of Kirkwall and St Ola}, a servant in Egilsay, Orkney, emigrated from Kirkwall, Orkney, to Savannah, Georgia, on the Marlborough, in September 1774, settled in Richmond County, Georgia. [PRO.T47.12] [PRO.AO13/34/123-4][Kirkwall OPR]

ALEXANDER, JOHN, an Anglican minister appointed to Sunbury, Georgia, during 1766. [SPCKpp, London]

ALEXANDER, L. S., born in Scotland during 1811, a bagman, wife Margaret born in Scotland during 1811, children Sarah born in Scotland in 1841 and James born in Alabama in 1843, settled in Alabama. [C]

ALEXANDER, WILLIAM, in Halifax, St George's parish, Georgia, pro.5 May 1760 Georgia.

ALEXANDER, WILLIAM, land grant in Augusta, Georgia, on 7 June 1757, [CRG#28/1.116]; possibly later a partner in Panton, Leslie and Company, Indian traders in Florida, Loyalist, settled in the Bahamas during 1783, husband of Mary Cleland, died in October 1799. Pro. 30 September 1796 Bahamas, [IT#21, 45][Bahama Gazette, 8.10.1799]

ALEXANDER, WILLIAM, wife and 3 children, embarked at Wick, Caithness, on the Marlborough, Captain George Prissick, in September 1774 bound for Georgia, an indentured servant. [PRO.AO13/34/123-4]

ALLAN, CHRISTOPHER, from Kirkwall, an indentured servant who embarked on the Marlborough, Captain George Prissick, bound for Georgia in September 1775. [PRO.AO13.34/123-4]

ALLAN, ROBERT, baptised on 4 August 1805, in the parish of Ruthven, Angus, son of Robert Allan {1778-1858} and Elizabeth Lindsay {1779-1842}, died in New Orleans on 17 June 1830. [Dundee, Constitution Road, g/s][Ruthven OPR]

ALLARDICE, JOHN, emigrated to Savannah, Georgia, on the snow Kinnoull, Captain Alexander Alexander, and was granted 100 acres between the Savannah and the Saludy Rivers on 30 May 1768. [Ga.Co.Journal#34.148/151]

ALLISON, JAMES, born in 1756, a cooper and gauger, died 2 June 1807. [Savannah Death Register][Savannah Republican: 4 June 1807]

ANCRUM, GEORGE, in Louisiana by 23 February 1764. [GaGaz#47]

ANDERSON, ALEXANDER, a farmer from Monymusk, Aberdeenshire, settled in East Florida by 1767. [NAS.NRAS.777.bundle#402] [NAS.GD345.916.4]

ANDERSON, ELIZABETH, land grant in Savannah, Christchurch parish, Georgia, on 1 July 1760, [CRG#28/1.324][Grant book B, #414]

ANDERSON, FLORA, born during 1749 in Scotland, an indentured servant who emigrated from London to Georgia on the Mary in February 1774. [PRO.T47.9/11]

ANDERSON, GEORGE, granted 500 acres in St John's parish, Georgia, on 7 January 1772. [Grant Book-I.487]

ANDERSON, GEORGE, of the town of Georgia(!), Captain of the Georgia, died at sea, pro. November 1777 PCC

ANDERSON, GEORGE, born 1798, son of George Anderson and Agnes Kerr, died in New Orleans on 7 October 1827. [Inverkeiller g/s]

ANDERSON, HUGH, gentleman in Bridgecastle, Cromarty, emigrated from Inverness or Cromarty to Georgia on the Two Brothers, Captain William Thomson, with wife Elizabeth, sons Alexander and Moore, and daughter Catherine, with servants, arrived on 27 June 1737; settled in Savannah, appointed Inspector of Public Gardens and of Mulberry Plantations in Georgia 4 August 1735; reference to on 9 December 1738. died possibly in Charleston, South Carolina, on 21 November 1748. [AGA#59] [SPC.43.226][PRO.CO.5.670.287][SCGaz#686]

ANDERSON, JAMES, born in 1716, a joiner, emigrated from Inverness to Georgia on the Prince of Wales, Captain George Dunbar, on 20 October 1735, landed on 10 January 1736, resident on his brother John's lot in Savannah 1738, [ESG#62]; a settler in Georgia on 9 December 1738. [AGA#59]

ANDERSON, JAMES, land grant of 500 acres in St George's parish, Georgia, on 21 May 1762. [PRO.CO.5.648.E68][CRG#28/1.423]

ANDERSON, JAMES, granted 10,000 acres in East Florida during 1766. [PC.Col.V.590]

ANDERSON, JAMES, a carpenter in Christ Church parish, Georgia, pro.6 January 1769 Georgia

ANDERSON, JAMES, jr., a merchant in Forres, Morayshire, died in Augusta, North America, on 19 July 1823. [BM.14.624][DPCA#1104]

ANDERSON, MALCOLM, born in Sleat, Skye, Inverness-shire, during
1788, emigrated to North Carolina 1799, moved to Savannah,
Georgia, 1811, to North Carolina in 1799, died in Savannah on 11
October 1814. [Savannah Republican, 27 October 1814]

ANDERSON, MARGARET, born during 1754 in Alloa,
Clackmannanshire, emigrated from Greenock to New York or to
Georgia on the Christy. [PRO.T47/12]

ANDERSON, MARY, born in Scotland during 1777, settled in Walton
County, Florida. [C]

ANDERSON, MATHEW, born in Scotland during 1814, a machinist,
settled in Mobile, Alabama, wife Lucinda born in Alabama during
1818, daughter Amanda born in Alabama during 1837. [C]

ANDERSON, THOMAS, from Dundee, settled in New Orleans, dead by
1835. [NAS.SH]

ANDERSON, THOMAS, born in 1795, son of George Anderson and
Agnes Kerr, Inverkeillor, Angus, died in New Orleans on 1 August
1835. [Inverkeillor g/s]

ANDERSON, WILLIAM, born in Dumfries, a planter in St Joseph's
parish, Georgia, pro.7 February 1772 Georgia.

ANDERSON, WILLIAM, born in 1789, emigrated to USA in 1806, a
theatrical performer in Augusta, Georgia. [1812]

ARCHER, WILLIAM, born in Perthshire during 1778, {probably son of
William Archer and Elspeth Watson, baptised on 8 July 1777 in
parish of Kinclaven}, a saddler, died in Savannah, Georgia, on 18
October 1805. [Savannah Death Register][Kinclaven OPR]

ANDERSON, WILLIAM, born in Scotland during 1820, a sailor, settled
in Alabama. [C]

ARBUCKLE, HUGH, born in Scotland 1808, a farmer in Goliad, Texas.
[C]

ARKLES, GEORGE, born in 1780, a grocer, died on 30 September 1806. [Savannah Death Register]

ARMOUR, JOHN, born in Scotland during 1824, a clerk, settled in Mobile, Alabama. [C]

ARMSTRONG, ALEXANDER, born in Scotland in 1821, a herd in Briscoe County, Texas. [C]

ARNOTT, DAVID, born in 1755, a smith, emigrated from Newcastle to Georgia on the Georgia Packet, during September 1775. [PRO.T47.9/11]

ARNOT, DAVID, born around 1763, a smith and indentured servant of Thomas Brown in Richmond County, Georgia, during 1783. [PRO.AO13.34]

ARNOT(?), THOMAS, born in Scotland during 1825, a baker, settled in Alabama. [C]

ARTHUR, JAMES, born in Scotland 1805, wife Walker (!) born in Ireland 1815, son John born in Ireland 1842, settled in Harrison County, Mississippi. [C]

ATKINSON, GEORGE, died 4 February 1822 in Darien, Georgia. [Statesman and Patriot: 18 February 1828]

AUCHENLECK, JOHN, writer and accountant, emigrated from Inverness to Georgia 20 October 1735 on the Prince of Wales, master George Dunbar, arrived 10 February 1736. [ESG#2]

AULD, A., born in Scotland 1804, a merchant, settled in Alabama. [C]

AULD, ALEXANDER, born in Scotland 1805, a merchant, wife Elizabeth born in Alabama 1801, daughter Catherine (born in Alabama), settled in Mobile, Alabama. [C]

BABCOCK, MARGARET, born in Scotland 1810, settled in Warren County, Mississippi. [C]

BAILLIE, ALEXANDER, granted 100 acres in St John's parish, Georgia, on 1 May 1756. [Grant Book-B.83]

BAILLIE, ELIZABETH, land grant near Savannah on 5 May 1767. [Grant book F, #220]

BAILLIE, GEORGE, a merchant in Savannah, Georgia, during 1763, [Ga.Gaz.#15]; Loyalist – settled in Edinburgh 1789, later in Coats, Haddington, East Lothian, 1794. [NAS.RD3.279.116] [PRO.AO13.1.332]

BAILLIE, HARRIET, daughter of George Baillie, married Lieutenant Colonel Wardrope, late of the 47th Regiment, on St Simon's Island, Georgia, on 8 March 1812. [SM.74.565]

BAILLIE, JOHANNA, wife of George Baillie, died on St Simon's Island, Georgia, on 9 July 1812. [SM#74.886]

BAILLIE, JOHN, merchant in Edinburgh, granted 400 acres in Georgia on 18 October 1733. [PRO.CO.5.668/670.106]; letter to brother Thomas in 1734, [NAS.GD170.3558]; land grant of 500 acres in Ogeechee District on 9 December 1756, [PRO.CO.5.646.C10][Grant book A, #304]; grant of wharf lot #2 on the Bay, Savannah, on 9 December 1756. [Grant Book A, #305]

BAILLIE, JOHN, died in McIntosh County, Georgia, on 22 April 1820. [BM.7.705]

BAILLIE, KENNETH, son of John Baillie, imported one male indentured servant from Inverness to Georgia on the Two Brothers, Captain William Thomson, 19 November 1737, arrived there 14 January 1738; an Ensign in a Troop of Rangers at the Siege of St Augustine in 1740, captured by the Spanish and imprisoned in Havanna, Cuba, and in St Sebastian, Spain, granted 350 acres in Midway District 5 February 1757, 500 acres there 7 June 1757, 100 acres in St John's 1 May 1759, and 200 acres in Midway 1 May 1759; a

planter in St John's parish, Georgia, pro.2 September 1766 Georgia
[refers to Andrew Darling a merchant in Sunbury, Georgia, John
Irvin a surgeon in Sunberry, John Brown a merchant {whose
brother Samuel Brown was an Indian trader in the Choctaw
nation}, his partners William Irwin a merchant in Savannah,
William Struthers an Indian trader, and John McGillevray a
merchant in Mobile]. [Grant Book A-382/3; A.404, B.73, B.82]
[Caledonian Mercury#3365][Ga.Gaz.#129,242][CRG#28/1.59,61;
30.8]

BAILLIE, ROBERT, granted 500 acres in Newport on 30 September
1757. [Grant Book A.459][CRG#28/1.113]; Lieutenant Robert
Baillie, land grant in St Andrew's parish in February 1762,
[CRG#28/1.418]; a planter in Georgia 1745-1775, died in Florida
in September 1782. [PRO.AO13.384]

BAILLIE, THOMAS, gentleman in the Orkney Islands, emigrated to
Georgia in 1735. [PRO.CO.5.670.219]; granted 500 acres in
Georgia on 3 September 1735. [PRO.CO.5.668]; reference on 9
December 1738, [AGA#59]; granted 300 acres in Savannah
District on 5 February 1757; land grant of 100 acres in
Christchurch parish on 4 July 1758; land grant in Savannah on 7
September 1762. [PRO.CO.5.646.C10] [Grant book A,
#173/174/175/298; Grant book B, #37; Grant book C, #7; Grant
book D, #204] Ga.Gaz.#80][CRG#28/1/49, 437]

BAILLIE, THOMAS, (2), settler in Georgia on 9 September 1738.
[AGA#59]

BAIN of LOCHAIN, JOHN, born in 1694, emigrated from Inverness to
Georgia on 20 October 1735 on the Prince of Wales, master
George Dunbar, arrived on 10 January 1736, an indentured servant.
[ESG#3]

BAIN, JOHN MACINTOSH, settled at New Inverness, Georgia, by
1739. [Ga.Col.Rec.3.427]; petitioned Oglethorpe re slavery 3
January 1739. [AGA#65]

BAIN, WILLIAM, born in 1749, a weaver in Wick, Caithness, emigrated from Caithness to Savannah, Georgia, on the Marlborough, an indentured servant, settled in Richmond County, Georgia. [PRO.T47.12][PRO.AO13.34/123-4]

BAIRD, JAMES, in Sunbury, Georgia, deceased by September 1763. [Ga.Gaz.#23]

BAKER, Mrs CHRISTIAN, born in Scotland in 1790, a farmer's wife in Jackson County, Florida, 1850. [C]

BALFOUR, ROBERT, land grant in Savannah, Georgia, for a meeting house 16 January 1756. [Grant book A, #97]

BALFOUR, ROBERT, baptised on 1 February 1803, youngest son of Reverend William Balfour (1767-1828) and Mary Mein (died 1852) in Bowden, Roxburghshire, died in Savannah, Georgia, on 13 September 1837. [S#1864][AJ#4691][F.2.172]

BALLANTYNE, JOHN, from Charleston, South Carolina, to Savannah, Georgia, in 1732. [AGA#41]

BALLENTINE, RICHARD, born in Scotland during 1814, settled in Alabama, died at The Alamo on 6 March 1836. [DRTL]

BAND, GEORGE, a planter, born in Scotland in 1792, settled in Warren County, Mississippi. [C]

BARBER, THOMAS, baptised on 2 August 1829 in Bellie, Banffshire, son of Thomas Barber and Madelina McLeod, died in Andersonville, Georgia, 9 September 1864. [Bellie g/s]

BARLOW, Mrs NANCY, born in Scotland in 1790, wife of Elias Barlow a chairmaker, settled in Montgomery County, Georgia. [C]

BARNES, R., born in Scotland in 1818, a sailor, settled in Mobile, Alabama. [C]

BARR, ALEXANDER, born in Glasgow, a shopkeeper, died in Savannah, Georgia 10 December 1801. [Colonial Museum and Savannah Advertiser, 11.12.1801]

BARRIE, JAMES, born in Moneydie, Perthshire, in 1785, died in Savannah, Georgia, on 10 October 1817. [Savannah g/s]

BARRIE, ROBERT, a surgeon in Pensacola, West Florida, later assistant surgeon in HM Hospital in St Augustine, East Florida, pro. August 1775. PCC.

BARRIE, ROBERT, son of Robert Barrie a surgeon, in Pensacola, Florida, in 1791, grandson of Isabella Forsyth in Sanquhar, Dumfries-shire. [NAS.SH]

BARRON, ALEXANDER, born in 1789, to New York in 1810, a house carpenter in Savannah, Georgia, in 1812, [1812]

BARTLETT, A., a carpenter, born in Scotland in 1800, settled in Adams County, Mississippi. [C]

BASSETT, H., born in Scotland in 1788, a carpenter, wife Sarah born in Pennsylvania in 1789, settled in Mobile, Alabama. [C]

BEAN, ALEXANDER, born around 1752, a shoemaker, with his wife Christina born in 1757 emigrated from Newcastle to Georgia on the Marlborough, September 1775, settled in Friendsborough, Georgia. [PRO.T47.9/11]

BEGGS, THOMAS, born in Ayrshire in 1770, a merchant, died in Savannah, Georgia, 11 September 1806. [Savannah Death Register]

BELL, ANDREW, an indentured servant and blacksmith in Georgia in 1735.

BELL, CATHERINE, born 1817, wife of William Roy, died in New Orleans on 27 May 1858. [Cupar, Fife, g/s]

BELL, GEORGE, proposed to establish a colony in Florida around 1712. [NAS.GD95.10, item 38]

BELL, HENRY, land grant in St Paul's parish, Georgia, 4 January 1763, [CRG#28/1.444]?

BELL, JEANETTE, born in 1770, settled in Carroll County, Georgia, before 1850. [C]

BELL, JOHN M., born in 1825, baptised on 6 August 1825 in the parish of St Mungo, Dumfries-shire, son of George Bell and Isabella Moffat in Kinmount, Cummertrees, Dumfries-shire, died in Savannah, Georgia, on 22 July 1847. [Cummertrees g/s][St Mungo OPR]

BELL, WILLIAM, (?), land grant in Savannah, Georgia, on 7 February 1758, [CRG#28/1.236][Grant book A, #583]

BELL, WILLIAM, born in 1808, son of John Bell and Janet Davidson in parish of Middlebie, Dumfries-shire, settled in New Orleans as a merchant in 1830, died on 30 November 1838. [Pennersaughs g/s]

BENNOCH, ALEXANDER, born in 1790, settled in Augusta, Georgia, around 1809, a merchant, died 4 October 1812. [Augusta Chronicle: 9.10.1812] [1812]

BENNOCH, PETER, born in 1786, a merchant, to USA in 1805, a merchant in Augusta in 1812. [1812]

BERTRAM, ALEXANDER, baptised in Cranshaws, Berwickshire, on 19 June 1796, son of John Bertram, died in Augusta, Georgia, on 27 November 1827. [Cranshaws OPR] [Georgia Courier, 29.11.1827][Edinburgh Advertiser#6695.63]

BEWS, JOHN, born in 1742, a laborer in Stromness, Orkney, emigrated from Kirkwall, Orkney, to Savannah, Georgia, on the Marlborough, as an indentured servant, settled in Richmond County, Georgia, husband of Christian Smith. [PRO.T47.12][PRO.AO13.34/123-4]

BIRRELL, WILLIAM, born in 1793, baptised 10 June 1793 in parish of Graitney, Dumfries-shire, son of Richard Birrell and Jean Richardson in Gretna, Dumfries-shire, settled in Savannah, Georgia, died there 16 October 1821. [Graitney g/s][Graitney OPR]

BISSETT, Hon. ALEXANDER, Senator for Glynn County, Georgia, died 28 November 1791, buried in St Paul's churchyard. [Georgia Gazette: 8.12.1791]

BISSET, Captain ROBERT, granted 5,000 acres in East Florida in 1767. [PC.Col.V.591]

BLACK, ALEXANDER LESLIE, born 1813, baptised in Forres, Morayshire, on 16 June 1813 eldest son of Charles Black, town clerk of Forres, and Ann Leslie, died in New Orleans on 9 October 1837. [AJ#4692][Forres OPR]

BLACK, DAVID, born in 1755, a book-binder, emigrated via Whitby to Savannah, Georgia, on the Marlborough in August 1774. [PRO.T47.9/11]

BLACK, DAVID, born on 5 May 1803, son of Reverend James Black {1754-1826} and Isabella Paterson {died 1814} in Penninghame, Wigtownshire, died in New Orleans in May 1840. [F.2.375]

BLACK, WILLIAM, born in 1772, a millwright, died on 10 July 1800. [Georgia Gazette: 17.7.1800]

BLACKBURN, ANDREW, a merchant in Glasgow, granted 500 acres in Georgia in October 1751. [PRO.CO5.669][admitted as a merchant burgess and guildsbrother of Glasgow on 27 October 1741 as the eldest son of John Blackburn merchant burgess and guildsbrother of Glasgow, {Glasgow Burgess Roll}]

BLAIR, DAVID, from Giffordland, Ayrshire, emigrated to Georgia in 1736. [PRO.CO.5.670.286] [SPC.43.148]; granted 500 acres in Georgia on 4 August 1736. [PRO.CO.5.668]

BLUE, DANIEL, born in 1757, emigrated to USA in 1790, half pay British subaltern and corn planter with wife and 7 children in Camden County, Georgia, 1812. [1812]

BOGLE, ROBERT, a merchant from Glasgow, died in New Orleans in February 1826. [EA][admitted as a merchant burgess and guildsbrother of Glasgow on 19 March 1801 as the eldest son of the deceased Allan Bogle a merchant burgess and guildsbrother of Glasgow, {Glasgow Burgess Roll}]

BONTHRON, ANDREW, born in 1777, son of Alexander Bonthron and Elspet Coit, baptised on 24 July 1777 in Moonzie, Fife, died in New Orleans 17 August 1813. [Moonzie g/s][Moonzie OPR]

BOULDRIDGE, JAMES, an indentured servant, embarked on the Marlborough, Captain George Prissick, in Kirkwall, Orkney, bound for Georgia in September 1774. [PRO.AO3.34/123-4]

BOWIE, JOHN, born in Dalhousie, Midlothian, a carpenter, died in Georgia on 17 September 1801. [GaGaz#311, 24.9.1801]

BOWMAN, JOHN, jr., son of Lord Provost Bowman of Glasgow, settled in East Florida in 1769, [NAS.NRAS#771.295]; land grant of 100 acres in Christchurch parish, Georgia, on 7 July 1772, [Grant book I, #678]; in Savannah, purchased land on Skiddaway Island, in Christchurch parish, from Anna Jean, wife of John Simpson of Savannah in 1774, which he sold when in Glasgow to Alexander Ferguson of Craigdarroch in June 1775. [NAS.GD77/167, 168]

BOYD, ALEXANDER, son of William Boyd, formerly of South Leith, Edinburgh, later in Savannah, Georgia, pro. December 1804 PCC

BOYD, CHARLES, wife Margaret Floyd her will probate 18 October 1793 refers to an estate in Scotland, her children Mary, Charles, Eston, Ann and James Boyd; executors - her sons, Charles Boyd sr., and Richard Floyd, (Will Book A, Chatham County, Georgia.)

BOYD, THOMAS, from Pitcon, Ayrshire, emigrated to Georgia in 1736,
[PRO.CO.5.670.286] [SPC.43.148]; granted 500 acres in Georgia
on 4 August 1736. [PRO.CO.5.668]

BOYD, THOMAS, born in 1779, a merchant, died 12 September 1808.
[Savannah Death Register]

BRASS, THOMAS, born in 1749, a weaver in Birsay, Orkney, emigrated
from Kirkwall, Orkney, to Savannah, Georgia, on the Marlborough
in September 1774, an indentured servant, settled in Richmond
County, Georgia. [PRO.T47.12][PRO.AO13.34/123-4]

BREMNER, ROBERT, granted 5,000 acres of land in East Florida in
1767. [PC.Col.V.591]

BRIBNER, WILLIAM, an indentured servant from Kirkwall, Orkney,
embarked on the Marlborough, Captain Thomas Walker, in
Kirkwall in September 1775 bound for Georgia.
[PRO.AO13.34/123-4]

BRIGGS, SAMUEL, born in 1747, a dyer, emigrated from Newcastle to
Georgia on the Georgia Packet in September 1775, settled in
Friendsborough, Georgia. [PRO.T47.12]

BRIGGS, ROBERT, emigrated to Savannah, Georgia, on the snow
Kinnoull, Captain Alexander Alexander, and was granted 100 acres
between the Savannah and the Saludy Rivers on 30 May 1768.
[Ga.Co.Journal#34.148/151]

BRISBANE, ROBERT, grant of 500 acres in Christ Church parish,
Georgia, on 2 October 1764. [Grant book E, #50]; '50 years in
South Carolina' died 17 December 1781. [RoyalGaGaz#2/2]

BROADSON, Mrs BRIDGET, born in Scotland in 1821, settled in
Mobile. [C]

BROCK, JAMES, born in 1754, a porter, emigrated from Kirkwall.
Orkney, to Savannah, Georgia, on the Marlborough,Captain
Thomas Walker, in September 1775, an indentured servant of

Thomas Brown, settled in Richmond County, Georgia. [PRO.T47.12][PRO.AO13.34/123-4]

BRODIE, JOHN, emigrated from Inverness to Savannah, Georgia, on the Two Brothers, Captain William Thomson, in July 1737, arrived on 16 November 1737, imported 10 men and 1 woman indentured servants. [SPC.44.6][PRO.CO.5.640.39][PRO.CO.5.667.192/3]

BROKEY, CHARLES, born in 1750, a gardener, emigrated from Newcastle to Georgia on the Georgia Packet in September 1775, settled in Friendsborough, Georgia. [PRO.T47.9/11]

BROOK, JAMES, from Kirkwall, Orkney, embarked on the Marlborough, Captain Thomas Walker, in Kirkwall bound for Georgia in September 1775, an indentured servant of Thomas Brown in Richmond County, Georgia, in 1783. [PRO.AO13.34]

BROUGH, GEORGE, born in 1739, a farmer in Evie, Orkney, with wife Barbara Leask {married on 24 December 1759 in Evie parish}, and children Thomas {baptised on 18 December 1760}, Christian {baptised on 19 November 1762}, James, and Helen {baptised on 28 December 1767}, emigrated from Kirkwall, Orkney, to Savannah, Georgia, on the Marlborough, Captain George Prissick, in September 1774, an indentured servant of Thomas Brown, settled in Richmond County, Georgia. [PRO.T47.9/11][PRO.AO13/34/123-4]

BROWN, ALEXANDER, (?), land grant in Christchurch, Georgia, on 5 February 1760, [CRG#28/1.312][Grant book B, #281/282]

BROWN, ANDREW, born 1789, a joiner from Crail, Fife, emigrated to America during 1830, settled in Natchez, died there on 28 January 1871. [EFR]

BROWN, ISABELLA, daughter of Lieutenant Colonel Brown, late of East Florida, married Lieutenant Sheriff, Royal Navy, in Nassau, New Providence, in March 1798. [GC#1056]

BROWN, JAMES, late of Georgia, married Margaret Finlay, daughter of Reverend John Finlay, in Paisley, Renfrewshire, on 19 March 1804. [CM#12879]

BROWN, JAMES, sr., formerly a merchant in Augusta, Georgia, died in Paisley, Renfrewshire, in 1810. [GM#80.590]

BROWN, JAMES, a clerk in Farmington, Georgia, died on 3 April 1851, cnf. 1856. [NAS.SC70.1.92]

BROWN, M., born in Scotland in 1821, a sailor, settled in Alabama. [C]

BROWN, STEPHEN, emigrated to Savannah, Georgia, on the snow Kinnoull, Captain Alexander Alexander, and was granted 100 acres between the Savannah and the Saludy Rivers on 30 May 1768. [Ga.Co.Journal#34.148/151]

BROWN, THOMAS, born in 1763, millwright, died on 5 December 1803. [Savannah Death Register]

BROWN, WALTER, a merchant in Georgia, 1780. [NAS.RD4.259.758]

BROWN, WILLIAM, Customs Controller in Savannah, Georgia, 1768-, a Loyalist in 1776, settled in Edinburgh in 1783. [PRO.AO13.38.37]; grant of 400 acres in Christ Church parish on 1 January 1771, [Grant book I, #232]

BROWNING, GEORGE W., born in Scotland 1805, a physician, settled in De Soto County, Louisiana, by 1850. [C]

BRUCE, DAVID, granted 20,000 acres in East Florida in 1769. [PC.Col.V.592]

BRUCE, JAMES, Collector of Customs in Pensacola, West Florida, in 1765. [PRO.CO5.602.68][NLS#MS119]

BRUCE, JAMES, born in Scotland in 1813, a clerk, wife Jane born in Scotland in 1812, settled in Alabama. [C]

BRUCE, JAMES, born in Scotland 1820, settled in Gadsden County, Florida. [C]

BRUCE, ROBERT, born in Scotland in 1794, a sailor, and his wife Mary born in Scotland in 1799, settled in Mobile. [C]

BRUCE, THOMAS, land grant in Great Ogeechee, Georgia, on 7 February 1758, [CRG#28/1.236][Grant book A, #577]

BRUCE, THOMAS, co-owner and master of the schooner the Fair Susannah, built in New England during 1754, registered in Georgia on 31 March 1757, arrived in Savannah from St Kitts with a cargo of 6 negroes on 17 August 1756. [PRO.CO5.709]; land grant in Savannah on 13 April 1761, [CRG#28/1.365]

BRYCE, THOMAS, born in 1798, settled in Carroll County, Georgia, before 1850. [C]

BRUCE, THOMAS, an overseer, born in Scotland in 1822, settled in Warren County, Mississippi. [C]

BRYDEN, WILLIAM, born in Scotland in 1804, a clerk, wife Emma born in England in 1814, settled in Alabama. [C]

BRYDIE, DAVID, granted 500 acres in St John's parish, Georgia, on 6 November 1770, also 150 acres there on 1 January 1771. [Grant Book I.177/234][Duke University, David Brydie Mitchell pp]

BUCHANAN, ARCHIBALD, born in 1740, a pewterer in Edinburgh, emigrated from Greenock to New York or to Georgia on the Christy in May 1775. [PRO.T47.12]

BUCHANAN, MOSES, a shoemaker, born in Scotland 1822, Almira Buchanan born in Florida 1832, settled in Gadsden County, Florida. [C]

BUDGE, WILLIAM, born in 1753, a joiner, emigrated from Newcastle to Georgia on the Georgia Packet in September 1775, settled in Friendsborough, Georgia. [PRO.T47.12]

BULLOCH, ANN GRAHAM, widow of James Bulloch, in Mulberry
    Grove, Georgia, sister Elizabeth - widow of James Jackson vintner
    in Inverness, nephews John and Thomas, sons of Reverend Thomas
    Chisholm in Kilmorack, executors John Stuart, Superintendent of
    Indian Affairs in South Carolina, and cousin George Cuthbert,
    witnesses Christopher Dawson, a planter, and Mary, wife of
    George Cuthbert of Drakies, Georgia. Pro. 26 June 1764 Georgia

BULMAN, GEORGE, born in 1729, a carpenter, with wife Elizabeth
    born in 1739, and children George born in 1770 and Diana born in
    1771, emigrated from Newcastle to Georgia on the Georgia Packet
    in September 1775, settled in Friendsborough, Georgia.
    [PRO.T47.9/11]

BUNCLE, GEORGE, in Georgia on 9 December 1738, [AGA#59]

BURGESS, JOSEPH, with wife Margaret, emigrated from Inverness to
    Georgia on the Prince of Wales, master William Dunbar, on 20
    October 1735, arrived on 10 February 1736, [ESG#66]; settled at
    Darien, New Inverness, by 1739. [Ga.Col.Rec.3.427]; petitioned
    Oglethorpe re slavery on 3 January 1739. [AGA#65]; killed at the
    Siege of St Augustine in June 1740. [ESG#66]

BURN, HUGH, planter in Christchurch parish, Georgia, son of Elizabeth
    Burn in Stirling, Scotland, [will refers to sister Elizabeth Burn,
    Hugh son of brother Alexander Burn in Charleston, South Carolina;
    executors Joseph Clay, merchant in Savannah, Joseph Weatherly
    and William Gibbons planters in Christchurch parish.] Pro. 30
    October 1767 Georgia

BURNETT, D., born in Scotland in 1821, a ship carpenter, wife Agnes
    (?) born in Scotland in 1827, settled in Mobile, Alabama. [C]

BURNET, JOHN, granted 150 acres in St John's parish, Georgia, on 25
    September 1760 and 57 acres there 25 September 1760. [Grant
    Book C.312/314][CRG#28/1.369]

BURNETT, WILLIAM, from Dumfries, a physician in West Florida around 1775. [NAS.RS23.21.335]

BURNEY, WILLIAM, born in 1739, and his wife born in 1751, arrived in Fort Miro, Louisiana, 8 May 1797. [NWI.2.231]?

BURNEY, WILLIAM, his son, born in 1769, his wife born in 1771, sons John born in 1789, James born in 1791, and William born in 1796, arrived in Fort Miro, Louisiana, on 8 May 1797. [NWI.2.230]?

BURNS, PATRICK O., born in Scotland in 1828, a gardener, settled in Harrison County, Mississippi. [C]

BURNSIDE, JAMES, a settler in Georgia 9 December 1738. [AGA#59]; loan to on 29 October 1740, [CRG#30.122]; land grants in Savannah and on Rotten Pusem Island on 28 March 1758, [CRG#28/1.237][Grant book A, #593/594]

BURNSIDE, ROBERT, born 1783, arrived in USA on 28 September 1803, a teacher in New Orleans. [1812]

BURROUGHS, CALVIN, born in Scotland in 1830, a laborer, settled in Alabama. [C]

CADENHEAD, JOHN, a trader among the Lower Creeks in 1735. [SPAWI.1735#157.vii]

CALDER, ALEXANDER, born in parish of Watten, Caithness, in 1733, a wright in Wick, Caithness, with wife Henrietta Bain {married in parish of Reay, on 30 July 1758}, and children Katherine {baptised on 4 August 1759, in Watten}, Robert {baptised on 25 July 1761, in Bower}, John, James, Christian {baptised on 6 January 1770, in Watten} and Peggy, emigrated from Caithness to Savannah, Georgia, on the Marlborough in September 1775, an indentured servant of Thomas Brown, settled in Richmond County, Georgia. [PRO.T47.12][PRO.AO13.34/123-4][Watten OPR]

CALDER, WILLIAM, born in 1721, emigrated from Inverness to Georgia on 20 October 1735 on the Prince of Wales, master

George Dunbar, arrived on 10 January 1736, an indentured servant, later soldier of the Highland Independent Company on 6 May 1741. [ESG#7]

CALLENDAR, ALEXANDER, granted 10,000 acres of land in West Florida in 1767. [PC.Col.V.593]

CALLENDAR, JOHN, of Craigforth, granted 20,000 acres in East Florida in 1767. [PRO.CO5.542][PC.Col.V.591]

CAMERON, ALEXANDER, 'came from Frederica', Georgia, on 25 April 1740. [CRG#30.296]

CAMERON, ALEXANDER, in Medway, St Andrew's parish, Georgia, in 1763. [Ga.Gaz.#34]

CAMERON, ALEXANDER, born in Scotland, British Army Ensign at Fort Prince George, South Carolina, in 1763, married a Cherokee, Deputy Superintendent for the British Indian Department in the South, based in Pensacola, West Florida, died in Savannah, on 27 December 1781, ['The Cherokees', Oklahoma, 1963] Savannah, Georgia. [Pro February 1784 PCC][RoyalGaGaz#2/3]

CAMERON, ANGUS, jr., soldier of the Black Watch, imprisoned in the Tower of London on a charge of mutiny, transferred to Oglethorpe's Regiment in Georgia in 1743. [GHS, Cate Collection, folder #45, mf.3172]

CAMERON, CHARLES, son of Donald Cameron in Kilmally, Captain of the 71st Regiment, died in Savannah, Georgia. [Pro. January 1782 PCC]

CAMERON, DONALD, soldier of the Black Watch, imprisoned in the Tower of London on a charge of mutiny, transferred to Oglethorpe's Regiment in Georgia in 1743. [GHS, Cate Colln. 45/3172]

CAMERON, DONALD, jr., soldier of the Black Watch, imprisoned in the Tower of London on a charge of mutiny, transferred to

Oglethorpe's Regiment in Georgia in 1743, transferred to an Independent Company in 1749. [GHS, Cate Colln. 45/3172]

CAMERON, DUNCAN, soldier of the Black Watch, imprisoned in the Tower of London on a charge of mutiny, transferred to Oglethorpe's Regiment in Georgia in 1743, transferred to an Independent Company in 1749. [GHS, Cate Colln. 45/3172]

CAMERON, Captain EWAN, a Highlander, executed by the Mexicans in Texas on 25 April 1843. [Inst.of Texan Cultures, San Antonio]

CAMERON, JANET, born in 1715, 4 year indentured servant, emigrated from Inverness to Georgia on 19 November 1737 on the Two Brothers, Captain William Thomson, arrived on 14 January 1738. [ESG#8]

CAMERON, JOHN, born in 1723, an indentured servant, emigrated from Inverness on the Two Brothers, Captain William Thomson, to Georgia in July 1737, arrived on 20 November 1737. [ESG#8]

CAMERON, JOHN, born in 1721, an indentured servant, emigrated from Inverness on the Two Brothers, Captain William Thomson, to Georgia in July 1737, arrived on 20 November 1737, a Ranger on 6 May 1741. [ESG#8]

CAMERON, JOHN, born in 1714, 4 year indentured servant, embarked in Inverness on the Two Brothers, Captain William Thomson, for Georgia on 19 November 1737, arrived there on 14 January 1738. [ESG#8]

CAMERON, JOHN, jr., soldier of the Black Watch, imprisoned in the Tower of London on a charge of mutiny, transferred to Oglethorpe's Regiment in Georgia in 1743. [GHS, Cate Colln. 45/3172]

CAMERON, JOHN, born in Scotland in 1785, a gardener, wife Margaret born in England in 1784, and daughter Elizabeth born in England in 1826, settled in Alabama. [C]

CAMERON, JOHN, born in Scotland in 1822, a carpenter, wife Ann
born in Scotland in 1827, settled in Alabama, children Elizabeth
and Allen (both born in Alabama). [C]

CAMERON, RICHARD, born in 1697, servant to Francis Scott,
emigrated from Gravesend on the Anne, Captain Thomas Shubrick,
on 6 November 1732, arrived in Georgia on 1 February 1733,
"absconded at Palacholas". [ESG#8/110]

CAMPBELL, ARCHIBALD, planter in southern Georgia in 1741.
[CRG#30.343]

CAMPBELL, ARCHIBALD, baptised on 11 April 1813, son of
Archibald Campbell {1781-1843}, a sawyer in Perth, and Margaret
Watt {1791-1854}, died in New Orleans on 5 October 1839. [Perth
OPR][Perth, Greyfriars, g/s]

CAMPBELL, Sir ARCHIBALD, a soldier in Georgia 1778-1779.
[NAS.NRAS#0028, pp.1.3.6.7.19.83]

CAMPBELL, DANIEL, planter in southern Georgia in 1741,
[CRG#30.343]

CAMPBELL, DANIEL, master of the British built brigantine Betsey,
registered in Savannah on 11 October 1762, arrived in Savannah
from St Croix on 6 April 1763. [PRO.CO5.709]

CAMPBELL, DANIEL, born in Scotland in 1780, Jenny Campbell born
in Scotland in 1800, Archibald Campbell born in North Carolina in
1829, and Mary Campbell born in North Carolina in 1830, settled
in Walton County, Florida. [C]

CAMPBELL, DOUGAL, in Mobile, 1764. [NLS#MS119]

CAMPBELL, DUGALD, of Skerrington, died in New Orleans on 24
October 1827. [SM#57.818]

CAMPBELL, EDWARD, born in Kintyre, Argyllshire, in 1757, married
Mary McLellan {died 1816 in South Carolina}, emigrated from

Greenock to South Carolina in 1788, settled in Florida in 1819, died in Escambia County, Florida, in February 1837. [NCSA.2.70]

CAMPBELL, EDWARD, born in Scotland in 1821, a merchant, settled in Alabama. [C]

CAMPBELL, ELIZABETH, born in 1810, daughter of David Campbell {1788-1848} and Mary Porter {1785-1868}, died in New Orleans on 1 September 1838. [Buittle g/s]

CAMPBELL, JAMES, granted 500 acres in Georgia in April 1752. [PRO.CO5/669]

CAMPBELL, JAMES, Indian trader in Augusta, on 20 November 1756. [PRO.CO5/646, C17]

CAMPBELL, JAMES, in New Orleans and in Arkansas in 1764. [NAS.NRAS#0631]

CAMPBELL, JAMES, born in Glasgow in 1776, a cooper, died in Savannah, Georgia, in 13 June 1810. [Savannah Death Register]

CAMPBELL, JAMES, born in 1794, emigrated to USA in 1810, a clerk in Augusta, Georgia, in 1812, [1812]

CAMPBELL, JAMES, Petershill, married Miss Martin, East Florida, on 7 July 1794. [SM#56.441]

CAMPBELL, JAMES, born in Scotland in 1797, a merchant, wife Mary born in 1813, children Douglas, a clerk, James, a student, Hellen, Archibald, Charles, (born in Alabama) with children Jane and Susan (born in Scotland), settled in Alabama. [C]

CAMPBELL, JANE, baptised 20 April 1821 in parish of Drymen, Stirlingshire, daughter of Archibald Campbell {1790-1838} and Jean Graham {1789-1854} in Drymen, Stirlingshire, died in Nashville, Tennessee, on 19 May 1849. [Drymen/Denny g/s][Drymen OPR]

CAMPBELL, JEAN, a mantua maker in Savannah, Georgia, on 20 August 1766. [Ga.Gaz.#152]

CAMPBELL, JENETTE, born in Scotland in 1815, children John born in 1832, Isabella born in 1830, and Andrew born in 1834 all in Louisiana, settled in Adams County, Mississippi. [C]

CAMPBELL, JOHN, born in 1717, a woodcutter, an indentured servant, embarked in Inverness on the Loyal Judith, Captain John Lemon, for Georgia on 21 September 1741, arrived there on 2 December 1741. [PRO.CO.5.668] [ESG#8][CRG.30.197/199]

CAMPBELL, JOHN, sr., soldier of the Black Watch, imprisoned in the Tower of London on a charge of mutiny, transferred to Oglethorpe's Regiment in Georgia in 1743. [GHS, Cate Colln. 45/3172]

CAMPBELL, JOHN, jr., soldier of the Black Watch, imprisoned in the Tower of London on a charge of mutiny, transferred to Oglethorpe's Regiment in Georgia in 1743. [GHS, Cate Colln. 45/3172]

CAMPBELL, JOHN, emigrated possibly via London on the brigantine Africa in 1772, settled in Pensacola, Florida, before 1773. [PCCol#5.378]

CAMPBELL, JOHN, born in 1780, a rigger, died on 26 October 1807. [Savannah Death Register]

CAMPBELL, MARTIN, an Indian trader in Augusta, Georgia, on 15 June 1756. [PRO.CO5/646, C15]

CAMPBELL, RANDALL, born in Scotland in 1778, a farmer in Montgomery County, Georgia. [C]

CAMPBELL, ROBERT, granted 20,000 acres in East Florida in 1767. [PC.Col.V.591]

CAMPBELL, Captain ROBERT, born in Greenock, Renfrewshire, in 1776, died in Georgia in 1818. [Colonial Museum and Savannah Advertiser, 1.4.1818]

CAMPBELL, SAMUEL, granted 20,000 acres in East Florida in 1766. [PCCol.V.590]

CAMPBELL, WILLIAM, a merchant in Montrose, Angus, emigrated from Gravesend to Georgia on the Mary Anne in 1737. [SPC.1737.107]

CAMPBELL, Lord WILLIAM, sailed to England on 30 April 1763; granted 20,000 acres in East Florida in 1766. [GaGaz#6][PCCol.V.590]

CARGILE, ADAM, and wife Janet, embarked on the Marlborough, Captain George Prissick, in Kirkwall, Orkney, bound for Georgia, in September 1774, an indentured servant of Thomas Brown in Georgia. [PRO.AO13.34.123/4]

CARGILL, DAVID, in New Orleans, died on 10 February 1846. [NAS.SH]

CARNEGIE, JAMES, died in Augusta, Georgia, on 30 September 1788. [Georgia State Gazette: 4.10.1788]

CARNOCHAN, DAVID, born in 1774, to USA in 1811, a distiller in McIntosh County, Georgia, in 1812, [1812][possibly baptised on 11 April 1773 in parish of Rerrick, son of Robert Carnochan and Catherine Black][Rerrick OPR]

CARNOCHAN, JANE, born in Galloway, settled in McIntosh County, Georgia, married William McMasters, from Galloway, on 9 April 1826. [Daily Georgian, 11.4.1826]

CARNOCHAN, JOHN, born in Dumfries in 1778, son of John Carnochan {1737-1790} and Mary Murray, emigrated to Nassau, the Bahamas, later settled in Georgia, married Harriet F. Putnam, father of John Murray Carnochan born in 1812, died in 1841. [BLG.2602]

CARNOCHAN, WILLIAM, born in 1774 in Gatehouse of Fleet, Stewartry of Kirkcudbright, baptised on 18 November 1774 in the parish of Girthon, son of J. Carnochan and Mary Murray, settled in Darien, Georgia, in 1810, died there on 28 November 1825. [Daily Georgian, 3.12.1825]; a sugar planter in McIntosh County, Georgia, in 1812, [1812] [Girthon OPR]

CARR, ALEXANDER M., born in Scotland in 1810, a broker, wife Maria born in Georgia in 1816, children James, Mary and George, (all born in Alabama, settled in Alabama by 1843. [C]

CARR, MARK, a planter and a soldier, settled in St Patrick's parish, Glynn county, Georgia, pro. 1767 Georgia

CARREY, JOHN, born in Scotland in 1802, a plasterer, settled in Alabama. [C]

CARRICK, JAMES, born in Stirling, son of William Carrick and Margaret Gardiner, and Adelaida Segand, born in New Orleans, daughter of Pablo Segand and Maria Francisco Conard, were married in Louisiana 19 March 1797. [LGS]

CARRIGEL, JOHN, from Aukland, Orkney, embarked on the Marlborough, Captain Thomas Walker, in September 1775 bound for Georgia, an indentured servant of Thomas Brown in Richmond County, Georgia, in 1783. [PRO.AO13.34/123-4]

CARRUTHERS, JAMES, born in 1776 in Wamphrey parish, Dumfries-shire, by 1815 a merchant in Savannah, Georgia, died in Augusta, Georgia, on 9 September 1820. [Colonial Museum and Savannah Advertiser, 19.9.1820]; cnf 1822 [NAS.SC70.1.26][Wamphrey g/s] [NAS.CS17.1.39/42/552]

CARRUTHERS, JOHN, born in 1770 in Wamphrey parish, Dumfries-shire, settled in Savannah, Georgia, by 1815, died in Saratoga on 24 August 1824. [Wamphrey g/s]

CARRUTHERS, JOSEPH, born in 1783, settled in Savannah in 1804, died there on 19 October 1823. [Daily Georgian: 28.10.1823][Wamphrey g/s][possibly baptised on 16 February 1784 in the parish of Applegarth, Dumfries-shire. {Applegarth OPR}]

CARSON, JOHN, born in Scotland in 1820, a clerk, wife Mary born in Kentucky in 1827, settled in Mobile, Alabama. [C]

CARSON, ROBERT, sergeant of the 22nd Foot, died in Mobile, West Florida, pro. April 1766 PCC

CARSON, WILLIAM, born in Scotland in 1812, a clerk, settled in Alabama. [C]

CARSWELL, SAMUEL, born in 1762, his wife born in 1763, daughter Jean born in 1787, sons Robert born in 1792 and Matthew born in 1794, arrived in Louisiana on 19 April 1797. [NWI.2.228]?

CATHERWOOD, ROBERT, appointed a Member of the Council of East Florida on 7 June 1771, in St Augustine, East Florida, pro.September 1787 PCC [PC.Col.V.5654][APC.Col.1766-1783#564]

CHALMERS, GILBERT, emigrated to Savannah, Georgia, on the snow Kinnoull, Captain Alexander Alexander, and was granted 100 acres between the Savannah and the Saludy Rivers on 30 May 1768.[Ga.Co.Journal#34.148/151]

CHISHOLM, JAMES, born in 1771, a baker, died on 8 October 1804. [Savannah Death Register]

CHISON, ALEXANDER, a mechanic, born in Scotland in 1800, Flora Chison born in North Carolina in 1824, and John born in Florida in 1847, settled in Walton County, Florida. [C]

CHRISTIE, ADAM, petitioned the Council of West Florida for 40,000 acres in West Florida to settle 100 families from Scotland, on 13

June 1774. [PRO.CO5.630]; a merchant in Pensacola in 1778. [NAS.CS16.1.173]

CHRISTIE, ROBERT, a merchant from Culross, Fife, husband of Margaret Sands, in Florida in 1667. [PC.4.297]

CHRISTIE, THOMAS, born in 1700, a merchant, land grant on 26 October 1732, embarked on the Anne, Captain Thomas Shubrick, at Gravesend on 6 November 1732, arrived in Georgia on 1 February 1733, a bailliff there, granted 200 acres in Georgia on 16 February 1740, [PRO.CO.5.668]; reference on 9 December 1738, [AGA#59]; settled in Savannah, may have left colony in 1740. [ESG9/107]; thought to be the author of "A Description of Georgia, by a gentleman who has resided there upwards of 7 years" {London, 1741}, [CRG.30.172][ESG#107]

CHRISTIE, THOMAS, land grant in St Andrew's parish, Georgia, on 7 July 1760, [CRG#28/1.374]

CHRISTIE, WILLIAM, born in 1776, died in October 1829. [Georgia Republican: 3.10.1829]

CLARK, ALEXANDER, son of Daniel Clark, settled at New Inverness by 1739. [Ga.Col.Rec.3.427]; petitioned Oglethorpe re slavery on 3 January 1739. [AGA#65]

CLARK, DANIEL, from Castle Stewart, Petty parish, Inverness, an Indian trader in Augusta, Georgia. [Pro.August 1757 PCC] [Pro.13 May 1757 Georgia][will refers to friends Alexander Petrie and wife, John McQueen, wife and daughter Anne; George Summers and wife; Alexander, son of Mary Dicks; Lauchlan McGillvray; Alexander McGillvray and wife; Robert Brisbane; John McGillivray; James Parsons; William Struthers; Rev. Morrison of the Scotch Meeting House in Charleston; Alexander Clark in Petty, Inverness; brother in law Alexander Clark merchant in Inverness and his daughter Margaret; executors Alex Petrie, Laurence McGillivray, John McQueen, and James Parsons]; a merchant in Augusta, Georgia. [Georgia Misc. Bonds, O.pp147/148]; in New Inverness, petitioned Oglethorpe re slavery on 3 January 1739.

[AGA#65][CRG.3.427]; 1760, 1766. [NAS.CS16.1.107, 125]
[pro. August 1757 PCC][NAS.CS16.1.107]

CLARK, DONALD, (1), settled in New Inverness, Georgia, by 1739.
[Col.Rec.Ga.3.427]; petitioned Oglethorpe re slavery on 3 January
1739. [AGA#65]; land grant in Darien on 28 March 1758.
[CRG#28/1.237]

CLARK, DONALD, [2], settled in New Inverness by 1739.
[CRG.3.427]; petitioned Oglethorpe re slavery on 3 January 1739.
[AGA#65]

CLARK, E., born in Scotland in 1824, a bagman, settled in Mobile,
Alabama. [C]

CLARK, HUGH. land grants of 500 acres in Sapola District, Georgia, on
11 February 1757, and in St Andrew's parish, Georgia, on 7 July
1761. [PRO.CO.5.646.C10][CRG#28/1/49, 360]

CLARK, JAMES, born in 1765, a Protestant, an innkeeper in St
Augustine, East Florida, in 1786. [FHR#18][1786 Census of St
Augustine]

CLARK, JOHN, a settler in Georgia on 9 December 1738. [AGA#59]

CLARK, JOHN, born in 1758 in Petty, Inverness-shire, {possibly
baptised in 1758 at Kingussie son of Malcolm Clark and Marjory
MacPherson} emigrated to South Carolina, a teacher in South
Carolina and Georgia, later a Baptist missionary in Georgia 1789-
1833, died in St Louis 1833. [TSA][Kingussie OPR]

CLARK, JOHN, born in 1779, son of .... Clark and Margaret Scott,
settled in Louisiana, died in Maxwelltown, Dumfries-shire, on 9
April 1866. [Dumfries g/s]

CLARK, JOHN, son of William Clark in Creebridge, Kirkcudbrightshire,
settled in New Orleans 18.... [Monigaff g/s]

CLARKE, R.C., born in Scotland in 1814, a carpenter, settled in Alabama. [C]

CLARK, WILLIAM, land grant of 500 acres in Sapola District, Georgia, on 11 February 1757. [PRO.CO.5.646.C10][CRG#28/1/50]

CLARK, ..., died in St Andrews, Amelia, Georgia, in 1737. [SPC.1737#596][PRO.CO5.640.13]

CLEMENTS, WILLIAM, born in Scotland in 1764, a mariner, died in Savannah, Georgia, on 24 October 1809. [Savannah Death Register]

CLUNAS, ALEXANDER, born in 1717, an indentured servant, embarked on the Two Brothers master William Thomson in Inverness bound for Georgia in July 1737, arrived there on 20 November 1737, a servant at Darien on 6 May 1741. [ESG#10]

COBB, JOHN, born in 1744, a butcher, emigrated from Newcastle to Georgia on the Georgia Packet in September 1775. [PRO.T47.9/11]

COCHRAN, Lieutenant Colonel JAMES, father of Maryann, Betty and Caroline, settled in Georgia before 1737, [PRO.CO.5.670.334]; granted 500 acres in Georgia on 25 November 1737 and on 15 March 1738. [PRO.CO.5.668][SPAWI.1738#109]

COCHRAN, JAMES, baptised on 5 July 1752 in parish of Errol, Perthshire, son of James Cochran and Isobel Gairn, steward of HM transport ship Betsy, died in Savannah, Georgia. Admin. January 1781 PCC [Errol OPR]

COCHRAN, ROBERT, born in Kirkcudbright on 9 May 1788, eldest son of Robert Cochran and Elizabeth Guthrie, a merchant in New York, later settled in Natchez, Mississippi, died in Albany, New York, on 21 January 1849. [ANY#2.172]

COCHRANE, WILLIAM W., an agent, born in Scotland in 1823, wife Aliza A. born in Mississippi in 1829, settled in Adams County, Mississippi. [C]

COCK, RALPH, born in 1737, a linen-weaver and indentured servant, with his wife, emigrated via Whitby to Savannah on the Marlborough in August 1774, an indentured servant of Thomas Brown in Georgia. [PRO.T47.9/11][PRO.AO13.34/123-4]

COGACH, JOHN, born in 1708, a labourer and cowherd, an indentured servant, embarked from Inverness on the Loyal Judith, Captain John Lemon, for Georgia on 21 September 1741, arrived in Georgia on 2 December 1741 with wife Anne Mackay, son Angus born in 1734, daughter Christiana born in 1725, daughter Isabel born in 1728, and son William born in 1730. [PRO.CO.5.668] [ESG#11][CRG.30.7/199]

COLQUHOUN, ANGUS, born in Argyll in 1782, settled in Montgomery County, Georgia, before 1812. [NCSA.2.71]

COLTHRED, JOHN, emigrated from Inverness to Georgia on the Two Brothers, Captain William Thomson, in July 1737, arrived in Georgia on 13 November 1737. [SPC.43.161]

COLTHRED, WILLIAM, a settler in Georgia, reference to on 9 December 1738, [AGA#59]

COMYN, THOMAS, merchant, granted 10,000 acres of land in West Florida in 1769, [PC.Col.V.593]; born 1756, settled with his family in Michael Street, Pensacola, West Florida, in 1786. [FHR#18] [Spanish Census of Pensacola, 1784-1820]

CONWAY, LAWYER(?), a raftman, born in Scotland in 1829, settled in Warren County, Mississippi. [C]

COOLING(?), GEORGE, servant to Patrick Tailfer, emigrated on 14 October 1735, arrived in Georgia on 1 February 1736. [ESG#69]

COOPER, P., born in Scotland in 1829, a sailor, settled in Alabama. [C]

COOPER, ROBERT, a blacksmith, born in Scotland in 1810, settled in Warren County, Mississippi. [C]

CORBETT, WILLIAM, born in 1769, emigrated to USA in 1807, a merchant in Washington, in Georgia 1812. [1812]

CORGILL, JOHN, from Harra, Orkney, embarked on the Marlborough, Captain Thomas Walker, in Kirkwall, Orkney, in September 1775, bound for Georgia, an indentured servant of Thomas Brown in Richmond County, Georgia, in 1783. [PRO.AO13.34/123-5]

CORRIGIL, ADAM, born in 1742, a farmer in Evie, Orkney, with wife Janet, and children Katherine, William and Robert, emigrated from Kirkwall, Orkney, to Savannah, Georgia, on the Marlborough, in September 1775. [PRO.T47.12]

CORRIGIL, ELIZABETH, born in 1755, a servant in Kirkwall, emigrated from Kirkwall, Orkney, to Savannah, Georgia, on the Marlborough, Captain Thomas Walker, in September 1775, settled in Richmond County, Georgia, as an indentured servant of Thomas Brown. [PRO.T47.12][PRO.AO13.34/123-4]

COTTON, ANNE, born in 1718, a single woman, an indentured servant, embarked from Inverness on the Loyal Judith, Captain John Lemon, for Georgia on 21 September 1741, arrived there on 2 December 1741. [PRO.CO.5.668] [ESG#11][CRG.30.197/199]

COULL, JOHN, servant of Patrick Tailfer before 1740. [ESG#69]

COUPAR, JOHN, born on 24 April 1759, son of Reverend John Coupar {1706-1787} and Sarah MacKill {died 1796} in Lochwinnoch, Renfrewshire, settled in Hopeton, St Simon's Island, Georgia, in 1804, father of James H. Coupar and William A. Coupar, died 1850. [University of North Carolina, Coupar pp][F#3/153]

COUTTS, JAMES, granted 10,000 acres in East Florida in 1766. [PCCol.V.590]

COUTTS, THOMAS, granted 10,000 acres in East Florida in 1766. [PCCol.V.590]

COWAN, JOHN, born in Kirkcudbright in 1789, baptised there on 27 October 1789, son of David Cowan and Jean Craig, to USA in 1803, a merchant's clerk in Savannah in 1812, died in Savannah, Georgia, on 7 September 1820. [Colonial Museum and Savannah Advertiser, 14.9.1820][1812][Kirkcudbright OPR]

COWPER, BASIL, President of the St Andrew's Society of Savannah 1774-1775. [SSS#88]

COWPER, MARY, a widow in Savannah, pro.August 1822 PCC

CRAIG, Mrs BEATRICE, born in Scotland in 1805, husband E. Craig born in Pennsylvania, settled in Adams County, Mississippi. [C]

CRAIG, MARGARET, embarked on the Marlborough, Captain George Prissick, in Kirkwall, Orkney, bound for Georgia in September 1774, an indentured servant of Thomas Brown there. [PRO.AO13.34/123-4]

CRAIG, R. S., a clerk, born in Scotland in 1814, settled in Adams County, Mississippi. [C]

CRAIG, WILLIAM, a servant in Georgia around 1740. [ESG#69]

CRAWFORD, ALEXANDER, overseer on John Milligan's plantation on the Little Ogeechee River, murdered on 28 March 1763. [GaGaz.7.4.1763]

CRAWFORD, ALEXANDER, granted 5,000 acres in East Florida in 1767. [PC.Col.V.591]

CRAWFORD, JOHN, granted 500 acres in Georgia in October 1751. [PRO.CO5.669]

CRAWFORD, JOHN, British consul in New Orleans in 1838. [NAS.GD121.82/105]

CRAWFORD, ROBERT, born in 1759, a yeoman, emigrated from Newcastle to Georgia on the Georgia Packet in September 1775, [PRO.T47.9/11]

CRAWFORD, WILLIAM, granted 500 acres in October 1751. [PRO.CO5/669]

CRAWFORD, WILLIAM, born in 1759, died on his plantation at Little Satilla, Glynn County, Georgia, on 20 October 1809. [DPCA#398] [Savannah Republican: 26.10.1809] Pro. 11 November 1809 Chatham County, Georgia. [Will Book E] (will refers to his brother John, his sister Barbara in Scotland, his sister Betty Crawford or Nicol; executors John Cooper, planter in St Simon's, and Richard M. Stites, subscribed 20 June 1809)

CRAWFORD and LINDSAY, GEORGE, Earl of, granted 20,000 acres in West Florida on 13 May 1767. [PRO.C05.613.410]

CREIGHTON, ALEXANDER, grant of 250 acres in Christ Church parish, Georgia, on 6 March 1770. [Grant book G, #540]

CRERICH, MARGARET, wife of James Clark an innkeeper, in St Augustine, East Florida, in 1786. [FHR#18]

CRIGHTON, ALEXANDER, in St Augustine, East Florida, 1817. [NAS.CS17.1.37/386]

CROCKATT, JOHN, appointed warden of St Philips, Georgia, on 15 April 1751; appointed a member of the Council of Georgia, on 2 March 1752. [SCGaz#883/927]

CROOKSHANKS, ROBERT, servant to Farquhar McGillvray, emigrated from Inverness on the Prince of Wales, Captain George Dunbar, on 20 October 1735, arrived in Georgia 10 January 1736, blind by 1739, in Darien on 6 May 1741. [ESG#69]

CROSBIE, JANE, born in 1770, died on 16 September 1806. [Savannah Death Register]

CUMMING, DAVID, born in 1799, a clerk, wife Janet born in 1799, children George born in 1824 an engineer, David born in 1825 a carpenter, Janet born in 1825, Catherine born in 1827, Jane born in 1829, Mary born in 1830, Alexander born in 1831, Christine born in 1833, Ogan (?) born in 1839, James born in 1842, all born in Scotland and all settled in Alabama. [C]

CUMMING, GEORGE S., born in Scotland in 1812, a merchant, wife Ann born in England in 1816, children George, Charles, and Martin, (all born in Alabama), settled in Alabama. [C]

CUMMING, JAMES, a merchant in the firm of Inglis and Cumming, a Baptist, died on 21 September 1820. [Colonial Museum and Savannah Advertiser: 10.10.1820]

CUNNINGHAM, DAVID, land grant in Savannah on 30 September 1757, [CRG#28/1.113]; land grant on Savannah wharf on 2 October 1759, [CRG#28/1.314]; in Savannah, on 29 December 1763. [Ga.Gaz. #39][Grant book A, #457; Grant book B, #306;]

CUNNINGHAM, GEORGE, son of Henry Cunningham, in East Florida, grandson of John Cunningham of Balbougie, Fife, in 1771. [NAS.SH]; son of Henry Cunningham surgeon in Edinburgh then in East Florida, on 3 March 1772. [NAS.CS16.1.148]

CUNNINGHAM, Dr HENRY, son of John Cunningham of Balbougie, Fife, a surgeon from Edinburgh, a physician in St Augustine, East Florida, died there on 23 February 1771, pro.10 April 1771 Georgia, (will refers to wife Margaret, son George Sackville Cunningham and daughter Esther Cunningham); cnf 23 November 1792 Edinburgh [NAS.CC8.8.129][SM#33.331] [NAS.CS16.1.134/141]

CUNNINGHAM, KEITH, born in Scotland in 1807, a carpenter, wife Jane born in Scotland in 1814, settled in Alabama. [C]

CUNNINGHAM, Mrs MARGARET, widow of Dr Henry Cunningham in East Florida on 5 November 1772, [deed refers to John Graham late of Savannah, Georgia; Charles Innes clerk to HM Signet; Dr Lewis Johnston in Edinburgh]. [NAS.RD2.244/2.149]

CUNNINGHAM, ROBERT, born in 1779, a merchant, died on 12 September 1804. [Savannah Death Register]

CUNNINGHAM, WILLIAM, late of St Augustine, East Florida, died in Nassau, the Bahamas, pro. September 1791 PCC

CURRIE, ALEXANDER, born in Galloway in 1775, baptised in parish of Rerrick, Kirkcudbrightshire, on 19 May 1775, son of David Currie and Catherine Goldie, settled in McIntosh County, Georgia, died in Savannah on 12 February 1813. [Old Colonial Cemetery, Savannah, g/s][Rerrick OPR] [Savannah Republican: 16.2.1813]

CURRY, A., (male), born in Scotland in 1781, a planter, with John Curry born in North Carolina in 1788, a planter, John Curry born in 1827 in Mississippi, Mary Curry born in 1829 in Mississippi, A. (female), born in Mississippi in 1832, and Edward Curry born in 1833 in Mississippi, settled in Jefferson County, Mississippi. [C]

CURRY, GEORGE, an Indian trader in Augusta, arrived in Georgia in 1736. (?) [ESG#70]

CURRIE, GEORGE, second son of William Currie in Greenhead, Roxburghshire, died in New Orleans in January 1829.[PA#96] [EEC#18655]

CURRIE, JOHN, born in Galloway in 1762, settled in Savannah, Georgia, died on 27 September 1799. [Old Colonial Cemetery, Savannah, g/s] [CM, 1.10.1799]

CURRY, MARY, born in Scotland in 1788, with Mary Curry born in North Carolina in 1823, settled in Jefferson County, Mississippi. [C]

CUSHNY, THOMAS, born on 31 March 1812, baptised on 19 April 1812 in Peebles, son of Arthur Cushny and Alison Minto, died in Natchez, Georgia, in October 1837. [Peebles OPR][Peebles g/s]

CUTHBERT, GEORGE, a farmer from Inverness, emigrated from Inverness on the Prince of Wales, Captain George Dunbar, on 20 October 1735, arrived in Georgia on 10 January 1736, settled in Darien, a cattle hunter with 6 servants 1738/1739. [ESG#70]

CUTHBERT, GEORGE, land grants on the Great Ogeechee River, Georgia, on 16 January 1756, [Grant book A, #62/63]; land grant in Savannah on 5 April 1757, land grant of 600 acres in Christ Church parish, Georgia, on 4 January 1763. [PRO.CO.5.648.E48][CRG#28/1/59, 443] [Grant book A, #381; Grant book D, #267; Grant book E, #253]; died in Savannah on 20 April 1768. [GaGaz#3/2]

CUTHBERT, JAMES, of Castlehill, baptised in Inverness on 21 August 1732 son of George Cuthbert and Marjory McIntosh, physician, son of George Cuthbert and Mary Macintosh, with wife Anne, and sons George, Lewis, Graeme and Joseph, daughter Elizabeth, settled in Drakies, Christchurch parish, Georgia. Pro. 20 October 1770 Georgia, [refers to John Graham in Savannah, and Alexander Inglis, merchant in Savannah, executors][NAS.RD4.210.774]; subscribed towards a Presbyterian Meeting House in Savannah in 1769. [Ga.Gaz.#38, 291]; land grants in Christ Church parish in 1769, [Grant book G, #251/264] [NAS.CS17.1.2][Inverness OPR]

CUTHBERT, JOHN, of Drackies, Inverness, born in 1704, emigrated from Inverness to Georgia on the Prince of Wales, Captain George Dunbar, on 20 October 1735, arrived in Georgia on 10 January 1736, [PRO.CO.5.670.219]; granted 500 acres in Josephstown, Georgia, on 3 September 1735, later moved to Darien alias New Inverness. [PRO.CO.5.668]; Ranger Captain in 1738. [CRG, 10.5.1738]; appointed Commander of Fort St Andrews by Oglethorpe in 1736; signed a treaty with the Creek Indians on 11 August 1739, died on 16 November 1739. [SPC.43.453][ESG#70]

CUTHBERT, JOHN, settled in New Inverness by 1739. [Ga.Col.Rec.3.427]; petitioned Oglethorpe re slavery on 3 January 1739. [AGA#65]

CUTHBERT, JOHN, absconded from Georgia to Carolina in August 1742. [ESG#70]

CUTHBERT, JOSEPH, in Savannah, Georgia, eldest son of Dr James Cuthbert, grand-nephew of Alexander Cuthbert of Castlehill, Inverness, 1783, 1785, 1786. [NAS.RS.Inverness, 143] [NAS.CS17.1.2] [NAS.RD4.238.237][NAS.SH]

CUTHBERTSON, JOHN, born in Scotland 1820, settled in De Soto, Louisiana, by 1850. [C]

CUTLER, MARSHALL, born in Scotland in 1800, a carpenter, settled in Alabama. [C]

DADE, Mrs MARY, born in Scotland 1806, husband R.R.Dade a printer born in Virginia 1793, settled in Alabama before 1829, children Agnes, Frank, Lucy, William, Susan, Robert, and Catherine (all born in Alabama). [C]

DALLAS, DUNCAN, born 1720, a servant, emigrated from Inverness on the Two Brothers, Captain William Thomson, to Georgia 24 June 1737, arrived 20 November 1737, schoolmaster at Highgate, in England 1741, schoolmaster and Registrar of Savannah 1741. [ESG#14]

DALRYMPLE, THOMAS, born 1787, to USA 1811, a merchant's clerk in Savannah 1812, [1812]

DALZIEL, ROBERT, born in 1824, son of William Dalziel and Margaret Currie, died in Memphis on 3 October 1864. [Fenwick, Ayrshire, g/s]

DANSKIN, JAMES, granted 10,000 acres in West Florida 1767. [PC.Col.V.593]

DARLING, ANDREW, granted 24 acres in St John's parish, Georgia, on 3 July 1770. [Grant Book H.41]; a merchant in St John's parish, Sunbury, pro.5 June 1772 Georgia.

DARLING, KENNETH BAILLIE, granted 125 acres in St John's parish, Georgia, on 4 May 1773. [Grant Book I.970]

DAVIDSON, ADAM, born 1791, to USA 1811, a merchant in Savannah 1812, [1812]

DAVIDSON, ALEXANDER, born in 1800, son of Thomas Davidson {1758-1846}, died in Savannah, Georgia, on 25 December 1825. [Kilbride g/s, Isle of Arran]

DAVIDSON, DUNCAN, granted 10,000 acres in East Florida in 1767. [PCCol.V.590]

DAVIDSON, EDWARD, possibly baptised 1 July 1721 son of Francis Davidson and Janet Farquhar in Inverness-shire, a 5 year indentured servant, embarked from Inverness on the Two Brothers, Captain William Thomson, for Georgia on 19 November 1737, arrived on 14 January 1738.[ESG#12]

DAVIDSON, HENRY, granted 10,000 acres in East Florida in 1767. [PC.Col.V.590]

DAVIDSON, JAMES, born in Scotland 1805, a planter, settled in De Soto parish, Louisiana, by 1850. [C]

DAVIDSON, JOHN, born in Scotland 1801, a planter, settled in De Soto parish, Louisiana, by 1850. [C]

DAVIDSON, JOHN, born in Scotland during 1800, a farmer, wife Margaret born in Scotland 1808, settled in Cocke County, Tennessee. [C]

DAVIDSON, ROBERT T., born 1793, died in Texas on 30 June 1838. [Anwoth, Kirkcudbrightshire, g/s]

DAVIDSON, WILLIAM, born in Kilmarnock, Ayrshire, died in Georgia on 14 December 1801. [Colonial Museum and Savannah Advertiser, 18.12.1801][GaGaz#3/3]

DAVIDSON, ..., in Fredericia, Georgia, in 1737. [SPC.1737.596]

DAWSON, THOMAS, servant to Patrick Houston, arrived in Georgia on 1 August 1734, possibly on the snow Hope of Leith, Captain Greig. [ESG#70]

DAWSON, WILLIAM, granted 100 acres in St John's parish, Georgia, on 3 January 1775. [Grant Book M.868]

DAWSON, WILLIAM, from Perth, a minister in Pensacola, West Florida, cnf 17April 1770 Edinburgh. [NAS.CC8.8.121]

DAWSON, WILLIAM ALFRED, from Mobile, Alabama, married Jane Ogilvy, second daughter of Sir William Ogilvy of Carnousie, Banffshire, in Edinburgh, on 12 August 1842. [AJ#4936]

DEMPSTER, GEORGE, servant to Patrick Houston, arrived in Georgia on 1 August 1734, possibly on the snow Hope of Leith, Captain Greig, died in August 1738. [ESG#70]

DEMPSTER, GEORGE, a cooper and indentured servant, absconded from his master W. Stirling in June 1734. [SCGaz#22]

DEMPSTER, GEORGE, granted 20,000 acres of land in West Florida in 1766. [PC.Col.V.593]

DEMPSTER, JAMES, born in Cupar, Fife, during 1760, died in Savannah on 19 October 1802. [Colonial Museum and Savannah Advertiser: 10.12.1802][Georgia g/s]

DENHOLM, ROBERT, merchant in Savannah, son of James Denholm of Birthwood and Jean Weir, [refers to his brother and executor John Denham a bookseller in London; John Newal of Barsheugh; John Syme WS; James Denham of Birthwood, his wife Jean Weir, and their children John, Thomas, Alexander, David and Jean; Neil Stewart mason and builder in Causewayside, Edinburgh.] cnf 11 December 1786 Edinburgh. [NAS.CC8.8.127/1]

DENNESTONE, JAMES, granted 500 acres in Georgia in October 1751. [PRO.CO5/669]

DENNY, WALTER, (?), planter in southern Georgia in 1741, [CRG#30.343]; land grant in Vernonburgh, parish of Christchurch, Georgia, on 4 December 1759, [CRG#28/1.372][Grant book C, #359]

DENOON, JOHN, born in 1715, an indentured servant, emigrated from Inverness to Georgia on 20 October 1735 on the Prince of Wales, master George Dunbar, arrived on 10 January 1736. [ESG#13]

DICK, JOHN, born in 1761, a laborer, emigrated via Newcastle to Georgia on the Georgia Packet in September 1775, settled in Friendsborough, Georgia. [PRO.T47.9/11]

DICK, WILLIAM, born in 1799, son of William Dick {1765-1816} a machinemaker in Dundee, and Euphemia Drummond {1771-1835}, died in Montgomery, Alabama, in January 1832. [Dundee, Howff, g/s]

DICKSON, ALEXANDER, former Major of the 16th Regiment, attorney for his father David Dickson, for 6,000 acres at Houma Chita on the Mississippi in 1774. [PRO.CO5.613.257]

DICKSON, DAVID, of Hartree, Peeblesshire, former Captain of the 64th Foot, granted 6,000 acres at Houma Chita on the Mississippi before 1774. [PRO.CO5.613.257]

DOIG, ALEXANDER, born in Scotland in 1820, an engineer, settled in Alabama. [C]

DOIG, WILLIAM, born in 1779, a house carpenter, died on 21 September 1807. [Savannah Death Register]

DON, JOHN, born in Edinburgh in 1771, died in Augusta, Georgia, on 10 August 1810. [Augusta Chronicle, 11.8.1810]

DONALD, Mrs ANNE, died in New Orleans on 1 May 1858. [Howff g/s, Dundee]

DONALD, JAMES, a Scottish Loyalist from Virginia petitioned the Council of West Florida for land on the Pearl River on 26 December 1776, [PRO.CO5.634]; a merchant in St Augustine, East Florida, trading to the Mississippi, on 31 October 1776. [NAS.NRAS.0159.C4]

DONALD, ROBERT, a Scottish Loyalist from Virginia, petitioned the Council of West Florida for land on the Pearl River, West Florida, on 26 December 1776, [PRO.CO5.634]; a merchant in Pensacola, West Florida, then in Ayr, cnf 10 February 1791 Glasgow

DONALD, W., born in Scotland in 1813, settled in Adams County, Mississippi. [C]

DONALDSON, GEORGE, in Mobile around July 1767. [NLS#MS119]

DONALDSON, ROBERT, from Fyvie, Aberdeenshire, a planter in St Andrew's parish, Georgia. pro.10 October 1769 Georgia, (will refers to wife Christian, his sister Margaret Jamieson in Fyvie, executors Robert Baillie and George McIntosh)

DONAN, A., a blacksmith, born in Scotland in 1814, son S.F. born in Mississippi in 1849, settled in Adams County, Mississippi. [C]

DOUGLAS, COLIN, of Mains, died in Sunbury, Georgia, on 28 April 1820. [S.4.173][EA#5890]

DOUGLAS, COLIN, a raftman, born in Scotland in 1815, settled in Warren County, Mississippi. [C]

DOUGLAS, DAVID, granted a lot in Savannah in 1736, a settler in Georgia on 9 December 1738, [AGA#59]; settled on the Ogeechee River by 1739, later petitioned for land on Wilmington Island [PRO.CO.5/667], possibly in Charleston, SC, in 1741. [ESG#72]

DOUGLAS, DAVID, Justice of the Peace in Augusta, Georgia, on 2 March 1758, [PRO.CO5/646, C16]; land grant of 500 acres in St George parish, Georgia, on 7 July 1761.[PRO.CO.5.648, E46] [CRG#28/1.361]; at Morton Hall, near Savannah, in July 1763, died on his plantation on 9 October 1763. [Ga.Gaz.#15/28]; in Augusta, pro.19 December 1763 Georgia

DOUGLAS, GEORGE, born in 1713, a laborer, an indentured servant, embarked from Inverness on the Loyal Judith Captain John Lemon, for Georgia on 21 September 1741, arrived on 4 December 1741, with wife Margaret Monro born in 1712, and daughter Isabel born in 1739. [PRO.CO.5.668][ESG#14][CRG.30.197/199]

DOUGLAS, JANET, sister of David Douglas, possibly in Savannah in 1736. [ESG#72]

DOUGLAS, JOHN, born in 1755, a gardener, emigrated via Newcastle to Georgia on the Georgia Packet in September 1775, settled in Friendsborough, Georgia. [PRO.T47.9/11]

DOUGLASS, JOHN, formerly in St Augustine, East Florida, late in Crooked Island, Bahamas, pro June 1820 PCC

DOUGLAS, JOHN, born in Scotland in 1823, a merchant, settled in Mobile, Alabama. [C]

DOUGLAS, JOHN, born in Scotland in 1822, a clerk, settled in Alabama. [C]

DOUGLAS, SAMUEL, probably from Galloway, formerly in Savannah, Georgia, late of Jamaica, pro. April 1823 PCC [reference to William Douglass, Samuel McClymont, Hugh McClymont, Samuel Douglass, James Gordon, Alexander Gordon, Reverend James Black in Penningham, Wigtownshire, Reverend John Sibbald in Kirkmabreck, Kirkcudbrightshire, and William McCulloch]

DOUGLAS, WILLIAM, servant to Patrick Tailfer, arrived in Georgia on 1 August 1734, possibly on the snow Hope of Leith, Captain Greig. [ESG#72]; a surgeon and an indentured servant to Dr Patrick

Tailfer in Georgia, found murdered on 9 November 1735. [SCGaz#100]

DOUGLASS, WILLIAM, born in Scotland 1795, a merchant, Mary born in Scotland 1815, William born in Scotland 1842, Narcissa born in Louisiana 1844, and Alexander born in Alabama 1848, settled in Autauga County, Alabama. [C]

DOUGLAS, Lieutenant Colonel ...., granted 10,000 acres of land in West Florida instead of land in East Florida, in 1776. [PC.Col.V.594]

DOW, ROBERT, born on 26 May 1753, son of Reverend Robert Dow {1707-1787} and Janet Adie, a physician from Greenock, Renfrewshire, later in New Orleans, in 1843. [NAS.SH][F.3.79]

DOWAN, J., born in Scotland in 1800, settled in Adams County, Mississippi. [C]

DOWNIE, DAVID, settled in Augusta, Georgia, in 1796, died there on 25 December 1816. [Augusta Chronicle: 1.1.1817]

DREGHORN, ROBERT, second son of Allan and Elisabeth Dreghorn in Govan, Lanarkshire, baptised in parish of Glasgow, on 7 August 1796, a merchant in Savannah, died in Savannah, Georgia, on 22 July 1823. [BM.14.374][EA.][Glasgow OPR]

DRON, WILLIAM, baptised on 17 September 1812 son of William Dron and Mary MacIntosh in Auchtermuchty, Fife, emigrated to USA in 1839, died in Augusta, Georgia, on 4 July 1879. [Fife Herald, 31.7.1879]

DRUMMOND, ANDREW, born in Scotland in 1818, settled in Warren County, Mississippi. [C]

DRUMMOND, DAVID, a mariner in Savannah pro.17 July 1771. Georgia

DRUMMOND, WALTER, born in 1765, to USA in 1801, a millwright in Savannah 1812, [1812]

DRYDEN, ADAM, born in 1746, a gardener and indentured servant, emigrated via Whitby, Yorkshire, to Savannah, Georgia, on the Marlborough in August 1774, an indentured servant of Thomas Brown there. [PRO.T47.9/11][PRO.AO13.34.123-4]

DRYSDALE, JAMES, servant of Hugh Anderson in Georgia around 1740. [ESG#72]

DUFF, ARCHIBALD, Advocate General of the Court of Admiralty of East Florida, 1774-. [Mowat#165]

DUNBAR, Captain GEORGE, granted 500 acres in Georgia on 3 September 1735, also on 28 May 1748. [PRO.CO.5.668.283/6; CO.5.670.219]; son of James Dunbar, a merchant in Inverness, and Janet Dunbar; settled in Josephstown, Georgia, in 1733; master of the Prince of Wales which brought colonists from Inverness to Georgia in the 1730s; in Savannah on 25 June 1738, [PRO.CO5.640.126]; signed a treaty with the Creek Indians in 1739; Lieutenant of Oglethorpe's Regiment in 1741; executor of Sir Patrick Houstoun in 1762; land grant in Christchurch, Georgia, on 2 October 1759, [CRG#28/1.311][Grant book B, #275] [ESG#72]

DUNBAR, JOHN, born in 1705, a farmer in Inverness, emigrated from Inverness on the Prince of Wales, Captain George Dunbar, on 20 October 1735, arrived in Georgia on 10 January 1736, died in 1740. [ESG#72]

DUNBAR, JOHN, granted a lot in Savannah, went to England in December 1737. [ESG#72]

DUNBAR, JOHN, settler in Louisiana on 23 February 1764. [GaGaz#47]; in Pensacola during May 1766. [NLS#MS119]

DUNBAR, JOHN, merchant in Sunbury, Georgia, in 1769, [NAS.CS16.1.138]; son of George Dunbar of Leuchold, died in Sunbury, Georgia, on 19 June 1768. [SM#30.503][NAS.CS16.1.138]

DUNBAR, MARGARET, servant to William Bradley in Georgia around 1740. [ESG#72]

DUNBAR, PRISCILLA, baptised on 31 October 1711 in Inverness, daughter of James Dunbar, a merchant, and Janet Dunbar, emigrated from Inverness on 18 October 1735 on the Prince of Wales, Captain George Dunbar, to Georgia, landed at the Altamaha River in February 1736, married Sir Patrick Houstoun in 1741, died on 26 February 1775.Will, subscribed to on 10 June 1772, refers to daughter Ann, wife of George MacIntosh, eldest son Patrick, Miss Anne Stuart, sons James and John, Johnston and Simpson merchants in Charleston, witnesses Thomas Ross, James Simpson, William Ross and James Beverley, pro.9 March 1775 Georgia. [GaGaz.,17.5.1775] [Christ Church g/s][Inverness OPR]

DUNBAR, WILLIAM, born in 1749 in Morayshire, son of Sir Archibald Dunbar {1693-1769} and Anne Bain, educated in Aberdeen emigrated to Philadelphia, Pennsylvania, in 1771, an Indian trader at Fort Pitt, later a planter in Florida, Louisiana, finally a planter and merchant in Natchez, Adams County, Mississippi, and correspondent of the American Philosophical Society, husband of Dinah Clark, died there in 1810. [UNC.William Dunbar pp, MS#231] [NAS.GD188.12.5]

DUNCAN, ALEXANDER, Clerk of Common Pleas in West Florida in 1766, [PRO.CO324.51.285]; granted 20,000 acres in West Florida in 1767. [PC.Col.V.593]

DUNCAN, ALEXANDER, born in 1821 eldest son of Reverend Alexander Duncan minister of the Associated Congregation of Original Seceders in Dundee, died in Savannah, USA, on 23 September 1842. [AJ#4951]

DUNCAN, DONALD SHAW, baptised on 19 March 1804 in the parish of Greenock West, Renfrewshire, son of James Duncan a merchant in Greenock, {died 1823} and Elizabeth Shaw {died 1806}, settled in St Louis, Mississippi. [Greenock g/s]

DUNCAN, GEORGE, emigrated from Inverness to Georgia on the Two Brothers, Captain William Thomson, in July 1737, landed in Savannah, Georgia, on 16 November 1737. [PRO.CO.5.690.169][SPC.44.153]

DUNCAN, GEORGE, born in 1703, a 4 year indentured servant, embarked for Georgia on 19 November 1737, arrived there on 14 January 1738. [ESG#14]

DUNCAN, JAMES, baptised in Balmerino, Fife, on 3 May 1772, son of William Duncan, a wright in Gauldry, and Agnes Sime, died in Savannah, America, in 1798. [Kilmany, Fife, g/s]

DUNCAN, JOHN, servant to Patrick Houston, possibly emigrated from Leith on the snow Hope of Leith, Captain Greig, arrived in Georgia on 1 August 1734, later a servant to A. Johnson on 21 January 1735. [ESG#72]

DUNCAN, JOHN, in New Hanover, south of the Altamaha River, Georgia, in 1759. [CRG#28/1.189]

DUNCAN, ROBERT, born in 1790, a mariner, died in Georgia on 12 September 1804. [Savannah Death Register]

DUNCAN, THOMAS, a raftman, born in Scotland in 1820, settled in Warren County, Mississippi. [C]

DUNCAN, Sir WILLIAM, 20,000 acre land grant before 1776.[PCCol]

DUNCANSON, WILLIAM, an Anglican minister sent to Georgia in 1761, appointed to Christchurch parish, in Savannah in June 1762. [SPCK pp. London: American MS 11231, #52][FPA,26.3.1763]

DUPRAS, Mrs CHRISTINE, born in Scotland in 1810, settled in Alabama before 1834. [C]

DYSON, DUNBAR SMITH, born in Kirkcudbrightshire in 1806, settled in New York by 1831, died in New Orleans on 22 December 1848. [ANY.2.27]

EATTON, MARGARET, wife of Richard Floyd, in Christchurch, Georgia, in 1774. [NAS.SH]

EATTON, THOMAS, (?), land grant in Savannah on 27 November 1761, [CRG#28/1.371][Grant book C, #353; Grant book D, #353]

EDMONDS, JAMES, born in Govan, Lanarkshire, in 1794, baptised on 5 June 1794 in parish of Glasgow, son of James Edmonds and Elisabeth Dreghorn, died in Georgia on 2 November 1821. [Augusta Herald, 6.11.1821][Glasgow OPR]

EDWARD, JAMES, in Natchez, married Charlotte Bruen Farrand, eldest daughter of James Farrand of New York, in New York on 2 September 1839. [EEC#19963]

EKSON, Mrs SARAH, born in Scotland in 1826, husband Captain H. Ekson born in Switzerland in 1822, settled in Mobile, Alabama. [C]

ELIBANK, Lord PATRICK, landowner in West Florida in 1766. [NAS.GD32.25.109]

ELLIOT, ANDREW, formerly in Senegambia, late of Savannah, pro. January 1775 PCC?

ELLIOT, JAMES, born in 1739, a husbandman and an indentured servant, with his wife, emigrated via Whitby to Savannah on the Marlborough in August 1774, a servant of Thomas Brown there. [PRO.T47.9/11][PRO.AO13.34.123-4]

ELLIOT, JOHN, Governor of West Florida, died in June 1769. [SM#21.391]?

ELLIOT, JOHN, born in 1803, from Kelso, Roxburghshire, died in Tuscumba, Alabama, on 21 September 1839. [EEC#19976]

ELPHINSTONE, WILLIAM, an apothecary, with wife Anne, embarked on 28 September 1733, arrived on 14 January 1734, dead by 27 January 1734. [ESG#14]

EUNSON, GEORGE, baptised on 27 January 1756 in Kirkwall, son of John Eunson and Isabel Johnston, a shoemaker in Kirkwall, emigrated from Kirkwall, Orkney, to Savannah, Georgia, on the Marlborough,Captain George Prissick, in September 1774, settled in Richmond County, Georgia, as an indentured servant to Thomas Brown. [PRO.AO13.34.123-4] [PRO.T47.12]

EWAN, WILLIAM, an indentured servant, arrived in Georgia in 1735, granted 50 acres on Skidoway Island, in 1737, [PRO.CO5.639.225]; a settler in Georgia on 9 December 1738, [AGA#59]; land grant in Little Ogeechee on 28 March 1758, [Grant book A, #592]; land grant in Darien on 28 March 1758, [CRG#28/1.237]; vendue master in 1760. [CRG#28/1.276]; land grants in St George's parish on 3 November 1761, in Christchurch on 3 August 1762, in Savannah on 7 September 1762, [CRG#28/1.367, 434, 437] [Grant book A, #591; Grant book D, #177/201/219]

EWING, ALEXANDER, born in 1846 son of James Lindsay Ewing, died in Mobile on 8 February 1849. [AJ#5283][EEC#21792]

EWING, ALEXANDER, born in Scotland in 1813, a merchant, wife Roberta and daughter Mary born in Alabama, settled in Mobile. [C]

EWING, JOHN, an indentured servant, emigrated via Gravesend on the Mary Ann, Captain Thomas Shubrick, to Georgia on 13 August 1737, [PRO.CO5.639.325/327]

EWING, J.L., born in Scotland in 1815, a merchant, wife Martha and son James born in Alabama, settled in Alabama. [C]

EWING, MARGARET, born in Scotland in 1820, settled in Mobile, Alabama. [C]

EWING, ROBERT, born in Glasgow in 1796, died in Georgia on 18 July 1824. [Georgia Republican: 27.7.1824][possibly baptised on 1 December 1793 in parish of Barony, Glasgow, son of Alexander Ewing and Margaret Robertson, {Barony OPR}]

EWING, W., born in Scotland in 1800, a clerk, settled in Alabama. [C]

FACHRIE, JAMES, born in Greenock, Renfrewshire, in 1773, a ship's captain, died in Savannah, Georgia, on 17 July 1809. [Savannah Death Register]

FADER (?), ALEXANDER, born in Scotland in 1832, a laborer, settled in Jefferson County, Mississippi. [C]

FAIRLEY, JAMES, a merchant in Virginia then in Pensacola, in 1781. [NAS.CS16.1.181]

FALCONER, JOHN, in Mobile, 1766. [NLS#MS119]

FALCONER, WILLIAM, a storekeeper at Coles Creek, Natchez, who died at New Feliciano, born in Logie, Aberdeenshire, son of Sylvester Falconer, pro.17 November 1794 Natchez, [refers to brother Cosmo Falconer in Edinburgh, George Fitzgerald and David Ross merchants in Natchez, his executors]

FARRELL, Mrs MATILDA, born in Scotland in 1828, wife of Edward Farrell an upholsterer born in Ireland in 1828, settled in Alabama. [C]

FARLEY, SARAH, formerly in Edinburgh, then in Savannah, Georgia, pro. October 1814 PCC [reference to Robert Cooper, Sarah Drysdale, Elizabeth Irvine, and Rachel Johnston]

FARQUHAR, GEORGE, emigrated to Savannah, Georgia, on the snow Kinnoull, Captain Alexander Alexander, allocated 100 acres between the Savannah and Saludy Rivers by the Council of Georgia on 30 May 1768. [GaCouncil Journal#34.148/151]

FARQUHARSON, ROBERT, born in 1777, son of James Farquharson in Ballintruan, Banffshire, died in Nashville, Tennessee, on 28 June 1856. [Inveravon g/s]

FAWCETT, CHARLES, born in 1781, a seaman, died on 10 October 1805. [Savannah Death Register]

FENTON, JAMES, granted 10,000 acres in East Florida in 1767. [PC.Col.V.590]

FENTON, RICHARD, born in 1748, a canvas weaver, with his wife and children, emigrated via Whitby to Savannah on the Marlborough in August 1774, [PRO.T47.9/11]

FERGUSON, ALEXANDER, of Craigdarroch, purchased Skiddoway Island, parish of Christchurch, Georgia, in Glasgow June 1775. [NAS.GD77.168]

FERGUSON, ANN, born in Scotland in 1820, settled in Alabama. [C]

FERGUSON, DANIEL, born in 1750, a butcher, died on 2 February 1805. [Savannah Death Register]

FERGUSON, GEORGE, a servant, born in 1724, embarked in Inverness on the Two Brothers, Captain William Thomson, for Georgia in July 1737, arrived on 20 November 1737. [ESG#15]

FERGUSON, HENRY, St George, Georgia, Loyalist in 1783. [PRO.AO13.34.479]

FERGUSON, HENRY, youngest son of Archibald Ferguson, 22 St James Square, Edinburgh, died in New Orleans, on 22 October 1859. [CM#21904][possibly baptised on 21 March 1839 in the parish of St Cuthbert's, Edinburgh, son of Archibald Ferguson and Agnes Anderson, {St Cuthbert's OPR}]

FERGUSON, ISABEL, in Goose Creek, Winchester District, South County, Tennessee, sister of John Ferguson in Kilbride, Ayrshire, in 1815. [NAS.NRAS.0396]

FERGUSON, JAMES, born 1789, emigrated to USA in 1807, a grazier in Attakapas, Louisiana. [1812]

FERGUSON, JAMES, from Texas, married Marie, daughter of Gottfried H.Heslet, in Stuttgart, Germany, on 28 October 1848. [EEC#21735]

FERGUSON, MARY, born in Scotland in 1821, settled in Montgomery County, Georgia. [C]

FERGUSON, ROBERT, son of Robert Ferguson a mason in Duns, Berwickshire, settled in New Orleans before 1 June 1848. [NAS.SH]

FERGUSON, ROBERT OLIPHANT, born 1824, late of Thornhill, Muthill, Perthshire, died in New Blaufels, Texas, on 22 August 1850, his infant daughter Euphemia died there on 6 September 1850. [EEC#22034]

FERGUSON, THOMAS, a servant, arrived in Georgia on 8 June 1737. [ESG#73]

FERGUSON, THOMAS, born 1783, emigrated to USA in 1805, a grazier in Attakapas, Louisiana. [1812]

FERGUSON, WALTER, a brickmaker, born in Scotland in 1829, wife Tabitha born in Tennessee in 1824, settled in Warren County, Mississippi. [C]

FERGUSON, WILLIAM, master of the scout boat in Georgia, around 1740. [ESG#73]

FERGUSON, WILLIAM, born in Scotland in 1787, a planter in Choctaw County, Alabama, son Lewis a laborer born in 1828, daughter Mary born {both born in Mississippi}, children David born in 1829, John born in 1833, George born in 1837, Benjamin born in 1839, and Nancy, {all born in Alabama} [C]

FEVEND{?}, ROBERT, born in Scotland in 1822, a merchant settled in Rodney, Jefferson County, Mississippi. [C]

FINDLAY, ALEXANDER, born in Aberdeen, settled in Savannah in 1767, an Anglican minister appointed to St George's parish, Georgia, in 1770. [SPCK pp, London]; together with James Seymour granted 300 acres in Christ Church parish, Georgia, on 1 August 1769. [Grant book G, #387]

FINLAY, JOHN, servant to William Bradley, emigrated from Inverness to Georgia on 20 October 1735 on the Prince of Wales, master George Dunbar, arrived in February 1736. [ESG#15]

FINDLAY, KENNETH, born in 1763, died in Tuscaloosa in 1828. [Macon Telegraph: 11.2.1828]

FINDLAY, ROBERT, and company, trading from Glasgow on the Orangefield with Pensacola, West Florida, 1777. [JCTP]

FINDLAY, ROBERT, born on 17 January 1808 at Water of Leith, Edinburgh, emigrated via Liverpool to New York on the America in 1828, settled in Philadelphia as a joiner, moved to Georgia in 1838, died in Macon County, Georgia, in November 1859. [SGen.36.4.140]

FINDLAY, THOMAS, born in 1813, son of James Findlay {1780-1852} and Barbara Marshall {1794-1868}, died in New Orleans in 1840. [Aberdeen, St Clement's, g/s]

FINLAY, WILLIAM ACHISON, writer, embarked for Georgia on 11 September 1733, arrived there on 16 December 1733, settled at Fort Argyll. [ESG#15]; received payment in November 1735. [PRO.CO5.668.194]; a constable among the Creek Indians in 1742, [CRG#30.256]

FINLAYSON, ANGUS, Indian trader in Jacksonville, Telfair County, Georgia, on 1 September 1821. [Telfair County Debt Suits Book BB]

FINLAYSON, JOHN, Indian trader in Jacksonville, Telfair County, Georgia, on 1 September 1821. [Telfair County Debt Suits Book BB]

FIRTH, JOHN, from Harra, Orkney, an indentured servant of Thomas Brown in Richmond County, Georgia, in 1783. [PRO.AO13.34]

FISHER, DONALD, son of James Fisher in Kilchrennan, Argyll, emigrated to America in 1816, Principal Instructor of Jefferson College, Washington, Mississippi, 1821-1823, died in Jamaica in 1826. [SGen.1.4.21]

FLEMING, BEATRICE, daughter of ....Fleming and Margaret Boswell in Edinburgh, widow of J. Thomson in Georgia, in 1806. [NAS.SH]

FLEMING, MILLAR, born in Glasgow, a merchant, died in Lexington, Oglethorpe County, Georgia, on 25 September 1810. [Georgia Express: 6.10.1809][EA#4900][probably the Millar Hount Fleming baptised on 1 January 1788 in the parish of Govan, Lanarkshire, son of John Fleming and Margaret Ross, {Govan OPR}]

FLEMING, T.S., born in 1816, died in Nashville, USA, on 15 June 1849. [Buittle, Kirkcudbrightshire, g/s]

FLETCHER, WILLIAM, from Edinburgh, settled in Augusta, Georgia, died in 1836, cnf.1856. [NAS.SC70.1.90]

FLETT, C.L., born in Scotland in 1813, a clerk, settled in Alabama. [C]

FLOYD, Mrs MARGARET, wife of Richard Floyd in Christchurch, Georgia, in 1774. [NAS.SH]

FLOOD, SOPHIA, born in Scotland in 1790, settled in Mobile, Alabama. [C]

FLUCKER, MARY, born in Scotland in 1818, settled in Alabama. [C]

FOGG, JOHN, a merchant, born in Scotland in 1823, settled in Adams County, Mississippi. [C]

FORBES, C.G., in Mobile in 1844. [NAS.GD121.114]

FORBES, DONALD, soldier of the Black Watch, imprisoned in the Tower of London on a charge of mutiny, transferred to Oglethorpe's Regiment in Georgia in 1743, settled in Georgia. [GHS, Cate Colln. 45/3172]

FORBES, HUGH, absconded from his master W. Stirling in June 1734. [SCGaz#22]

FORBES, HUGH, servant to William and Hugh Stirling, emigrated from Inverness on the Prince of Wales, Captain George Dunbar, on 20 October 1735, arrived in Georgia on 10 January 1736. [ESG#74]

FORBES, JAMES, a merchant in New York, son of Dr James Forbes in Aberdeen, died on passage from Savannah on 26 September 1818. [AJ#3700][S.2.100]

FORBES, JOHN, born in 1715, a servant to John Cuthbert of Drakies, settled in Georgia. [ESG#74]

FORBES, JOHN, late a merchant in Charleston, died in Savannah on 22 March 1775. [GaGaz#2/2]

FORBES, Reverend JOHN, eldest son of Archibald Forbes of Deskrie, Aberdeenshire, graduated from King's College, Aberdeen, an Anglican minister in St Augustine, East Florida, 1764-1783; married Dorothy Murray on 2 February 1769, father of James Grant Forbes, John Murray Forbes, and Ralph Bennett Forbes; Judge of the Admiralty Court of East Florida 1771-1776, appointed member of the Council of East Florida on 7 June 1771, Acting Chief Justice of East Florida 1776-1779, died on 17 September 1783. [PC.Col.V.564][Mowat#162/165/166] [EMA#28][HF] [APC.Col.1766-1783#564][JCTP#84.138]

FORBES, JOHN, baptised on 20 December 1767 son of James Forbes and Sarah Gordon in Gamrie, Banffshire, emigrated to St Augustine, East Florida, in 1784, partner in Panton, Leslie and Company, Indian traders in Florida, pro.2 October 1820 Mobile. [Will Book 1, Mobile County Court House]

FORBES, THOMAS, son of James Forbes and Sarah Gordon in Gamrie, Banffshire, an Indian trader in East Florida, partner in firm of Panton, Forbes and Company of St Augustine, East Florida, in 1775, a Loyalist, settled in Nassau, the Bahamas, in 1783, married Elizabeth Ann Yonge on 9 July 1789, he died in Nassau on 13 February 1808. [IT#21] [GM#78.364]

FORBES, WILLIAM, a farmer, born in Scotland 1770, settled in Gadsden County, Florida. [C]

FORREST, JAMES, born in 1778, baptised on 28 January 1778 in the parish of Annan, eldest son of John Forrest and Janet Turnbull in Annan, Dumfriesshire, died in Savannah, Georgia, on 5 February 1820. [EA.5876.175][Anwoth g/s][Annan OPR]

FORREST, MARY, born 1839, daughter of Robert Forrest, died in New Orleans during 1853. [Carluke, Lanarkshire, g/s]

FORRESTER, JOHN, an Episcopalian householder in St Augustine, East Florida, in 1787. [1787 Census of St Augustine]

FORRESTER, ROBERT, born in Scotland 1815, a teacher, Margaret born in Mississippi in 1822, Arabella born in Mississippi 1845, and John born in Mississippi in 1848, settled in Wayne County, Mississippi. [C]

FORSYTH, CATHERINE, born in 1722, a 4 year indentured servant, embarked for Georgia on 19 November 1737, arrived there on 14 January 1738, dead by 1741. [ESG#16]

FORSYTH, MARGARET, born in 1721, a 4 year indentured servant, embarked for Georgia on 19 November 1737, arrived there on 14 January 1738. [ESG#16]

FORSYTH, WILLIAM, soldier of the Black Watch, imprisoned in the
    Tower of London on a charge of mutiny, transferred to
    Oglethorpe's Regiment in Georgia in 1743, transferred to an
    Independent Company there in 1749, settled in Georgia. [GHS,
    Cate Colln. 45/3172]

FORTH, JOHN, from Harra, Orkney, an indentured servant who
    embarked on the Marlborough, Captain Thomas Walker, in
    Kirkwall bound for Georgia in September 1775.
    [PRO.AO13.34.123-4]

FOSTER, GEORGE, emigrated from Inverness to Savannah, Georgia, on
    the Two Brothers, Captain William Thomson, in July 1737, arrived
    in November 1737, settled in Fredericia, Georgia. [SPC.43.161]

FRASER, ALEXANDER, soldier of the Black Watch, imprisoned in the
    Tower of London on a charge of mutiny, transferred to
    Oglethorpe's Regiment in Georgia in 1743. [GHS, Cate Colln.
    45/3172]

FRASER, ALEXANDER, Lieutenant and Adjutant of the 71st Regiment,
    died in Savannah, Georgia, {brother Thomas Fraser at Dalcaitick,
    Scotland}, pro. December 1783 PCC

FRASER, ANNE, born in 1706, a 4 year indentured servant, embarked
    for Georgia on 19 November 1737, arrived on 14 January 1738.
    [ESG#16]

FRASER, CATHERINE, born in 1725, a 4 year indentured servant,
    embarked for Georgia on 19 November 1737, arrived on 14
    January 1738. [ESG#16]

FRASER, DONALD, servant to A. Johnson, arrived in Georgia on 7 May
    1734. [ESG#74]

FRASER, DONALD, of Abercour, servant to Patrick Grant, emigrated
    from Inverness on the Prince of Wales, Captain George Dunbar, on
    20 October 1735, arrived in Georgia on 10 January 1736.[ESG#74]

FRASER, DONALD, born in 1721, from Inverness, servant to Alexander Macintosh, emigrated from Inverness on the Prince of Wales, Captain George Dunbar, on 20 October 1735, arrived in Georgia on 10 January 1736. [ESG#74]

FRASER, DONALD, born in 1719, from Inverness, a servant to John Cuthbert of Drakies, emigrated from Inverness on the Prince of Wales, Captain George Dunbar, on 20 October 1735, arrived in Georgia on 10 January 1736. [ESG#74]

FRASER, DONALD, born in 1716, from Kingussie, Inverness-shire, servant to John Macintosh, emigrated from Inverness on the Prince of Wales, Captain George Dunbar, on 20 October 1735, arrived in Georgia on 10 January 1736. [ESG#74]

FRASER, DONALD, settled in Georgia by 1768, Customs Collector of Sunbury, Georgia, Loyalist, settled in Jamaica by 1783. [PRO.AO.P13.35.80/101]

FRASER, DONALD, born in Inverness-shire in 1781, died in 1827, buried in Midway Cemetery, Georgia. [Midway g/s]

FRASER, GEORGE, a planter in Abercorn, Georgia, pro. 30 July 1755 Georgia

FRASER, GEORGE, a physician in Savannah, pro.15 December 1775 Georgia

FRASER, HENRIETTA, born in 1725, a 5 year indentured servant, embarked for Georgia on 19 November 1737, arrived on 14 January 1738. [ESG#17]

FRASER, HUGH, a tailor, an indentured servant, embarked on 15 June 1733, arrived on 29 August 1733, dead by January 1738 [ESG17]; a settler in Georgia 9 December 1738, [AGA#59]

FRASER, HUGH, born 1722, a 5 year indentured servant, embarked on 19 November 1737, arrived on 14 January 1738. [ESG#17]

FRASER, HUGH, a planter in southern Georgia in 1741, [CRG#30.344]

FRASER, JAMES, soldier of the Black Watch, imprisoned in the Tower of London on a charge of mutiny, transferred to Oglethorpe's Regiment in Georgia in 1743. [GHS, Cate Colln. 45/3172]

FRASER, JAMES, in Augusta, Georgia, storekeeper for Mr William Yeoman of Charlestown, South Carolina, in 1749. [PRO.CO.5.668.305]; appointed Conservator of the Peace in Augusta, Georgia, on 16 July 1750. [PRO.CO.5.669.28]

FRASER, JAMES, born in Greenock, Renfrewshire, in 1759, died in Darien, Georgia, on 18 December 1828. [Georgia Republican, 29.12.1828]

FRASER, JAMES, born in 1793, to USA in 1807, a merchant in Augusta 1812, [1812]

FRASER, JANET, born in 1723, a 4 year indentured servant, embarked for Georgia on 19 November 1737, arrived on 14 January 1738, at Darien on 6 May 1741. [ESG#17]

FRASER, JOHN, born in 1720, an indentured servant, embarked in Inverness on the Two Brothers, Captain William Thomson, for Georgia in July 1737, arrived on 20 November 1737, a servant in Darien on 6 May 1741. [ESG#17]

FRASER, JOHN, born in 1713, an indentured servant, embarked in Inverness on the Two Brothers, Captain William Thomson, for Georgia in July 1737, arrived on 20 January 1737. [ESG#17]

FRASER, Reverend JOHN, a graduate of Edinburgh University, an Anglican minister in East Florida in 1769, died in New Smyrna, East Florida, in 1772. [FPA#308][Mowat#166]

FRASER, JOHN, on St Simon's Island, Georgia, Royal Marines Lieutenant on half pay, husband of Mrs Anne Sarah Fraser, pro. January 1841 PCC

FRASER, MARGARET, at Darien, Georgia, on 6 May 1741. [ESG#17]

FRASER, SIMON, land grant of 150 acres in St Andrews parish, Georgia, on 3 February 1762. [CRG#28/1.416] [PRO.CO.5.648.E68]

FRASER, Major SIMON, born in 1758, fought in the Revolution, died in Liberty County, Georgia, on 26 October 1812. [Savannah Republican: 5.11.1812]

FRASER, SIMON, son of Alexander Fraser the Sheriff-Clerk of Haddingtonshire {now East Lothian}, died in Gibsonport, Mississippi, on 23 October 1819. [EA#5853.423][AJ#3757][S.2.100]

FRASER, THOMAS, servant to Patrick Houston, possibly emigrated from Leith on the snow Hope of Leith, Captain Greig, arrived in Georgia on on 1 August 1734, in Georgia in 1746. [ESG#74]

FRASER, THOMAS, granted 2 lots and 50 acres of land in Vernonburgh, Georgia, on 4 December 1759. [Grant book B, #278/339] [PRO.CO.5.648.E28][CRG#28/1.317]

FRASER, WILLIAM, servant of A. Johnson, arrived in Georgia on 7 May 1734. [ESG#74]

FRASER, WILLIAM, soldier of the Black Watch, imprisoned in the Tower of London on a charge of mutiny, transferred to Oglethorpe's Regiment in Georgia in 1743. [GHS, Cate Colln. 45/3172]

FRASER, Dr WILLIAM, died in Darien, Georgia, in 1828. [Statesman and Patriot: 10.1.1829]

FRASER, ..., an Indian trader, killed while travelling to Mobile in 1768. [GaGaz#3/1]

FULTON, SAMUEL, granted 900 acres of land in St Andrews parish, Georgia, on 3 February 1762. [PRO.CO.5.648.E67][CRG#28/1.416]

FYFFE, ALEXANDER, a storekeeper and Indian trader in Savannah on 11 June 1761, [SCGaz#1406]; a merchant in Savannah, youngest son of James Fyffe of Dron, near Dundee, died in Charleston, South Carolina, in May 1766, [GaGaz#1/1]; pro. 29 December 1766 Georgia. [refers to sisters Magdalene and Elizabeth Fyffe in Dundee, his executors: nephew James, son of John Fyffe merchant in Dundee; Patrick Crighton NP in Dundee; George Johnson; James Anderson NP, witnesses Robert Dick, James Jobson and William Smith all writers in Dundee][Ga.Gaz.#13, 271]

FYFFE, ELIZABETH, from Dundee, settled in St George's parish, Georgia, by 14 November 1777. [GSA: Misc. Bonds KK2.489]

FYFFE, MAGDALENE, from Dundee, settled in St George's parish, Georgia, by 14 November 1777. [GSA: Misc. Bonds KK2.489]

FYFFE, RACHEL, servant to Patrick Houston, possibly emigrated on the snow Hope of Leith, Captain Greig, arrived in Georgia on 1 August 1734. [ESG#74]

GAIRDNER, JAMES, born in Edinburgh in 1761, baptised on 4 May 1764 in the parish of St Cuthbert's, Edinburgh, son of Andrew Gairdner a merchant in Edinburgh and Rebecca Penman, married Mary Gordon, emigrated to Charleston, South Carolina, in 1780, a cotton planter in Georgia, died in 1830. [BLG#2696][NAS.SH][St Cuthbert's OPR]

GALBRAITH, ELIZABETH, married John Turner of Savannah, Georgia, in Luss, Dunbartonshire, on 17 August 1821. [EA#6025.127]

GALLOWAY, A., in Savannah, Georgia, around 1854. [NAS.NRAS.0744.39.15]

GALLOWAY, ALEXANDER, in Jackson, Mississippi, in 1858. [NAS.NRAS#0744.55/25, 26]

GALLOWAY, DAVID, in Savannah, Georgia, in 1854.
[NAS.NRAS#0744.39.15]

GALLOWAY, JAMES, a settler in Georgia on 9 December 1738,
[AGA#59]
In Savannah around 1740, with wife Elizabeth. [ESG#75]

GANNT, ROBERT, born in Scotland in 1799, a merchant, arrived in
Savannah late 1821 on the ship Pallas Captain Land. [USNA/par]

GARDENER, JAMES, a merchant in Augusta, Georgia, 1811.
[NAS.CS17.1.30/551]

GARDNER, ANNA, daughter of James Gardner, married Joseph P.
McKinne, a merchant in New York, in Augusta, Georgia, in 1813.
[Edinburgh Advertiser#5178.13]

GARDNER, JAMES CORBET, eldest son of James Gardner a perfumer
in Glasgow, died in Mobile on 19 June 1844. [SG#1324]

GARDNER, JAMES OGILVIE, son of James Ogilvie Gardner in
Edinburgh, died in Nashville, Tennessee, in February 1847.
[EEC#21496]

GARDNER, ROBERT, died on 30 July 1791. [Augusta Chronicle:
6.8.1791]

GARDNER, THOMAS, born Glasgow in 1772, baptised on 13
December 1772, son of James Gardner and Margaret Wilson, a
merchant in Savannah, Georgia, died in Sandhills, Augusta,
Georgia, on 20 August 1822. [BM.12.802][Georgia Republican:
27.8.1822][Glasgow OPR]

GARSON, ROBERT, born in 1725, a farm servant in Sandwick, Orkney,
emigrated from Kirkwall to Savannah, Georgia, on the
Marlborough, Captain Thomas Walker, in September 1775, settled
in Richmond County, Georgia, as an indentured servant to Thomas
Brown. [PRO.T47.12][PRO.AO13.34.123-4]

GAYR, GEORGE, servant to Anne Morrison, arrived in Georgia on 15 July 1734, possibly on the snow Hope of Leith, Captain Greig. [ESG#75]

GEDDES, JAMES, born in 1707 in Morayshire, son of Alexander Geddes and Margaret Innes, emigrated to Georgia in 1737. [SG.33.233] Possibly a servant of Edward Jenkins around 1740. [ESG#75]

GEDDES, JAMES, born in 1720, a 4 year indentured servant, embarked for Georgia on 19 November 1737, arrived on 14 January 1738. [ESG#17]

GEDDES, JOHN, born in 1721, a 4 year indentured servant, embarked for Georgia on 19 November 1737, arrived on 14 January 1738. [ESG#17]

GEIKIE, CATHERINE CAROLINA ELEANORA, born 11 August 1807, daughter of James Henry Geikie and Catherine Amelia Gamble, baptised on Colonel's Island, Glynn County, Georgia, on 24 March 1811. [Arbroath OPR]; daughter of James Geikie on St Simon's Island, Georgia, married Jonathan Duncan Gleig HEICS, in Arbroath, Angus, on 5 March 1832. [AJ#4395][FH#525]

GEIKIE, JAMES HENRY, son of William Geikie in Arbroath, Angus, settled in Georgia before 1809. [NAS.SH]; on Colonel's Island, Glynn County, Georgia, 1816. [NAS.CS17.1.35/259,479]

GEIKIE, HENRY, on Colonel's Island, Glynn County, Georgia, 1816. [NAS.CS17.1.37/105]

GIBBON, JAMES S., born in Scotland in 1822, a butcher, settled in Alabama. [C]

GIBBONS, THOMAS, President of the St Andrew's Society of Savannah 1798-1800. [SSS#88]

GIBSON, JAMES TAYLOR, baptised on 8 October 1805 son of John Gibson and Jean Taylor in Linlithgow, West Lothian, member of the firm of John Gibson and Company in New Orleans, died there on 12 February 1849. [SG#1804]

GIBSON, JOHN W., MD, married Martha Louisa Richardson, eldest daughter of Colonel Richardson, a planter in Liberty, Mississippi, there on 20 May 1828. [Scotsman#911.634]

GIBSON, JOHN, born in Scotland in 1805, a merchant, settled in Mobile, Alabama by 1845, married Rubanna born in Alabama in 1823, father of John and James, (both born in Alabama). [C]

GILCHRIST, CHONIE A., born in Scotland, settled in Alabama. [C]

GILCHRIST, WILLIAM, born in Scotland in 1800, a laborer, settled in Mobile, Alabama. [C]

GILES, ALEXANDER, born in 1780, baptised in Edinburgh on 23 June 1780, son of Arthur Giles and Ann Park, settled in New Orleans by 1830, died in 1852. [New Calton g/s][Edinburgh OPR]

GILES, ANNE MOIR, born in New Orleans on 11 March 1838, daughter of James Park Giles {1784-1848} and Ann Potter {1795-1867}, died in Edinburgh on 18 May 1889. [Greyfriars g/s, Edinburgh]

GILES, GRACE FRASER, born in Edinburgh on 4 August 1836, daughter of James Park Giles {1784-1848} and Ann Potter {1795-1867}, died in New Orleans on 11 September 1838. [Greyfriars g/s, Edinburgh]

GILLESPIE, JOHN, born in 1750, a farmer in Doune, Perthshire, emigrated from Greenock, Renfrewshire, to Georgia on the Georgia in July 1775. [PRO.T47.12]

GILLESPIE, THOMAS, born 1755, a farmer in Doune, Perthshire, emigrated from Greenock, Renfrewshire, to Georgia on the Georgia in July 1775. [PRO.T47.12]

GILLIS, DANIEL, born in 1770, emigrated to Wilmington, North Carolina, 1788, settled in Wayne County, Tennessee, before 1824. [NCSA.2.67]

GILLIS, FLORIDA, born in Scotland in 1790, Daniel Gillis, a farmer, born in North Carolina in 1818, and Nancy Gillis born in South Carolina in 1823, settled in Walton County, Florida. [C]

GILLIS, Mrs KATHERINE, born in Scotland in 1794, emigrated via South Carolina to Georgia, settled in Georgia during 1829, a farmer's wife in Montgomery County, Georgia. [C]

GILLIS, JOHN C., born in Scotland in 1780, emigrated via North Carolina to Georgia, a farmer in Montgomery County, Georgia. [C]

GILLIS, JOHN, a farmer, born in Scotland in 1814, Christian Gillis born in South Carolina in 1824, Angus Gillis born in Florida in 1844, Daniel Gillis born in Florida in 1847, and Norman Gillis born in Florida in 1849, settled in Walton County, Florida. [C]

GILLIS, NEIL, a farmer, born in Scotland in 1810, Martha Gillis born in Georgia in 1825, Elizabeth Gillis born in South Carolina in 1831, Daniel born in Florida in 1833, Catherine Gillis born in Florida in in 1835, Norman Gillis born in Alabama in 1837, Martha Gillis born in Alabama in 1839, and Florida Gillis born in Alabama in 1840, settled in Walton County, Florida. [C]

GILLIS, RODERICK, born in Scotland in 1779, emigrated to North Carolina, later a farmer in Montgomery County, Georgia.[C]

GILMORE, GEORGE, Presbyterian minister in Voluntown, Georgia, Loyalist, settled in St Johns and by 1786 in Halifax, Nova Scotia. [PRO.AO13.13.55.58]

GILMORE,(?) {"Gallimore"}, CHRISTOPHER, servant to Alexander Ross, emigrated on 31 October 1734, arrived in Georgia on 28 December 1734, died during 1740. [ESG#74]

GLAISTER, ROBERT, born in Greenock, Renfrewshire, in 1771, a ship's captain, died in Savannah, Georgia, on 8 October 1806. [Savannah Death Register]

GLASS, JOHN, born in 1723, a servant, emigrated from Inverness on the Prince of Wales, Captain George Dunbar, on 20 October 1735, arrived in Georgia on 10 January 1736. [ESG#75]

GLEN, ARCHIBALD, a servant to William and Hugh Stirling, possibly emigrated from Leith on the Hope of Leith a snow, Captain Greig, arrived in Georgia on 1 August 1734, [ESG#75]; a settler in Georgia, on 9 December 1738. [AGA#59]

GLEN, JOHN, in Savannah, subscribed towards a Presbyterian Meeting House in Savannah in 1769. [Ga.Gaz.#291]; President of the St Andrew's Society of Savannah 1795-1796. [SSS#88]

GLEN, WILLIAM, land grant in Savannah on 21 May 1762, [CRG#28/1.422][Grant book D, #93]

GOLDEY, JANE, born in 1783, settled in Savannah, died in September 1823. [Georgia Republican: 18.9.1823]

GOLDSMITH, Mrs MARGARET, born in Scotland 1831, husband Elbert born in Georgia 1824, a farmer, daughter Elizabeth born 1847 and Sarah born in 1849 both in Alabama, settled in Coosa District, Coosa County, Alabama. [C]

GORDON, ALEXANDER, botanist in New Orleans and Mobile around 1843. [NAS.GD121.79-82]

GORDON, ARTHUR, Attorney General of East Florida in 1771, appointed as a Member of the Council of East Florida on 31 July 1772, died aged 30 in December 1778. [APC.Col.1766-1783#565]

GORDON, DONALD, born in 1725, a servant, embarked in Inverness on the Two Brothers, Captain William Thomson, in July 1737 for Georgia in July 1737, arrived on 20 January 1737. [ESG#19]

GORDON, HUGH, born in 1753, a yeoman, emigrated from Newcastle to Georgia on the Georgia Packet in September 1775, settled in Friendsborough, Georgia. [PRO.T47.12]

GORDON, JAMES, born in 1718, a servant, emigrated from Inverness to Georgia on 20 October 1735 on the Prince of Wales, master George Dunbar, arrived on 10 January 1736. [ESG#19]

GORDON, JAMES, of Corestoun, jr., a merchant in Stromness, Orkney, later in Savannah, Georgia, in 1778, 1782. [NAS.CS16.1.171, 173; 2/282]

GORDON, JOHN, born in Scotland, a merchant in Fredericia, St Simon's Island, Georgia, and in Beaufort, South Carolina, a partner in McQueen, Gordon and Company in Charleston, South Carolina, in 1760, a partner with Grey Elliot in Beaufort, South Carolina, and in Sunbury, Georgia, 1762-1767, later partner in firm of Gordon and Netherclift in Charleston and Savannah, later moved to East Florida.["Indian Traders of the South Eastern Spanish Borderlands" Coker & Watson {Florida, 1986}]. He and Grey Elliot were granted 200 acres in St John's parish, Georgia, on 6 August 1765 and 100 acres there on 2 March 1773, and 200 acres on Bermuda Island, St John's parish, on 6 August 1765. [Grant Books E.195/6 and I.902]; land grant in Great Ogeechee, Georgia, on 13 May 1756, [Grant book A, #158]; land grants in Savannah on 5 February 1760 and on 1 July 1760, [CRG#28/1.315, 320, 329] [Grant book B, #317/368/416/544; Grant book C, #72]; purchased land near Savannah on 20 October 1760, [CRG#28/1.277]; a merchant and trader in East Florida in 1764, later in Charleston, South Carolina, in 1767. [NAS.NRAS, bundles 403/489]; bought land in East Florida 1766. [PRO.PC.Unbound.1766/3]

GORDON, JOHN, a Scottish Loyalist from Virginia, petitioned the Council of West Florida for land on the Pearl River, West Florida, 26 December 1776. [PRO.CO5.634]

GORDON, MARGARET, servant to Charles Pury in Georgia around 1740. [ESG#76]

GORDON, PETER, born 1706, an upholsterer, emigrated from Gravesend to Georgia on the Anne, Captain Thomas Shubrick, 6 November 1732, arrived 1 February 1733, land grant in Georgia 16 October 1734, bailiff in Savannah, left colony for England 12 April 1738, died 1740, with wife Catherine born 1704. [ESG#19/108][PRO.CO.5.668][SPAWI.1738#139]

GORDON, PHILIP, servant to John Penrose in Georgia around 1740. [ESG#76]

GORDON, WILLIAM, soldier of the Black Watch, imprisoned in the Tower of London on a charge of mutiny, transferred to Oglethorpe's Regiment in Georgia 1743. [GHS, Cate Colln. 45/3172]

GORDON, WILLIAM, an Anglican minister in West Florida 1767-1775, later in Virginia. [EMA#30]; Dr William Gordon, a chaplain in Mobile, West Florida, 1779. [JCTP#86.27]

GORDON, WILLIAM, born 1750, a merchant in Aberdeen, emigrated from Greenock, Renfrewshire, to Georgia on the Georgia in July 1775. [PRO.T47.12]

GORDON, WILLIAM, born 1810, third son of William Gordon a vintner in Montrose, Angus, a joiner, died in New Orleans on 27 September 1835. [AJ#4587]

GOVAN, JAMES, from Greenock, Renfrewshire, a glasscutter in Mobile, died during September 1849, cnf 1855. [NAS.SC70.1.87]

GOWANS, JOHN, son of Peter Gowans and Jean Clark in Crieff, Perthshire, settled in Tennessee by 1829. [NAS.SH]

GRAEME, WILLIAM, Member of the Assembly and Attorney General of Georgia, died in Savannah, Georgia, on 29 July 1770. [Scots Magazine# 32.458]; subscribed towards a Presbyterian Meeting House in Savannah 1769. [Ga.Gaz.#291]

GRAHAM, ALEXANDER, granted 20,000 acres in East Florida 1769. [PC.Col.V.592]

GRAHAM, or CUTHBERT, ANNE, widow of Patrick Graham received land grants in Hardwick, and in Josephstown, Savannah, Georgia, 5 April 1757, [CRG#28/1.57][Grant book A, #364/365/366]

GRAHAM, BRYCE, born 1795, baptised on 21 July 1795 in the parish of Hutton, son of John Graham and Agnes Beattie in Balstock, Hutton, Dumfries-shire, settled in Russel's Vail, Franklin County, Alabama, died 5 January 1839. [Hutton g/s][Hutton OPR]

GRAHAM, CATHERINE, born 1717, an indentured servant, embarked in Inverness 19 November 1737, arrived in Georgia 14 January 1738. [ESG#19]

GRAHAM, DAVID, 500 acres in Christ Church parish, Georgia, surveyed 16 November 1752. [Plat book C, #73]

GRAHAM, HENRY, born 1749, a yeoman, emigrated from Newcastle to Georgia on the Georgia Packet in September 1775. [PRO.T47.9/11]

GRAHAM, JAMES, grant of a wharf lot in Savannah on 1 July 1760, [PRO.CO.5.648.E46][CRG#28/1.365][Grant book C, #226]; merchant and Indian trader in Savannah, Georgia, married Sally, daughter of John Stuart, Superintendent of Indian Affairs in the Southern Department, in July 1767. [Scots Magazine# 29.557]

GRAHAM, JAMES, granted 710 acres in Newport, St John's parish, Georgia, on 7 February 1758, 1000 acres in St John's parish on 3 July 1770, and 1000 acres in St John's parish on 2 April 1771. [Grant Books - A.603 and I.49/50/282]

GRAHAM, JOHN, a settler in Georgia on 9 December 1738. [AGA#59]

GRAHAM, JOHN, baptised on 5 November 1733, son of Reverend Alexander Pyot {1700-1765} and Eleanor Stevenson {died 1742} in Whitekirk, Dunbar, East Lothian, emigrated to Georgia 1753, land grant in Savannah, Newport and Hardwick on 7 February 1758, land grant in St Matthew's on 2 October 1759, land grant in Christchurch on 5 February 1760, commissary and clerk of court in Georgia in 1763, planter, Lieutenant Governor of Georgia 1776, Loyalist, died in Naples 1795. John Graham and Company dissolved on 31 December 1768; President of the St Andrew's Society of Savannah 1770-1771. [Ga.Gaz.#280][SSS#88] [NAS.GD2.244/2.149] [CRG#28/1.238, 314, 316] [HOG125][F.1.408] [NAS.GD110.999/1046] [NAS.GD105][Grant book A, #604; Grant book B, #100/305; Grant book I, #266/267/405/406; Grant book M, #40]

GRAHAM, JOHN, granted 5,000 acres of land in East Florida during 1769. [PC.Col.V.592]

GRAHAM, MUNGO, granted land in town of Hardwick, Georgia, 1755. [CRG.VII.201/686]; land grant in Hardwick 6 December 1757, [CRG#28/1.233]; pro.3 December 1766 Georgia.

GRAHAM, PATRICK, apothecary in Redford, Crieff, Perthshire, emigrated to Georgia before 1736, [PRO.CO.5.670.284]; granted 100 acres in Savannah, Georgia 19 May 1736, [PRO.CO.5.668]; reference to 9 December 1738, [AGA#59]; appointed as an assistant surgeon and medicine dispenser to the poor in Savannah, 1747, [PRO.CO.5.668.239-240]; secured lands of the Creeks 1752 [PRO.CO.5.6689.113-119]; in Josephstown, Georgia, probate 27 August 1755 Georgia. [Refers to wife Ann Cuthbert, to his brother David and lands in Redford, Perthshire, sister Mary wife of John Grindlay, niece Ann daughter of brother Thomas Graham, Mungo Graham, witnesses Patrick and Isabel Mackay, George Cuthbert][ESG#76][Plat book C, #73]

GRAHAM, ..., Captain Lieutenant of the Highlanders, killed in Georgia 20.10.1763. [GaGaz#29]

GRANDISON, ISABELLA, born in Scotland 1780, settled in Warren County, Mississippi. [C]

GRANT, Sir ALEXANDER, granted 20,000 acres in East Florida 1766.
[PCCol.V.590]

GRANT, ALEXANDER, from Leatham, embarked on the Marlborough,
Captain Thomas Walker, in Caithness during September 1775
bound for Georgia, an indentured servant to Thomas Brown there.
[PRO.AO13.34.123-4]

GRANT, ANDREW, merchant in Edinburgh, emigrated from Leith to
Georgia in March 1734, possibly on the snow Hope, master Greig,
[SCGaz, 11.5.1734]; arrived in Georgia during June 1734,
[ESG#76]; settled in Ogychee, Georgia, [PRO.CO.5.670.108]
[NAS.RD2.171.33]; granted 400 acres in Georgia 18 October
1733. [PRO.CO.5.668]; a settler in Georgia 9 December 1738,
[AGA#59]; abandoned Stirling's Bluff and moved to Savannah
before September 1737, later moved to the Carolinas and then to
England, father of Joseph etc. [ESG#76]

GRANT, ARCHIBALD, servant to William and Hugh Stirling, arrived in
Georgia on 1 August 1734, possibly emigrated from Leith on the
snow Hope of Leith Captain Greig. [ESG#76]

GRANT, Sir ARCHIBALD, of Monymusk, Aberdeenshire, granted
20,000 acres in East Florida during 1767. [PC.Col.V.591]
[NAS.NRAS#0099;pp10, 16, 20]; 'sending a surveyor and
servants in July 1767' [AJ#1020]

GRANT, CHRISTIAN, born 1725, a 5 year indentured servant, embarked
19 November 1737, arrived 14 January 1738. [ESG#19]

GRANT, DANIEL, servant to Richard Kirchiner in Georgia around 1740.
[ESG#76]

GRANT, DONALD, a planter, died on the Great Satilla River Plantation
on 6 January 1821. [Georgia Republican: 13.1.1821]

GRANT, DUNCAN, granted 10,000 acres in East Florida 1766.
[PCCol.V.590]

GRANT, GILBERT, born 1732, a 9.5 year indentured servant, embarked 19 November 1737, arrived in Georgia 14 January 1738, soldier in the Independent Highland Company 6 May 1741. [ESG#19]; land grant in St Andrew's parish 4 December 1759, [CRG#28/1.330]

GRANT, JAMES, a servant to William Stephens in Georgia around 1740. [ESG#76]

GRANT, JAMES, land grant in St Matthew's parish, Georgia, 4.12.1759, [CRG#28/1.327]

GRANT, JAMES, from Ballindalloch, Banffshire, officer of the 1st Regiment (The Royal Scots) 1741-, to America as a Major of the 77th (Montgomery's Highlanders) in 1757, fought at Fort Duquesne and later in South Carolina, Governor of East Florida, 1763-1773. [NAS.RD4.210.541][NAS.RS29{Elgin}VIII.202] [NAS.GD25.sec.9/box27]

GRANT, JOHN, born 1717, servant to Patrick Grant, emigrated from Inverness on the Prince of Wales, Captain George Dunbar, on 20 October 1735, arrived in Georgia on 10 January 1736. [ESG#76]

GRANT, JOHN, born 1722, an indentured servant, embarked in Inverness on the Two Brothers, Captain William Thomson, for Georgia in July 1737, arrived on 20 January 1737. [ESG#19]

GRANT, JOHN, born 1726, a 9 year indentured servant, embarked for Georgia 19 November 1737, arrived 14 January 1738, soldier in the Independent Highland Company on 6 May 1741. [ESG#19]

GRANT, JOHN, born 1719, a laborer, an indentured servant, embarked from Inverness on the Loyal Judith, Captain John Lemon, for Georgia on 21 September 1741, arrived on 4 December 1741. [PRO.CO.5.668][ESG#19] [CRG.30.197/199]

GRANT, JOHN, soldier of the Black Watch, imprisoned in the Tower of London on a charge of mutiny, transferred to Oglethorpe's Regiment in Georgia 1743, settled in Georgia. [GHS, Cate Colln. 45/3172]

GRANT, JOHN, born 1737, a laborer and indentured servant, emigrated from London to Georgia on the Mary in February 1774, [PRO.T47.9.11]

GRANT, JOHN, baron of the Exchequer in Scotland, granted 20,000 acres in East Florida 1767. [PRO.CO5.542][PC.Col.V.591]

GRANT, LUDOWICK, a servant to William Stephens later (?) a trader in the Cherokee nation around 1740. [ESG#76]

GRANT, MARGARET, in Darien on 6 May 1741. [ESG#76]

GRANT, PATRICK, of Aberlour, Banffshire, born 1717, a farmer, emigrated from Inverness on the Prince of Wales, Captain George Dunbar, on 20 October 1735, arrived in Georgia on 10 January 1736, settled in Savannah, killed in a duel 1740. [ESG#76]

GRANT, PETER, born 1727, a 5 year indentured servant, embarked for Georgia 19 November 1737, arrived 14 January 1738. [ESG#19]

GRANT, PETER, a servant to Thomas Causton around 1740. [ESG#76]

GRANT, WILLIAM, born 1727, a 10 year indentured servant, embarked for Georgia 19 November 1737, arrived 14 January 1738. [ESG#20]

GRAY, ALEXANDER, of Brora, Sutherland, eldest son of William Gray of Lairg, Sutherland, emigrated to Georgia by 1761, died ca. 1766. [SGen.XLI.2]; land grant in Christchurch parish 11 September 1764. [Ga.Gaz.#78]

GRAY, ALEXANDER, a settler in Louisiana 23 February 1764. [GaGaz#47]

GRAY, ELIZABETH, servant to John Baillie, possibly emigrated from Leith on the snow Hope of Leith, Captain Greig, arrived in Georgia on 1 August 1734, married George Sims 10.3.1735, died 1740. [ESG#77]

GRAY, JAMES, grant of a town lot in Augusta 5.6.1759.
[PRO.CO.5.648.E68][CRG#28/1.419]; land grant of 100 acres in
St George parish, Georgia, 7 December 1762
[PRO.CO.5.648.E48] ; land grant in Christchurch parish 11
September 1764. [Ga.Gaz.#78]

GRAY, JOHN, born 1691, a 3 year indentured servant, embarked for
Georgia 19 November 1737, arrived 14 January 1738. [ESG#20]

GRAY, JOHN, youngest son of William Gray of Lairg, Sutherland, to
Georgia 1746 as Ensign of Oglethorpe's Regiment, later Ensign of
Mackay's Independent Company in America, received land grants
in Georgia ca1759, Captain of an Independent Company and
Governor of a Fort in Georgia, pro 22.8.1770 PCC. [reference to
brother Robert Gray in Creich, Scotland] [SGen.XLI.2]

GRAY, MARGARET, born 1717, single woman, an indentured servant,
embarked from Inverness on the Loyal Judith, Captain John
Lemon, for Georgia on 21 September 1741, arrived there
4.12.1741. [PRO.CO.5.668][ESG#20][CRG.XXX.197/199]

GRAY, RODERICK, son of David Gray in Millbrae, died in Mobile,
West Florida, 18 May 1820. [BM#7#583][EA#5907]

GRAY, WILLIAM, planter in Augusta, Georgia, 1739-, petitioned the
Trustees 16 February 1748. [PRO.CO.5.668.305]; possibly an
agent with the Chichesaw and Utchea Indians around 1740.
[ESG#77]

GREEN, ALEXANDER, born in Scotland 1828, a sailor on a cutter in
Mississippi. [C]

GREENE, H., born in Scotland 1807, a bagman, wife Margaret born in
Ireland 1820, emigrated to America, children William H. born in
New York 1845, Elizabeth born in Alabama 1847, and Thomas
born in Alabama 1849, settled in Alabama. [C]

GREGG, Captain ..., from Dundee, in Georgia 1.1765. [Ga.Gaz.#94]

GREGORY, JAMES, arrived in Georgia via England 20 August 1766. [Ga.Gaz.#130, 227]

GREIG, JOHN WHITTET, born on 11 September 1813, son of Alexander Greig, Writer to the Signet, {1776-1857} and Jane Whittet {1785-1862}, died in New Orleans on 17 January 1848. [Edinburgh, St Cuthbert's, g/s][EEC#21620][SG#1693]

GREIG, ROBERT, born 1811, son of David Greig {1786-1859} and Anna ... {1786-1848}, in Kinghorn, a machinist, settled in Mobile, Alabama, by 1840, married Mary .... born in Alabama 1820, father of Carrie, Louisa, Catherine, Ann, Robert and Mary [all born in Alabama]. [C][Kinghorn, Fife, g/s]

GREIG, WILLIAM, born in Scotland 1828, an engineer, settled in Mobile. [C]

GRELLING, JOHN, emigrated to Savannah, Georgia, on the snow Kinnoull, Captain Alexander Alexander, and was granted 100 acres between the Savannah and the Saludy Rivers on 30 May 1768.[Ga.Co.Journal#34.148/151]

GRIERSON, JAMES, 1767, [NLS#MS119]; settled in Augusta, Georgia, before 1776, Loyalist Militia Captain 1773, father of James, Thomas, David, Katherine, and George, died in St Paul, Georgia, pro. 2.1789 PCC. [PRO.AO13.35.247/258; AO13.6.15/32]

GUNN, DONALD, a farmer, born in Scotland 1767, Mary Gunn born in Scotland 1781, William, a laborer, born in Florida 1824, settled in Walton County, Florida. [C]

GUNN, GEORGE, born 1723, a 6 year indentured servant, embarked for Georgia 19 November 1737, arrived 14 January 1738. [ESG#21]

GUNN, WILLIAM, born in 1710, servant of Mackay of Scourie, emigrated from Inverness on the Prince of Wales, Captain George Dunbar, on 20 October 1735, arrived in Georgia on 10 January 1736. [ESG#77]

GUTHRIE, THOMAS, born in 1732, a farmer in Stromness, Orkney, with wife Jean, and children Margaret, Helen, Adam, Thomas, John, Jean, and Janet, emigrated from Kirkwall, Orkney, to Savannah, Georgia, on the Marlborough, Captain George Prissick, in September 1774, indentured servants to Thomas Brown in Georgia. [PRO.T47.12][PRO.AO13.34.123-4]

HALCRO, MAGNUS, born on 5 November 1729 in Orphir, Orkney, son of Robert Halcro and Katherine Seater, emigrated with wife Elizabeth and son Hugh, from Kirkwall to Savannah, Georgia, on the Marlborough, Captain George Prissick, in September 1774, settled in Richmond County, Georgia, as indentured servants of Thomas Brown. [PRO.T47.12][PRO.AO13.34.123-5]

HALL, ALEXANDER, born 1776, a shoemaker, died on 4 September 1804. [Savannah Death Register]

HALL, H. H., an engineer, born in Scotland 1821, settled in Warren County, Mississippi. [C]

HAMIGAR, JAMES, born in 1739, a sailor in Evie, Orkney, emigrated from Kirkwall to Savannah, Georgia, with wife Jean, on the Marlborough, in September 1774, settled in Richmond County, Georgia. [PRO.T47.12]

HAMILTON, ARCHIBALD, patroon of the Trustees perigua at Fredericia, Georgia, 1739. [ESG#77]

HAMILTON, HENRY, granted 100 acres in St John's parish, Georgia, and in Savannah, 16 January 1756. [Grant Book A, #16/17]: pro.23 October 1760 Georgia

HAMILTON, HUGH, in Pensacola, Lieutenant of HM Forces, pro. April 1793 PCC

HAMILTON, JAMES, in St Simon's, died in Philadelphia on 12 April 1829. [BM#26.268][EEC#18322]

HAMILTON, JAMES, in New Orleans, married Jane Duncan, eldest daughter of W. Duncan a writer in Hamilton, Lanarkshire, in Wishaw, Lanarkshire, on 9 October 1832. [FH#554]

HAMILTON, JOHN, of Bargeny, granted 10,000 acres in East Florida 1765. [ActsPCCol.4.813]

HAMILTON, JOHN, born in 1788, a mariner, died on 27 August 1809. [Savannah Death Register]

HAMILTON, PAUL, grant of 500 acres in Georgia 24 September 1735. (?) [ESG#77]

HAMILTON, THOMAS, land grant in Savannah on 27 November 1761, [CRG#28/1.372][Grant book C, #377]

HAMILTON, WILLIAM, born in Scotland 1815, a clerk, wife Caroline born in Scotland 1829, son William born in New York, settled in Mobile, Alabama. [C]

HAMMOND, M.P., born in Scotland 1814, a merchant, settled in Alabama, married by 1843 to P. A. .... born in Alabama 1822, father of St. J., Alice, and A. {all born in Alabama}. [C]

HANBY, JOHN, born 1774, a grocer, died on 17 October 1806. [Savannah Death Register]

HANNAY, GEORGE of Kingsmuir, in St Augustine, East Florida, 1783. [NAS.CS17.1.2/388]

HARDIE, GEORGE, fifth son of Archibald Hardie a merchant in Bo'ness, West Lothian, died in Natchez, Georgia, on 7 September 1818. [S.97.18]

HARDIE, JAMES, a carpenter, born in Scotland 1808, wife Jane born in England 1809, children Mary born 1845 and Sarah born 1848 both in Mississippi, settled in Adams County, Mississippi. [C]

HART, JAMES, born Scotland 1807, a merchant, settled in Alabama. [C]

HARVEY, BAKIA, born 1758, a servant in Kirkwall, Orkney, emigrated from Kirkwall to Savannah, Georgia, on the Marlborough, Captain George Prissick, in September 1774, settled at Snowhill, near Augusta, Georgia, by 1775 as an indentured servant of Thomas Brown. [NAS.NRAS.1031.68][PRO.T47.12][PRO.AO13.34.123]

HAY, JAMES, born 1808, son of Alexander Hay and Jeannie Scott, died in New Orleans on 1 December 1835. [Kilconquhar, Fife, g/s]

HAY, JENOUR(?), servant in Georgia to Thomas Baillie around 1740. [ESG#78]

HAY, JOHN, born 1817, baptised in the parish of St Cuthbert's, Edinburgh, on 7 March 1817, son of Peter Hay {1786-1837} and Alison Bathgate {1795-1853}, died in Natchez 1844. [Edinburgh, New Calton, g/s] [St Cuthbert's OPR]

HAY, Mrs MARGARET, born in Scotland 1816, children Thomas C. born 1839, Charles born 1844, Emma born 1846, and Anna born 1846 – all in Mississippi, settled in Warren County, Mississippi. [C]

HAY, ROBERT, cooper in Edinburgh, emigrated from Cromarty to Savannah, Georgia, on the Two Brothers, Captain William Thomson, 1737, [PRO.CO.5.670.331][SPC.43.513]; arrived in Georgia 27 June 1737, [ESG#78]; granted 500 acres in Georgia on 5 October 1737 also on 15 March 1738. [PRO.CO.5.668] [SPAWI.1738.86, 109]

HEARD, JOHN, born in Scotland 1823, a stone mason, settled in Coosa District, Coosa County, Alabama. [C]

HEARD, THOMAS, born in Scotland 1827, a carpenter, settled in Coosa District, Coosa County, Alabama. [C]

HEARD, THOMAS, born in Scotland 1825, a carpenter, settled in Coosa District, Coosa County, Alabama. [C]

HEDDLE, ALEXANDER, born 1758, a farm servant in Shapinsay, Orkney, emigrated from Kirkwall to Savannah, Georgia, on the Marlborough, Captain George Prissick, in September 1774, settled in Richmond County, Georgia, as an indentured servant of Thomas Brown. [PRO.T47.12][PRO.AO13.34.123-5]

HEIBES(?), ELIZABETH, born in Scotland 1829, settled in Adams County, Mississippi. [C]

HENDERSON, A., born in Scotland 1760, a farmer, settled in Mobile, Alabama. [C]

HENDERSON, HENRY, born 1790, a pilot in Savannah 1812. [1812]

HENDERSON, JAMES, son of James Henderson a factor in Lochgelly, Fife, died at Fort Clark, Los Moras River, Texas, in April 1853. [FH,12.1.1854]

HENDERSON, JOHN, in Broomhead, Dunfermline, Fife, late of Georgia, 2 February 1787. [NAS.RS.Fife, #1635; RGS#124/2]

HENDERSON, STEPHEN, settled in New Orleans before 1831. [Dunblane, Perthshire, g/s]

HENIE, Mrs JANE, born in Ayrshire 1777, died in Georgia on 5 October 1815. [Georgia g/s]

HENIE, WILLIAM, born in Glasgow 1784, a mariner, died in Savannah, Georgia, on 5 October 1808. [Savannah Death Register]

HENNEN, CAROLINE LOUISE, daughter of Alfred Hennen, wife of William Mure HM Consul, died in New Orleans on 15 December 1851. [FJ#995][W#1293]

HENRY, Captain ARCHIBALD, born 1793, son of Thomas Henry of Buraston {1756-1845} and Lillias Henry {1772-1820}, died on the River Mississippi in March 1837. [Walls, Shetland, g/s]

HERON, Captain ALEXANDER, of Colonel Oglethorpe's Regiment, granted 500 acres in Georgiaon 26 April 1738. [SPAWI.1738#169, 171] [PRO.CO.5.668; CO.5.670.347][ESG#78]; Colonel Alexander Heron appointed Commander in Chief of HM Forces in Georgia 1747. [CRG#28/1.260]

HERON, ANDREW, in Augusta, Georgia, pro. February 1817 PCC

HERRIES, MICHAEL, a merchant from Glasgow, granted 500 acres in Georgia in October 1751. [PRO.CO5/669]; granted 5,000 acres in East Florida in 1767. [PC.Col.V.591]

HERRIES, ROBERT, granted 5,000 acres in East Florida during 1767. [PC.Col.V.591]

HEWETT, ANDREW, Captain of the Florida Rangers, 1782. [PRO.CO5/III]

HILL, WILLIAM, died in New Orleans on 12 November 1826. [BM#21.374][AJ#4123]

HILLS, JAMES, born in Berwickshire, settled in Savannah, Georgia, in 1804, died on 17 July 1829. [Georgia Republican, 20.8.1829]; born 1787, to US 1802, a merchant in Savannah 1812, [1812]

HISLOP, MARY, servant to Hugh Anderson arrived in Georgia before March 1735. [ESG#78]

HODGE, DAVID, in New Orleans, dead by 1819. [NAS.SH]

HONEY, WILLIAM, born in Scotland 1798, resident of a hotel in Harrison County, Mississippi. [C]

HOPE, JOHN, servant to Patrick Tailfer, arrived in Georgia on 1 August 1734, possibly emigrated from Leith on the snow Hope of Leith, Captain Greig. [ESG#78]

HORDAN, ALEXANDER, born in Scotland 1816, a shopkeeper, wife Margaret born in England 1822, settled in Alabama. [C]

HORN, JANET, born 1755, a servant in Wick, Caithness, emigrated from Kirkwall, Orkney Islands, to Savannah, Georgia, on the Marlborough in September 1775, settled in Richmond, Georgia. [PRO.T47.12]

HOUSTON, Lady ANN, in Georgia, 1818. [NAS.SH]

HOUSTOUN, Sir GEORGE, land grant in Great Ogeechee on 15 May 1756, [Grant book A, #225]; President of the St Andrew's Society of Savannah 1793-1795, [SSS#88]; died in Georgia 1795. [SM#57.682]

HOUSTOUN, JAMES, granted 500 acres in Georgia on 14 November 1733. [PRO.CO.5.668; CO5.670.125]; arrived in Georgia on 1 August 1734, possibly emigrated from Leith on the snow Hope of Leith, Captain Greig, died 1737[ESG#79]

HOUSTOUN, JAMES, clerk in Mr Causton's store, [ESG#79]; reference on 9 December 1738, [AGA#59]; land grant between Vernon and the Little Ogeechee Rivers on 7 November 1755, grant on Whitemarsh Island on 3 November 1761, [Grant book A, #18; Grant book C, #269]; grant of 285 acres in Christ Church parish, Georgia, on 3 November 1761. [PRO.CO.5.648.E46][CRG#28/1.367]; executor of Hugh Ross in Purrysburg on 29 March 1764. [Ga.Gaz.#52]; a laborer in Christchurch parish on 25 November 1774, pro. 25 November 1774 Georgia.

HOUSTOUN, JOHN, pro. 22 July 1796, Chatham County, Georgia. [Will Book A] (refers to his goddaughters Ann, Priscilla and Joanna Houstoun and Harriet Louisa Baillie in Scotland, to his niece Harriet Thompson Houstoun, and brother William in New Jersey, executors Patrick and James Edward Houstoun and John McIntosh, subscribed 2 May 1796.)

HOUSTOUN, Sir PATRICK, Bt., born 1698 in Paisley, Renfrewshire, son of Patrick Houstoun, educated at Glasgow University, a merchant in Glasgow, granted 500 acres in Georgia on 1 August

1733. [PRO.CO.5.668/670.101]; emigrated from Leith to Savannah, Georgia, in March 1734, possibly on the snow Hope, Captain Greig, [SCGaz, 11.5.1734]; letter, 2 April 1736, [NAS.GD18.5360.3]; married Priscilla Dunbar 1741, died in Georgia 5 February 1762, buried at Bonadventure, Georgia [PRO.CO.5.670.101]; land grant between the Vernon and the Little Ogeechee Rivers on 7 November 1755, in Savannah 15 May 1756, in Christ Church parish 2 October 1759, and on Ilay Island 2 October 1759, [Grant book A, #15/224; Grant book B, #273/274]; land grant in Darien on 7 June 1757, [CRG#28/1.14]; land grants in Christchurch on 2 October 1759, [CRG#28/1.311]; will subscribed on 11 February 1761 in Savannah, Georgia, reference to wife Priscilla Dunbar, executor brother in law Captain George Dunbar, witnesses Hugh Ross, Ann Stewart, and John Ross. [Pro. 15 April 1762. Will Book A, ff83/84]; Sir Patrick Houstoun, Baronet, President of His Majesty's Council of Georgia, died 5 February 1762, aged 64. [Christchurch g/s][NAS.GD18.5272/5360][ESG#79]

HOUSTOUN, ROBERT, land grant in Great Ogeechee on 3 December 1760, [Grant book D, #82]; land grant of 100 acres in St Phillip's parish, Georgia, on 21 April 1762. [PRO.CO.5.648.E68][CRG#28/1.418, 425]

HOUSTON, Dr WILLIAM, born 1695, matriculated at the University of St Andrews 2 February 1719, matriculated at the University of Leyden 6 October 1727, graduated as a doctor of physics of St Andrews and of Leyden; in Kingston {Jamaica?} in December 1730; surgeon on the South Sea Company's ship Don Carlos 1730, in Vera Cruz 5 March 1732; appointed as a botanist in Georgia 4 October 1732; ill in Portobello May 1733; died in Jamaica 14 August 1733.[PRO.CO670.100][GM#3.662][BM.Sloane MS#4051/4052]

HOWDEN, JOHN, born 1789, son of Archibald Howden and Joan Manderson in Scoonie, Fife, a merchant, died in Savannah, Georgia, 26 October 1806. [St Monance g/s][Scoonie g/s] [Savannah Death Register]

HUME, DAVID, son of George Hume a shoemaker in Lauder, Berwickshire, settled in Tennessee before 1838. [NAS.SH]

HUME, JAMES, born in Georgia on 27 March 1747, educated in Scotland, appointed as a Member of the Council of Georgia on 16 March 1772, Attorney General of Georgia, Lord Chief Justice of East Florida, a Loyalist, died in Leadervale, Earlstoun, Berwickshire, 12 April 1839. [EEC#119887]; land grants in Acton village, Christ Church parish, Georgia, 3 September 1771, 20 April 1772, 5 July 1774, [Grant book H, #74, Grant book I, #409, Grant book M, #54]; land grants together with John Hume, in Christ Church parish, on 5 July 1774 and on 1 November 1774, [Grant book M, #53/666][APC.Col.1766-1783#565]

HUME, JOHN, born in 1747, a farmer, emigrated from Newcastle to Georgia on the Georgia Packet in September 1775, settled in Friendsborough, Georgia. [PRO.T47.10]

HUME, JOHN, land grants, together with James Hume, in Christ Church parish 5 July 1774 and 1 November 1774, [Grant book M, #53/666]; land grant in Christ Church parish 2 March 1773, [Grant book I, #917]

HUME, WILLIAM, born 1735, a shipmaster in Glasgow, emigrated from Greenock to Georgia on the Christy in July 1775. [PRO.T47.12]

HUME, Reverend WILLIAM, born in Urr, Dumfries-shire, 1770, educated at the University of Edinburgh, 30 years in Nashville, Tennessee, died there on 23 May 1833. [SG#156]

HUNTER, ANDREW, born in Glasgow 1777, {possibly son of James Hunter and Ann McLeran baptised in Glasgow on 10 January 1776}, a cotton machine maker, died in Savannah, Georgia, 16 August 1807. [Savannah Death Register][Glasgow OPR]

HUNTER, PATRICK, apothecary in Savannah 1738, apothecary to the Orphan House 1740. [ESG#79]

HUNTER, WILLIAM, died in Savannah 10 August 1802. [GM#72.1064]

HUNTER, WILLIAM, born 1772, a master mariner, died 9 September 1804. [Savannah Death Register]

HURRY, JOHN, born 1738, a farmer in Stenness, Orkney, with wife Jean, and children William and Jean, emigrated from Kirkwall to Savannah, Georgia, on the Marlborough in September 1774. [PRO.T47.12]

HUTCHINS, WILLIAM, born in Scotland 1800, a merchant, arrived in Savannah late 1821 on the ship Georgia, Captain Varnum. [USNA/par]

HUTCHINSON, ALEXANDER, born in Scotland 1829, a clerk, settled in Alabama. [C]

HUTCHINSON, WILLIAM, born in Scotland 1800, a merchant, settled in Alabama. [C]

HUTCHISON, PETER, born in Scotland 1815, a seaman, wife Mary C. born in Scotland 1823, son Peter (born in England) and son William M. (born in Scotland), settled in Mobile, Alabama. [C]

IMRIE, DUNCAN, baptised on 4 April 1754 in the parish of Dundee, son of John Imrie and Barbara Geddie, a ships carpenter in Carolina then in St Augustine, East Florida, who died on a voyage from America to Holland, [refers to John Rankine a merchant in Dundee; John Simpson late a merchant in Charleston, South Carolina, then in London; William Chalmers town clerk of Dundee; Lieutenant Sutherland; William Rankine a merchant in Dundee; and John Rankine of Dudhope] cnf.26 September 1782 Edinburgh. [NAS.CC8.8.125][NAS.SH][Dundee OPR]

IMRIE, JOHN, from Dundee, a ships carpenter in St Augustine, East Florida, 1782. [NAS.SH]

INGLIS, ANDREW, a merchant in Savannah, 1770. [NAS.RD4.210.774]

INGLIS, JAMES, in Barrataria, Louisiana, dead by 1836. [NAS.SH]

INGLIS, JOHN, President of the St Andrew's Society of Savannah 1772-1773. [SSS#8]

INNERARITY, Mrs FRANCES, born in Scotland 1818, husband Dr J.F.Innerarity born in Alabama 1812, children J.W.G., Eliza J., and Louisa (all born in Spain), Frances, James, Ann and Emanuel (all born in Alabama), settled in Alabama. [C]

INNERARITY, [Inverarity] JAMES, born in Brechin, Angus, 18 August 1777, son of John Inverarity and Henrietta Panton, emigrated to West Florida in May 1796, a merchant there, died on 3 October 1847. [IT#18/19]

INNERARITY, [Inverarity] JOHN, baptised 7 August 1749, a tanner in Brechin, Angus, married Henrietta Panton in Brechin 26 July 1776, settled in Aberdeen, father of James, Barbara, Jean, Henrietta, and John, emigrated before 24 June 1792, a partner in firm of Panton, Leslie and Company, settled in Pensacola, West Florida and Savannah, Georgia, then by 1798 in London, husband of Henrietta Panton, died in Stockwell, London, 1805. admin.January 1805 PCC. [IT#18]

IRELAND, DAVID, a lawyer, settled in Virginia and in 1817 moved to Huntsville, Mississippi, travelled throughout America especially the Mississippi Valley prior to 1832. [NAS.NRAS#1252]

IRONS, GEORGE, born in Scotland 1836, a coachmaker, settled in Alabama. [C]

IRONS, JAMES, born in Scotland 1836, a coachtrimmer, settled in Alabama. [C]

IRVIN, ANDREW, co-owner of the brigantine Betsey, registered in Savannah 11 October 1762. [PRO.CO5.709]

IRVINE, JAMES, born 1758 son of Nicol Irvine, a farm servant in Evie, Orkney, emigrated from Kirkwall to Savannah, Georgia, on the Marlborough, Captain Thomas Walker, in September 1775, settled in Richmond County, Georgia. [PRO.T47.12][PRO.AO13.34.123]

IRVINE, Dr JOHN, born in Aberdeen 1742, a physician, died in Savannah, Georgia, 15 October 1808. [Savannah Death Register] [Colonial Museum and Savannah Advertiser: 18.10.1808]; in London 1793,1798, [NAS.CS17.1.12/78; 18/183]

IRVINE, JOHN, granted 500 acres in St John's parish, Georgia, on 2 April 1771. [Grant Book -I.286]

IRVINE, JOHN, born 1748, a weaver in Stromness, Orkney, emigrated from Kirkwall to Savannah, Georgia, on the Marlborough, Captain George Prissick, in September 1774, settled in Richmond County, Georgia, as an indentured servant of Thomas Brown. [PRO.T47.12][PRO.AO13.34.123-5]

IRWIN, Mrs JANE, born in Scotland 1810, daughters Margaret Catherine born in Scotland 1825 and 1832, children George and William born in Alabama 1833 and 1836, settled in Alabama. [C]

IRWIN, THOMAS, land grant in St George's parish, Georgia, on 5 January 1762, [CRG#28/1.375]

IRWIN, WILLIAM, a merchant in Savannah, pro.1765 Georgia

IRWIN, WILLIAM, born in Scotland 1837, settled in Mobile, Alabama. [C]

ISAAC, ROBERT, born in Glasgow 1780, settled in Savannah 1801, died in Georgia on 16 October 1827. [Colonial Cemetery, Savannah, g/s] [Georgia Republican, 16.10.1827]

ISBISTER, HUGH, born in February 1757 in Firth, Orkney, son of David Isbister and Janet Omand, a boatman in Stromness, emigrated from Kirkwall to Savannah, Georgia, on the Marlborough, Captain Thomas Walker, in September 1775, settled in Richmond County, Georgia, as an indentured servant of Thomas Brown. [PRO.T47.12][PRO.AO13.34.123-5]

JACKSON, PETER, born 1770, a carpenter, died on 4 April 1809. [Savannah Death Register]

JAFFRAY, ALEXANDER, born in Stirling 1777, {probably the
  Alexander Jaffrey baptised on 21 December 1776 in the parish of
  St Ninian's, Stirling, son of Alexander Jaffrey and Euphan Christie,
  {St Ninian's OPR}], a machinist, died in Savannah, Georgia,
  9.4.1810, buried in the Old Colonial Cemetery, Savannah.
  [Savannah Death Register] [Colonial Cemetery, Savannah, g/s]

JAMES, CATHERINE, born in Scotland 1834, settled in Alabama. [C]

JAMES, ELIZABETH, servant to Patrick Tailfer, arrived in Georgia on 1
  August 1734, possibly emigrated from Leith on the snow Hope of
  Leith, Captain Greig. [ESG#80]

JAMIESON, JOHN, partner in George Baillie and Company in Savannah,
  Georgia, dissolved 11.5.1768; resident in Coats, Haddington, East
  Lothian, by 1794, [deed refers to George Baillie, late a merchant in
  Georgia now in Coats, Haddington, East Lothian]. [Ga.Gaz.#242]
  [NAS.RD3.279.116]; land grant in Christ Church parish, Georgia,
  3.3.1772, [Grant book H, #72]

JARVIE, DAVID, servant of Joseph Wardrope, emigrated on 11 April
  1734, arrived in Georgia 2on 1 August 1734, possibly sailed from
  Leith on the snow Hope of Leith, Captain Greig, died in 1740.
  [ESG#80]

JOHNSON, ALEXANDER, born in Scotland 1815, a clerk, settled in
  Alabama. [C]

JOHNSON, GEORGE, servant to Patrick Tailfer, arrived in Georgia on 1
  August 1734, a sawyer, possibly emigrated from Leith on the snow
  Hope of Leith , Captain Greig. [ESG#80]

JOHNSON, JAMES, a merchant in Glasgow, granted land in Georgia on
  5 November 1751. [CRG]

JOHNSON, SAMUEL, born in Edinburgh 1787, died in Georgia on 13
  September 1820. [Colonial Museum and Savannah Advertiser,
  16.9.1820]

JOHNSTON, ANDREW, in Georgia, in December 1763. [Ga.Gaz.#38]

JOHNSTON, ANDREW, physician in Augusta, Georgia, Loyalist, British
Army surgeon 1779-1781, settled in Savannah, Georgia, during
1782. [PRO.AO13.6.15/32]

JOHNSTON, ANN, born 1755, a farm servant in Stenness, Orkney,
emigrated from Kirkwall to Savannah, Georgia, on the
Marlborough Captain George Prissick, in September 1774, settled
in Richmond County, Georgia, as an indentured servant of Thomas
Brown. [PRO.T47.12][PRO.AO13.34.123-5]

JOHNSTON, DAVID, tobacconist, eldest son of Thomas Johnston a
baker in Edinburgh, died in Savannah, USA, 15 September 1820.
[AJ#3818][S.4.215]

JOHNSTON, DAVID, born in Scotland 1768, arrived in Savannah late
1821 on the ship Georgia, Captain Varnum. [USNA/par]

JOHNSTON, GEORGE, Indian trader in Augusta 20 November 1756.
[PRO.CO5/646, C17]

JOHNSTONE, GEORGE, in Pensacola 1766. [NAS.NRAS#0631]

JOHNSTONE, GEORGE, 1764, [PCCol, Unbound pp/593]; Governor of
West Florida, 1783. [BM.Add.3441/103]

JOHNSTON, GEORGE MILLIGAN, of Corehead, MD, Member of the
American Philosophical Society of Philadelphia, former Surgeon
General to HM Garrison in Georgia and South Carolina, died in
Dumfries on 9 March 1799. [EA#3674.174][AJ#2671]

JOHNSTON, JAMES, born on 13 September 1685, second son of Lewis
Johnston and Janet Rankin, married Janet Nisbet in Dumfries 1722,
a physician in the Royal Navy, settled in Georgia around 1750,
father of Janet, Henriette, Lewis, Andrew, James, John, Marion,
Rachel, and Elizabeth. [History of the Johnstons - Supplement,
Glasgow, 1925]

JOHNSTON, JAMES, senior, born 1738, a printer, founded the Georgia
    Gazette on 7 April 1763, died on 4 October 1808. [Savannah
    Death Register]

JOHNSTON, JANET, born 1754, a servant in Evie, Orkney, emigrated
    from Kirkwall, Orkney, to Savannah, Georgia, on the Marlborough,
    Captain Thomas Walker, in September 1775, an indentured servant
    of Thomas Brown in Georgia. [PRO.T47.12][PRO.AO13.34.123]

JOHNSTON, JOHN, granted 20,000 acres in West Florida 1767.
    [PC.Col.V.593]; in Mobile in August 1767. [NLS#MS119]

JOHNSTON, JOHN, a gardener, born in Scotland 1810, wife Catherine
    born in England, children John born 1845 and Mary Jane born
    1848, both born in Louisiana, settled in Harrison County,
    Mississippi. [C]

JOHNSTON, LEWIS, a merchant in Edinburgh, son of James Johnston,
    emigrated before 1756, settled in St Kitts and in Georgia, father of
    Ann, Elizabeth, and Rachel, died in Georgia, [refers to William
    Johnston; John Wood; James Hume] pro.April 1798 PCC.
    [NAS.SH.1756]; land grant in Savannah on 13 April 1761.
    [CRG#28/1.365] ; land grants in Savannah, Christ Church parish,
    on 16 January 1756, 7 August 1759, 7 August 1759, 7 July 1761,
    and 7 August 1764, [Grant book A, #61, Grant book B,
    #261/262/263, Grant book C, #128, Grant book E, #27]; President
    of the St Andrew's Society of Savannah 1768-1769. [SSS#88]

JOHNSTON, NICOL, born in 1747, a farmer in Evie, Orkney, emigrated
    with wife Isobel Flett and daughter Janet from Kirkwall to
    Savannah, Georgia, on the Marlborough, Captain Thomas Walker,
    in September 1775, settled in Richmond County, Georgia, as an
    indentured servant of Thomas Brown. [PRO.T47.12/AO13.34.123]

JOHNSTON, ROBERT, born 1715, servant to Thomas Christie,
    emigrated via Gravesend on the Anne, Captain Thomas Shubrick,
    to Georgia on 16 November 1732, married Anne Syms there, land
    grant in Savannah on 20 December 1733, died on 23 July 1734.
    [ESG#107]

JOHNSTON, ROBERT, granted 10,000 acres in East Florida during 1767. [PC.Col.V.592]

JOHNSTON, THOMAS RIDOUT, granted 10,000 acres in East Florida during 1767. [PC.Col.592]

JOLLIFFE, MARY, born in 1719, a single woman, an indentured servant, embarked from Inverness on the Loyal Judith for Georgia on 21 September 1741, arrived there on 4 December 1741. [PRO.CO.5.668.45] [ESG#26][CRG.30.197/199]

JOLLY, MARTIN, son of an Edinburgh tailor burgess, appointed a Member of the Council of East Florida on 13 May 1767; land agent and Member of the Council of East Florida 7 June 1767-1776, returned from Georgia, died in Antigua Street, Edinburgh, on 16 December 1806. [SM#69.78][Mowat, 43/164] [PRO.CO5.556.141] [PC.Col.V.564][APC.Col.1766-1783#564]

JOLLY, ..., brother of Martin Jolly, a shoemaker in St Augustine, East Florida, before 1775. [PRO.CO5.556.141]

JOLLY, ..., brother of Martin Jolly, an overseer in East Florida before 1775. [PRO.CO5.556.141]

JONES, JOHN, born in Scotland 1793, a blacksmith, settled in Mobile, Alabama. [C]

JONES, WILLIAM, born in Leith during 1793, a mariner, died in Savannah, Georgia, on 21 July 1809. [Savannah Death Register]

JONES, WILLIAM, born in Scotland during 1789, a sailor, settled in Alabama. [C]

JUNES(?), THOMAS, born in 1762, a Calvinist merchant in St Augustine, East Florida, 1786. [1786 Census of St Augustine]

JUNIER, KENNETH, born in 1762, a mariner, died on 10 October 1807. [Savannah Death Register]

KEITH, ANN, wife of John McAlister in Queensborough, Georgia, pro August 1807 PCC

KEITH, CHARLES, from Georgia, Lieutenant of the Royal Navy, son of William Keith, pro. March 1818 PCC

KELLY, WILLIAM, born in Scotland 1810, wife Mitha born in Georgia 1815, daughter Georgia Ann born in Georgia 1848. [C]

KELSALL, ROBERT, a merchant in Georgia, 1780. ? [NAS.RD4.259.758]

KEMP, Dr GEORGE, physician, possibly from Haddington, East Lothian, settled in East Florida later in Nassau, pro. July 1789 PCC

KEMP, JOHN, a merchant in New Orleans before 1847. [NAS.SH]

KENN, WILLIAM M., born in Scotland 1827, a merchant settled in Rodney, Jefferson County, Mississippi. [C]

KENNEDY, DANIEL, in Georgia during 1761, [CRG#28/1.400]

KENNEDY, DONALD, soldier of the Black Watch, imprisoned in the Tower of London on a charge of mutiny, transferred to Oglethorpe's Regiment in Georgia 1743, settled in Georgia. [GHS, Cate Colln. 45/3172]

KENNEDY, DONALD, land grant in Sappelo, Georgia, on 30 September 1757, [CRG#28/1.115]; in Medway, St Andrew's parish, during 1763. [Ga.Gaz.#34]

KENNEDY, DUNCAN, soldier of the Black Watch, imprisoned in the Tower of London on a charge of mutiny, transferred to Oglethorpe's Regiment in Georgia in 1743. [GHS, Cate Colln. 45/3172]

KENNEDY, HUGH, land grants in Ebenezer, Georgia, on 30 September 1757 and in St Matthew's on 5 January 1762, [CRG#28/1.114,

375]; planter, died on 15 March 1804. [Savannah Death Register] [Colonial Museum and Savannah Advertiser: 18.10.1808]

KENNEDY, JANE, in East Florida, dead by 1818. [NAS.CS17.1.37/299]

KENNEDY, JOHN, in Georgia during 1761, [CRG#28/1.400]

KENNEDY, Reverend JOHN, an Anglican minister and schoolmaster in East Florida 1777-1781, [Mowat#166]; formerly in East Florida, then in Glasgow, [will refers to Coll McDonald; Alexander McDonald; Charles McPherson] pro. December 1802 PCC; [NAS.CS17.1.38/291]; 1809, 1819, [NAS.CS17.1.28/305;38/291]

KENNEDY, KENNETH, born 1791, emigrated to USA in 1812, a mercantile clerk in New Orleans, moving to Opelousas. [1812]

KENNEDY, WILLIAM, born in 1719, servant to John Cuthbert of Drakies, Inverness, a tailor, emigrated from Inverness on the Prince of Wales, Captain George Dunbar, on 20 October 1735, arrived in Georgia on 10 January 1736, moved to Carolina in August 1742, husband of Elizabeth. [ESG#81]

KENNEDY, WILLIAM, soldier of the Black Watch, imprisoned in the Tower of London on a charge of mutiny, transferred to Oglethorpe's Regiment in Georgia in 1743. [GHS, Cate Colln. 45/3172]

KENNEDY, WILLIAM, land grants in Ebenezer, Georgia, on 30 September 1757, and on 7 February 1758, [CRG#28/1.115, 237]

KENNEDY, WILLIAM, in Savannah, Georgia, 1799. [NAS.CS17.1.18/183]

KERR, CHRISTOPHER, born 1790, emigrated to USA in 1805, a mercantile clerk in New Orleans, moving to Opelousas. [1812]

KERR, GEORGE, born in 1757, settled in USA during 1795, half-pay captain in British service, with wife and 8 children in Savannah in 1812. [1812]; a merchant in St Mary's, Camden County, Georgia,

1802, 1811. [NAS.CS17.1.21/412; 24/85; 25/151;30/316,457]

KERR, JAMES, born in 1797, son of William Kerr and Isobel Cuthill in Kincardineshire, died in Mobile during 1831. [Fordoun g/s]

KETTLE, THOMAS YOUNG, born in Leuchars, Fife, on 27 November 1778, eldest son of Reverend Thomas Kettle and Sarah Young, settled in Savannah, Georgia, died there on 6 August 1832. [F.5.222][EEC#18861]

KIDD, G., land grant in Christchurch parish, Georgia, on 11 September 1764. [Ga.Gaz.#78]

KIDSLEY, ..., a gardener, born in Scotland during 1815, settled in Adams County, Mississippi. [C]

KINCAID, GEORGE, in Christ Church parish, Georgia, later in Exeter, Devon, brother of Patrick Kincaid and husband of Marion Kincaid, pro. October 1791 PCC

KINNAIRD, DAVID, servant of William and Hugh Stirling, arrived in Georgia on 1 August 1734, possibly emigrated from Leith on the snow Hope of Leith, Captain Greig. [ESG#81]

KINNEAR, JAMES, born on 6 March 1824, son of Archibald Kinnear and Jean Kinnear in Montrose, Angus, died in Beardstown, Perry County, Tennessee, on 3 March 1853. [Montrose, Rosehill, g/s] [Montrose OPR]

KIRK, DAVID, an overseer, born in Scotland during 1820, settled in Adams County, Mississippi. [C]

KIRKPATRICK, WILLIAM, a carpenter, born in Scotland during 1825, settled in Harrison County, Mississippi. [C]

KNOX, ROBERT, Crown Agent in East Florida 1772-1782. [Mowat#162]

KNOX, ROBERT DADE, in Wilkes County, Georgia, son of Robert Knox a merchant in Virginia, grandson of John Knox, carpenter burgess of Renfrew, on 13 March 1829. [NAS.RD5.398.456][NAS.SH]

KNOX, WILLIAM, land grants in St Matthew's parish, Georgia, on 1 July 1760, in Savannah on 4 July 1758, 19 March 1759, 25 September 1760, in St Matthew's parish, Georgia, on 13 April 1761, in St Phillip's parish, Georgia, on 5 January 1762, [CRG#28/1.324, 331, 361, 374][Grant book B, #22/493, Plat book C, #128]; Crown Agent of East Florida 1764-1770. [Mowat#162]

LAIRD, C.A., born in Scotland during 1820, a merchant, settled in Mobile, Alabama. [C]

LAIRD, MARY, wife of James Houstoun, died in Mobile Bay on 14 February 1858. [Port Glasgow g/s]

LAIRD, ROBERT, born in Scotland during 1814, a merchant, settled in Mobile, Alabama. [C]

LAIRD, WILLIAM, son of David Laird in Glasgow, [probably the William Laird baptised on 12 May 1814 in Barony parish, Glasgow, son of David Laird and Christian Anderson, {Barony OPR}], died in Mobile, Alabama, on 13 May 1849. [SG#1827]

LAMON, ISABELLA, born in Scotland 1802, died 17 January 1864, wife of A. McDonald, buried at Carolina Presbyterian Church, Elmore, Alabama. [Elmore g/s]

LASHLEY, LAUCHLIN, a farmer, born in Scotland during 1782, Nancy Lashley, born in North Carolina in 1801, Archy Lashley, a teacher, born in 1827, Anna Lashley, born in 1831, Mary Lashley, born in 1832, Daniel Lashley, born in 1834, Rachel Lashley, born in 1838, Abigail Lashley, born in 1841, and Thomas Lashley, born in 1843, children born in Telfair County, Georgia, resident there. [C]

LAUDER, JANE, died in Savannah during September 1823. [Georgia Republican: 11.9.1823]

LAUDER, MARY, in Augusta, Richmond County, Georgia. cnf. 12 December 1797 Edinburgh. [NAS.CC8.8.130]

LAURIE, DAVID, born in Scotland during 1803, a wagon maker, Isabel born in England in 1809, Isabel born in London in 1832, Ann born during 1837 in Adams County, Mississippi, Fortia born during 1839 in Louisiana, Margaret born during 1844 in Amite County, Mississippi, settled in Amite County, Mississippi. [C]

LAW, JOHN, born 1790, emigrated to USA in 1802, a carpenter in New Orleans. [1812]

LAW, JOSEPH, Edinburgh, to America in 1674, settled in Liberty County, Georgia. [BLG#2782]

LAWRIE, ROBERT BLACK, born in 1792, married Janet Thomson on 22 September 1821, resident in Canongate, Edinburgh, emigrated to USA in 1822, died in Apalatachicola, Florida, on 3 July 1838. [SGen#XV.4.85]

LAWSON, JOHN, granted 100 acres in St John's parish, Georgia, on 1 July 1760 and 200 acres there on 13 April 1761. [Grant Books B.440 and D.366] ?

LAWSON, JOHN, baptised on 23 August 1795 in Dundee, son of David Lawson and Jean Hynd {1768-1822}, died in New Orleans during 1822. [Dundee, Howff, g/s][Dundee OPR]

LEECH, WILLIAM, third son of Reverend John Leech of the Secession Church in Largs, Ayrshire, died in Vernon, Mississippi, during 1831. [AJ#4384]

LESLIE, JOHN, baptised on 13 October 1749 second son of Alexander Leslie of Balnageith, Morayshire, and Anna Duff, emigrated to America, an executor in Florida of James Duff who died in Jamaica in 1782, [Aberdeen University MS#2226/72/15]; a partner of Panton, Leslie and Company, merchants in St Augustine, East Florida, 1786, married Elizabeth Cain in 1789, he died in 1803; an

SCOTS IN GEORGIA AND THE DEEP SOUTH, 1735-1845

Episcopalian resident of St Augustine in 1786. [FHR#18][IT#19, 47][1786 Census of St Augustine]

LESLIE, JOHN, born in Scotland during 1815, a baker, settled in Alabama. [C]

LESLIE, PETER, baptised on 12 March 1777 in Forfar, Angus, son of John Leslie and Agnes Ferrier, a shopkeeper, died in Savannah, Georgia, on 15 August 1805. [Savannah Courier: 11.9.1805] [Savannah Death Register][Forfar OPR]

LESLIE, ROBERT, baptised on 3 February 1758 in Rothes, Morayshire, son of Alexander Leslie of Balnageith and Anna Duff, emigrated to America, partner in firm of Panton, Leslie and Company merchants in Florida by 1792. [IT#19][Rothes OPR]

LESLEY, ROBERT, born in 1757, a husbandman and indentured servant, emigrated via London to Georgia on the Mary in February 1774. [PRO.T47.9/11]

LEYS, GEORGE, born 1834, son of John Leys, a farmer in Scallie, and Mary Duthie, died in New Orleans on 20 October 1848. [Udny, Aberdeenshire, g/s]

LIDDELL, JOHN, a merchant, born in Scotland during 1815, settled in Adams County, Mississippi. [C]

LIDDLE, GEORGE, born during 1760, a yeoman, emigrated via Newcastle to Georgia on the Georgia Packet in September 1775, settled in Friendsborough, Georgia. [PRO.T47.9/11]

LIDDLE, WILLIAM, granted 200 acres in St John's parish, Georgia, on 3 August 1762. [Grant Book - D171][CRG#28/1.434]

LINAY, JOHN, born in 1743, a farmer in Evie, Orkney, emigrated with wife Isobel and children James and Ann, from Kirkwall to Georgia on the Marlborough, Captain George Prissick, in September 1774, settled in Richmond County, Georgia, as an indentured servant of Thomas Brown. [PRO.T47.12][PRO.AO13.34.123-5]

LINDSAY, JAMES, baptised on 2 November 1794 in parish of Falkland, Fife, son of John Lindsay and Margaret Jackson, a joiner, died in New Orleans on 28 August 1822. [Falkland, Fife, g/s][Falkland OPR]

LINNON, WILLIAM, born in 1756, emigrated via Newcastle to Georgia on the Georgia Packet in September 1775, settled in Friendsborough, Georgia. [PRO.T47.9/11]

LITHGOW, ROBERT, born in 1758, son of Mr Lithgow in Leith, settled in Glynn County during 1775, died on his estate on Colonel's Island, Georgia, on 11 October 1802. [Edinburgh Advertiser#4077.03] [Colonial Museum and Savannah Advertiser: 22.10.1802]

LITTLE, J., born in Scotland during 1805, settled in Harrison County, Mississippi. [C]

LITTLE, WILLIAM, born in 1764 son of James Little {1741-1807} and Mary … in Sibbaldie, Dumfries-shire, emigrated to New York before 1813, in Tennessee by 1822, died at Mount William, Tennessee, on 20 July 1828. [NAS.SH][Sibbaldie g/s]

LIVINGSTONE, A., a saddler, born in Scotland in 1814, settled in Adams County, Mississippi. [C]

LIVINGSTONE, A. C., son of Archibald Livingstone, {1781-1857}, a coastwaiter at the Isle of Whithorn, died in Jacksonville, Florida, aged 68. [Whithorn, Wigtownshire, g/s]

LIVINGSTONE, HUGH, planter in southern Georgia in 1741. [CRG#30.343]

LOCH, THOMAS, embarked on the Loyal Judith, Captain John Lennon, in Inverness bound for Georgia on 21 September 1741, arrived on 4 December 1741, settled at Frederica, Georgia. [ESG#30]

LOCHHEAD, JAMES, a gardener, born in Scotland during 1810, settled in Warren County, Mississippi. [C]

LOGAN, JOHN, born in 1793, emigrated to USA in 1810, a merchant's clerk in Savannah 1812. [1812]

LOOKUP, ALEXANDER, born in Dumfries during 1786, [possibly baptised in Dumfries on 12 May 1788 son of Alexander Lookup, {Dumfries OPR}], Convenor of the Seven Incorporations there, a magistrate there, and an elder of St Michael's church in Dumfries, died in Columbus, Texas, on 24 June 1849. [SG#1847]

LOSSLEY, or Mackay, CHRISTIAN, born in 1711, a widow, and her daughter Katherine Mackay born in 1735, embarked on the Loyal Judith, Captain John Lemon, in Inverness for Georgia on 21 September 1741, arrived on 4 December 1741. [PRO.CO.5.668][ESG30][CRG.XXX.197/199]

LOUDEN, JAMES F., born in Scotland during 1814, a clerk, wife Mary Jane born in Massachusetts during 1819, and children Cora, Alice and Mima, (all born in Alabama), settled in Alabama by 1842. [C]

LOUDEN, ROBERT, born in 1786, emigrated to USA in 1808, a weaver in Louisville 1812. [1812]

LOUDON, WILLIAM, possibly from Dunbartonshire, in Louisiana during 1847. [NAS.SH]

LOUGHERY, Mrs JANE, born in Scotland during 1815, husband P. born in Ireland during 1813, mother of Eneas and Jane-Ann (both born in Alabama), settled in Mobile, Alabama. [C]

LOUTTIT, THOMAS, born on 1 October 1764 son of Robert Louttit and Katherine Irvine in Stromness, Orkney, emigrated from Kirkwall to Savannah, Georgia, on the Marlborough, Captain George Prissick, in September 1774, settled in Richmond County, Georgia, as an indentured servant to Thomas Brown. [PRO.T47.12][PRO.AO13.34.123-5]

SCOTS IN GEORGIA AND THE DEEP SOUTH, 1735-1845

LOW, ALEXANDER, of Criggie, late merchant in Savannah, 20
December 1816. [NAS.RGS#155/7]

LOW, JAMES, master of the Georgia of Savannah, died on passage to
Liverpool on 29 July 1819. [S#136.19]

LUNAN, FRANCIS, baptised 5 May 1729 son of William Lunan in
Monymusk, a farmer from Monymusk, Aberdeenshire, settled in
East Florida during 1767. [NAS.NRAS.777, bundle 402]
[NAS.GD345.916.4][Monymusk OPR]

LUNDIE, ARCHIBALD, from Greenock, Renfrewshire, a merchant in
Savannah, Georgia, before 1776, a merchant in St Augustine, East
Florida, trading to the Mississippi on 31 October 1776, a Loyalist,
settled in the West Indies. [PRO.AO13.33.45][NAS.CS16.1.185]
[NAS.CS16.1.185][NAS.NRAS.0159.C4]

LYON, JOHN, a blacksmith, died in Savannah on 12 October 1779.
[Royal GaGaz#2/3]

MCADAM, JOHN, born 1786, emigrated to US 1809, a merchant in
Lexington 1812. [1812]

MACALESTER, JAMES, born 1765, his wife born 1772, daughter
Elisabeth born 1788 and son James born 1792, arrived in Louisiana
on 19 April 1797. [NWI.2.229]?

MCALLAN, HUGH, soldier of the Black Watch, imprisoned in the
Tower of London on a charge of mutiny, transferred to
Oglethorpe's Regiment in Georgia 1743. [GHS, Cate Colln.
45/3172]

MCALLUM, Mrs MARYANN, born in Scotland 1790, emigrated via
North Carolina, wife of Archibald McAllum a farmer, settled in
Montgomery County, Georgia. [C]

MCALPIN, ALEXANDER, born 1730s, settled in South Carolina 1760s,
married Mary Moore Haggard, settled in Georgia during 1770s,
died 1790. [SGen]

MCALPIN, ARCHIBALD, born in Glasgow 1772, [possibly the Archibald McAlpin baptised in Glasgow on 1 December 1776, son of Walter McAlpin and Mary Neil, {Glasgow OPR}] settled in South Carolina and then in Georgia, died in Savannah, Georgia, 1822.[Georgia for the Country, Savannah, 28.9.1822]

MCALPIN, DONALD, soldier of the Black Watch, imprisoned in the Tower of London on a charge of mutiny, transferred to Oglethorpe's Regiment in Georgia 1743. [GHS, Cate Colln. 45/3172]

MCALPIN, HENRY, emigrated to America with his wife Helen McInnes in 1804, settled in Georgia 1812. [Duke University, Wallace pp]

MCANDREW, ALEXANDER, born 1757, a yeoman, emigrated from Newcastle to Georgia on the Georgia Packet in September 1775. [PRO.T47.9/11]

MACANNON, MARGARET, born 1720, a 4 year indentured servant, embarked for Georgia 19 November 1737, arrived on 14 January 1737. [ESG#31]

MCARTHUR, Mrs ELIZABETH, born in Scotland 1805, wife of Duncan McArthur a farmer in Montgomery County, Georgia. [C]

MCARTHUR, NEIL, born in Scotland during 1790, a planter in Choctaw County, Alabama, wife Martha born in North Carolina during 1805, children Nathan a laborer born in 1829, Martha born in 1834, ... born 1836, and Ann born in 1838, {all in Alabama}. [C]

MACBEAN, ARCHIBALD, of Aberlour, Banffshire, born 1709, a farmer, emigrated from Inverness on the Prince of Wales, Captain George Dunbar, on 20 October 1735, arrived in Georgia on 10 January 1736, died 1740, wife Catherine Cameron, son Alexander died in 1740. [ESG#83]; emigrated from Inverness to Georgia on the Two Brothers, Captain William Thomson, in July 1737, [SPC.1737.248]; imported 2 male indentured servants on the Two Brothers, Captain Thomson, 1738, [CRG#30.7]; Indian trader, arrived in Georgia on 16 January 1738. [ESG#31]; settled at New Inverness by 1739. [CRG.3.427]; petitioned Oglethorpe re slavery on 3 January 1739. [AGA#65]

MCBEAN, D., born in Scotland during 1816, wife and child born in Mississippi, settled in Harrison County, Mississippi. [C]

MCBEAN, DAVID, born in Scotland during 1830, settled in Harrison County, Mississippi. [C]

MACBEAN, DUNCAN, born in 1720, servant to John Mackintosh, emigrated from Inverness on the Prince of Wales, Captain George Dunbar, on 20 October 1735, landed in Georgia on 10 January 1736. [ESG#83]

MACBEAN, ELIZABETH, born in 1701, a 4 year indentured servant, embarked for Georgia on 19 November 1737, arrived on 14 January 1738. [ESG#31]

MCBEAN, JAMES, born in Scotland during 1824, settled in Harrison County, Mississippi. [C]

MCBEAN, JOHN, land grant in Darien, Georgia, on 5 April 1757, [CRG#28/1.57]

MCBEAN, JOHN MCWILLIE, born in 1714, servant to John Spence, emigrated from Inverness on the Prince of Wales, Captain George Dunbar, on 20 October 1735, arrived in Georgia on 10 January 1736. [ESG#83]

MCBEAN, LAUCHLAN, from Inverness, a planter, settled in Augusta, Georgia, with sons William and John, before 1756. [SPC.1737.6]; an Indian trader, allocated a house and 500 acres of land in Fort Augusta on 14 June 1736, [ESG#83]; a planter in Augusta, Georgia, on 11 November 1756 Georgia

MACBEAN, MARGARET, born in 1728, a 7 year indentured servant, embarked for Georgia 19 November 1737, arrived 14 January 1738. [ESG#31]

MACBEAN, WILLIAM, born in 1714, an indentured servant, emigrated from Inverness to Georgia on 20 October 1735 on the Prince of Wales, master George Dunbar, arrived on 10 January 1736, a servant in Darien on 6 May 1741. [ESG#31]

MACBEAN, WILLIAM, born in 1724, an indentured servant, emigrated from Inverness on the Two Brothers, Captain William Thomson, for Georgia in July 1737, arrived on 20 January 1737, a servant in Darien on 6 May 1741. [ESG#31]

MACBEAN, WILLIAM, born in 1720, an indentured servant, emigrated from Inverness on the Two Brothers, Captain William Thomson, in July 1737, arrived in Georgia on 20 January 1737. [ESG#31]

MCBEAN, WILLIAM, granted 10,000 acres in East Florida during 1767. [PC.Col.V.590]

MCBEATH, GEORGE, born in 1756, a farm servant in Wick, Caithness, emigrated from Caithness via Kirkwall, Orkney, to Savannah, Georgia, on the Marlborough, Captain Thomas Walker, in September 1775, settled in Richmond County, Georgia, as an indentured servant of Thomas Brown. [PRO.T47.12][PRO.AO13.34.123-5]

MCBRIDE, ANTONY, a servant to William and Hugh Stirling, arrived in Georgia on 1 August 1734 possibly emigrated from Leith on the snow Hope of Leith, Captain Greig. [ESG#83]

MCBRIDE, CLEMENT, a raftman, born in Scotland in 1819, settled in Warren County, Mississippi. [C]

MCBRIDE, HENRY, servant to William and Hugh Stirling, arrived in Georgia on 1 August 1734, possibly emigrated from Leith on the snow Hope of Leith, Captain Greig. [ESG#83]

MCBRYDE, JOHN, a merchant in Georgia, son of John McBryde a farmer in Little Tongue, and Margaret Donnan, {18..?} [Whithorn g/s]

MCCALLUM, PETER, born in Scotland during 1769, a sailor, settled in Mobile, Alabama. [C]

MCCANDLESS, JAMES, born in Scotland in 1817, wife Jane born in Louisiana during 1817, settled in Warren County, Mississippi. [C]

MCCASKILL, DANIEL, born in Skye, Inverness-shire, during 1760, son of Murdoch McCaskill, emigrated to America before 1770, father of John, Alexander, Bruce and Murdoch, possibly died in Georgia. [MCF]

MCCASKILL, FINLEY, a farmer, born in Scotland during 1796, wife Mary McCaskill born in North Carolina, settled in Walton County, Florida. [C]

MCCASKILL, ISABEL, born in Scotland during 1783, Catherine McCaskill born in Florida during 1820, Christian born in Florida during 1831, settled in Walton County, Florida. [C]

MCCAY, JOHN, born 1775, emigrated to US during 1810, with his wife and 2 children, an umbrella maker in Savannah 1812. [1812]

MCCAY, J.S., born in Scotland during 1839, settled in Alabama. [C]

MCCLAIN, ANDREW, born in Scotland during 1826, a clerk, wife Sarah born in Georgia 1824, settled in Mobile, Alabama. [C]

MCCLARIN, M. (female), born in Scotland during 1790, with William Shaw a planter born in 1820, Mary Shaw born in 1829, William Shaw jr., born in 1848, and M.E.Shaw (female) born in 1849, and C. Paterson (female) born in 1839, all born in Mississippi, settled in Jefferson County, Mississippi. [C]

MACCLELLAND, JAMES, land grant in St Andrew's parish, Georgia, on 21 May 1762, [CRG#28/1.421]

MCCLELLAND, JOHN, land grant in Ogeechee on 5 February 1757, [CRG#28/1.53]; allocated a land grant in Christchurch parish, Georgia, on 11 October 1764. [Ga.Gaz.#80]

MCCLELLAND, MARY, a widow, land grant in St Andrew's parish, Georgia, on 21 May 1762, [CRG#28/1.421]

MCCOIG, JOHN, born in Scotland during 1797, a farmer, wife Mary born in South Carolina during 1797, sons John born in 1828, Neal born in 1832, and Malcolm born in 1833, all farmers born in South Carolina, settled in Cocke County, Tennessee. [C]

MCCOLLUM, ARCHIBALD, a farmer, born in Scotland during 1784, Sarah McCollum born in North Carolina during 1820, Robert McCollum born in North Carolina during 1825, Dougal McCollum born in Florida during 1828, and Margaret McCollum born in Florida during 1830, settled in Walton County, Florida. [C]

MCCULLOM, ARCHIBALD, soldier of the Black Watch, imprisoned in the Tower of London on a charge of mutiny, transferred to Oglethorpe's Regiment in Georgia during 1743. [GHS, Cate Colln. 45/3172]

MCCOLLUM, JOHN, land grant in Halifax, Georgia, on 7 June 1757, [CRG#28/1.116]

MACCOULL, ALEXANDER, born in 1711, servant to Mackay of Scourie, emigrated from Inverness on the Prince of Wales, Captain George Dunbar, to Georgia on 20 October 1735, arrived there on 10 January 1736. [ESG#87]

MCCREA, MARGARET, born in 1795, settled in Carroll County, Georgia, before 1850. [C]

MCCREDIE, ANDREW, born in Ayrshire during 1757, son of William McCredie of Pierceton and Barbara Wilson, a shipmaster and merchant in Savannah, Georgia, died there on 17 April 1807. [Savannah Death Register] [Colonial Museum and Savannah Advertiser, 24.4.1807] [ANY#1/338]

MCCRIMMON, ARCHY, born in Scotland during 1790, a farmer, Mary McCrimmon, born in Pulaski County, Georgia, during 1811, John McCrimmon, born in 1829, Margaret McCrimmon, born in 1832, William McCrimmon, born in 1834, Duncan McCrimmon, born in 1836, Farquhard McCrimmon, born in 1838, Catherine McCrimmon, born in 1840, Isabella McCrimmon, born in 1842, and Archibald McCrimmon, born in 1848, all born in Telfair County, Georgia, resident there. [C]

MCCULLOCH, JOHN, granted 926 acres in St Andrew's parish, Georgia, on 2 November 1762. [PRO.CO.5.648.E68][CRG#28/1.439]

MCCULLOCH, JOHN, died in Savannah on 10 November 1802. [Colonial Museum and Advertiser, 12.11.1802]

MCCULLOCH, WILLIAM, born in 1751, a barber, emigrated with wife Barbara born 1751, via Newcastle to Georgia on the Georgia Packet in September 1775, settled in Friendsborough, Georgia. [PRO.T47.9/11]

MCCULLOM, JAMES, a planter, born in 1824, wife Julia born in 1815, children Elizabeth born in 1843, T. G. born in 1846, Julia born in 1837 all children born in Mississippi, settled in Adams County, Mississippi. [C]

MCCULLUM, JOHN, a planter, born in Scotland during 1794, settled in Adams County, Mississippi. [C]

MCCULLOM, WILLIAM, born in Perth during 1778, a mariner, died in Savannah, Georgia, on 6 December 1806. [Savannah Death Register]

MCCURRIE, ANDREW, land grant of 100 acres in St George parish, Georgia, on 13 April 1761. [PRO.CO.5.648.E46][CRG#28/1.362]

MCDANIEL, ANGUS, a farmer, born in Scotland during 1802, Mary McDaniel born in North Carolina during 1806, Margaret McDaniel born during 1831, Allen McDaniel born during 1833, John McDaniel born during 1834, Sarah McDaniel born during 1836, Catherine McDaniel born during 1838, Duncan McDaniel born during 1840, Nancy McDaniel born during 1844, and John McDaniel born during 1847, all children born in Florida, settled in Walton County, Florida. [C]

MCDANIEL, CATHERINE, born in Scotland during 1797, Janet McDaniel born in North Carolina during 1820, Sarah McDaniel born in North Carolina during 1822, Christian McDaniel born during 1830, Isabel McDaniel born during 1832, Archibald McDaniel born during 1836, Norman McDaniel born during 1838, and Charles McDaniel born during 1840, all born in Florida, settled in Walton County, Florida. [C]

MCDANIEL, JOHN, a farmer, born in Scotland during 1790, Mary McDaniel born during 1829 in North Carolina, settled in Walton County, Florida. [C]

MCDANIEL, JOHN R., a farmer, born in Scotland during 1805, Nelly McDaniel born in North Carolina during 1815, settled in Walton County, Florida. [C]

MCDANIEL, MARGARET, born in Scotland during 1790, settled in Walton County, Florida. [C]

MCDANIEL, PETER, a farmer, born in Scotland during 1792, Sarah McDaniel born in North Carolina during 1800, Mary McDaniel born during 1829, Margaret McDaniel born during 1831, Norman McDaniel born during 1827, Daniel McDaniel born during 1834, Alexander McDaniel born during 1836, and Peter McDaniel born during 1838, all children born in Florida, settled in Walton County, Florida. [C]

MCDANIEL, PETER, a farmer, born in Scotland during 1800, Margaret McDaniel born in North Carolina during 1805, Neil McDaniel, a laborer, born during 1828, Sarah McDaniel born during 1832, John McDaniel born during 1836, Bell Ann McDaniel born during 1834, Margaret McDaniel born during 1839, Lilla McDaniel born during

1840, and Florida McDaniel born during 1843, all born in Florida, settled in Walton County, Florida. [C]

MCDERMID, MARY, born in Scotland during 1790, settled in Telfair County, Georgia, with Joseph C. Clements, a farmer, born in Montgomery County, Georgia, during 1818, Mary Ann Clements, born in North Carolina during 1817, Catherine Clements, born in 1844, and Daly Ann Clements, born in 1847, both in Irving County, Georgia. [C]

MCDEVITT, H. D., born in Scotland during 1822, an artist, settled in Mobile, Alabama. [C]

MCDONALD, ALEXANDER, soldier, emigrated with wife Mary McDonald, from Gravesend to Georgia on the Mary Ann, Captain Thomas Schubrick, on 16 August 1737, arrived in Georgia on 31 October 1737. [SPC.43.459][ESG#83]

MACDONALD, ALEXANDER, in Darien on 6 May 1741. [ESG#31]

MCDONALD, ALEXANDER, land grant in St Andrew's, Georgia, on 7 November 1758, [CRG#28/1.325]

MCDONALD, ALEXANDER, Captain of the Florida Rangers, 1782, [PRO.CO5/III]; in Aberdeen, Captain on half-pay of the Florida Rangers, [refers to cousin Mary, wife of William Patterson guardian of his only children Alexia, James, and Margaret McDonald; and aunts Jane Munro and Mary MacLain] pro.April 1805 PCC

MCDONALD, ALEXANDER, born in Scotland during 1811, a farmer, settled in Vermillion parish, Louisiana, by 1850. [C]

MACDONALD, ARCHIBALD, born in 1721, an indentured servant, emigrated from Inverness on the Two Brothers, Captain William Thomson, for Georgia in July 1737, arrived on 20 January 1737. [ESG#31]

MCDONALD, BARBARA, born in Skye, Inverness-shire, during 1767, daughter of John and Flora McDonald, wife of Roderick McDonald, settled in Putnam County, Georgia, died in Fayetteville, Georgia, on 17 December 1859. [Fayetteville County Cemetery]

MACDONALD, CHRISTIAN, born in 1720, a 4 year indentured servant, embarked for Georgia on 19 November 1737, arrived on 14 January 1738. [ESG#31]

MACDONALD, DONALD, born in 1719, emigrated from Inverness on the Prince of Wales, Captain George Dunbar, on 20 October 1735, arrived in Georgia on 10 January 1736, a servant in Darien in 1741, husband of Alvine Wood, father of Donald. [ESG#83]

MACDONALD, DONALD, born in 1725, an indentured servant, emigrated from Inverness on the Two Brothers, Captain William Thomson, for Georgia in July 1737, arrived on 20 January 1737. [ESG#31]

MACDONALD, DONALD, granted 200 acres on the South Branch of the South Newport River, Georgia, on 5 April 1757. [Grant Book A.433]; and in 1763. [Ga.Gaz.#34][CRG#28/1.111]

MACDONALD, DONALD, born on 17 August 1802, son of Roderick McDonald and Barbara MacDonald, died on 29 December 1834. [Fayetteville County Cemetery, Georgia]

MACDONALD, DONALD, possibly from Skye, a grocer in Thomasville, Florida, (?), in 1841. [NAS.NRAS#0427]

MACDONALD, DUGALD, born in 1701, an indentured servant, emigrated from Inverness to Georgia on the Two Brothers, Captain William Thomson, in July 1737, arrived on 20 January 1737. [ESG#31]

MCDONALD, DUNCAN, a reluctant recruit for Georgia, absconded from Fort George, near Inverness, on 27 May 1737. [SPC.43.323][PRO.CO5.639#244]

MCDONALD, D., born in Scotland in 1825, settled in Adams County, Mississippi. [C]

MACDONALD, ELIZABETH [or HELEN?], born in 1722, a 4 year indentured servant, embarked for Georgia on 19 November 1737, arrived on 14 January 1738, at Darien on 6 May 1741. [ESG#31]

MCDONALD, FLORA, born on 25 August 1792, emigrated to America, died in Fayetteville, Georgia, on 22 October 1857. [Fayetteville Cemetery]

MACDONALD, FLORENICA, born in 1721, a 1 year indentured servant, embarked for Georgia on 19 November 1737, arrived on 14 January 1738. [ESG#31]

MACDONALD, GEORGE, of Tar, born in 1722, a laborer, an indentured servant, emigrated from Inverness to Georgia on 20 October 1735 on the Prince of Wales, master George Dunbar, arrived on 10 January 1736. [ESG#32]

MACDONALD, GEORGE, born in 1720, a laborer, an indentured servant, embarked in Inverness for Georgia on the Loyal Judith, Captain John Lemon, on 21 September 1741, arrived there on 2 December 1741. [PRO.CO.5.668][ESG#32]

MCDONALD, GEORGE, in South Newport, Georgia, in 1763. [Ga.Gaz.#34]

MCDONALD, GEORGE, born in 1676, 'came with Oglethorpe', died in Liberty County, Georgia, in July 1786. [Gaz.StateGa#2/2] [PHGA#159]

MACDONALD, HUGH, of Tar, born in 1704, laborer, an indentured servant, emigrated from Inverness to Georgia on 20 October 1735 on the Prince of Wales, master George Dunbar, arrived on 10 January 1736. [ESG#32]

MCDONALD, JAMES, a servant in Georgia on 23 June 1734. [ESG#83]

MCDONALD, JAMES, born in Culloden, Inverness-shire, in 1766, died in Savannah, Georgia, on 10 September 1811. [Savannah Republican: 12.9.1811]

MCDONALD, JOHN, servant to John Baillie later to Andrew Grant, arrived in Georgia on 1 August 1734, possibly emigrated from Leith on the snow Hope of Leith, Captain Greig. [ESG#83]

MCDONALD, JOHN, servant to Donald McDonald in Georgia around 1740. [ESG#83]

MCDONALD, JOHN, settled in New Inverness by 1739. [Ga.Col.Rec.3.427]; petitioned Oglethorpe re slavery on 3 January 1739. [AGA#65]; land grant in Darien on 30 September 1757, [CRG#28/1.234]

MACDONALD, JOHN, born in 1709, laborer and hunter, an indentured servant, embarked on the Loyal Judith, Captain John Lemon, in Inverness for Georgia on 21 September 1741, arrived on 2 December 1741, a freeholder of Savannah, wife Marian Cadach {born in 1712, died in 1742}, children Donald born in 1739, Elizabeth born in 1735, and William born in 1737. [PRO.CO.5.668] [ESG#32] [CRG.30.197/199]

MCDONALD, JOHN, soldier of the Black Watch, imprisoned in the Tower of London on a charge of mutiny, transferred to Oglethorpe's Regiment in Georgia in 1743, settled in Georgia. [GHS, Cate Colln. 45/3172]

MCDONALD, Dr JOHN, born in 1799, died on 30 September 1821. [Georgia Republican: 4.10.1821]

MCDONALD, JOHN, born in Scotland in 1800, a laborer, settled in Alabama. [C]

MCDONALD, JOHN, born in Scotland in 1826, a boatman, settled in Mobile, Alabama. [C]

MACDONALD, NORMAN, born in 1709, a laborer, an indentured servant, embarked on the Loyal Judith, Captain John Lemon, in Inverness for Georgia on 21 September 1741, arrived on 2 December 1741, with wife Elizabeth Mackay born in 1712, and children Catherine born in 1732, and John born in 1735; land grant in Darien on 7 February 1758. [PRO.CO.5.668][ESG#32] [CRG#30.197/199][CRG#28/1.327]

MACDONALD, RACHEL, born in 1722, a 4 year indentured servant, embarked for Georgia on 19 November 1737, arrived on 14 January 1738, servant to William Stephens. [ESG#32/83]

MCDONALD, RANALD, born in 1723, servant of John Mackintosh of Kingussie jr., emigrated from Inverness on the Prince of Wales, Captain George Dunbar, on 20 October 1735, arrived in Georgia on 10 January 1736, settled at Darien, New Inverness, by 1739.[ESG#83] [GCR.3.427]; petitioned Oglethorpe re slavery on 3 January 1739. [AGA#65]; of the Highland Company of Rangers, possibly killed at Fort Moosa in June 1740 [ESG#83]

MCDONALD, WILLIAM, land grant of 200 acres in St George's parish, Georgia, on 3 August 1762. [PRO.CO.5.648.E71][CRG#28/1.433]

MACDONALD, WILLIAM, a merchant in Port Leon, Florida, in 1841. [NAS.NRAS#0427]

MCDONNELL, ALEXANDER, born in 1760, a Catholic and a farmer in St Augustine, East Florida, in 1786. [FHR#18][1786 Census of St Augustine]

MCDONNELL, RANDOLPH, born in 1741, a Catholic and a farmer in St Augustine, East Florida, husband of Catherine, in 1786. [FHR#18] [1786 Census of St Augustine]

MCDOUGAL, CHARLES, born in Scotland in 1766, a planter, Catherine McDougal, born in North Carolina in 1800, settled in Jefferson County, Mississippi. [C]

MCDOUGAL, JOHN, born in 1778, a shipmaster, died on 22 October 1806. [Savannah Death Register]

MCDOUGALL, WILLIAM, a planter in East Florida, died in 1774. [NAS.NRAS.0181; p.11]

MCDOUGALD, WILLIAM, son of William McDougald a merchant in Edinburgh, died in East Florida on 8 July 1774. [SM#36.562]

MCDOWAL, ..., emigrated to East Florida in 1766, an estate manager there. [NAS.NRAS#771, bundle 295]

MCDOWALL, THOMAS, born in Wigtownshire in 1792, baptised in June 1793 in the parish of Inch, son of John McDowal and Ann Beggs, settled in Augusta, Georgia, died at Salt Sulphur Springs, Virginia, on 9 July 1825. [Augusta Chronicle: 27.7.1825][Inch OPR]; to USA in 1811, a merchant's clerk in Savannah by 1812, [1812]

MCDUFFIE, ABBIGAIL, born in Scotland in 1780, with Edward G. McDuffie, a farmer born in North Carolina in 1812, Catherine McDuffie, born in North Carolina in 1813, Caroline McDuffie, born in 1840, Margaret McDuffie, born in 1842, Thomas McDuffie, born in 1844, Abbigail McDuffie, born in 1846, Josephine McDuffie, born in 1847, John McDuffie, born in 1849, all born in Telfair County, Georgia, resident there. [C]

MCDUFFIE, CATHERINE, born in Scotland in 1770, Malcom McDuffie, a farmer, born in North Carolina in 1773, Margaret McDuffie, born in North Carolina in 1810, Catherine McDuffie, born in Telfair County, Georgia, in 1834, and Angus McDuffie, born in Telfair County, Georgia, in 1843, settled in Telfair County, Georgia. [C]

MCDUFFIE, MURDOCH, Justice of the Peace for Telfair County in 1809, [Georgia Executive Minutes]; Indian trader on the Ocmulgee River, Telfair County, Georgia, in 1822, later settled near Jacksonville. [Telfair County Deed Book G#33; Irwin County Misc. Estate Records 1822-1855, pp15/29][GHR]

MACEEVER, EVANDER, born in 1719, an indentured servant, emigrated from Inverness on the Two Brothers, Captain William Thomson, in July 1737, arrived on 20 January 1737. [ESG#32]

MACEEVER, RODERICK, born 1719, a 4 year indentured servant, emigrated from Inverness for Georgia 19 November 1737, arrived 14 January 1738. [ESG#32]

MCFADZEAN, JOHN, born 1773, a blacksmith, died on 10 August 1805. [Savannah Death Register][Savannah Courier: 4.9.1805]

MCFARLAND, ALEXANDER, killed by Indians in 1814. [Savannah Republican: 8.2.1814]

MCFARLANE, DANIEL, servant to William and Hugh Stirling, arrived in Georgia on 1 August 1734, possibly emigrated from Leith on the snow Hope of Leith, Captain Greig. [ESG#83]

MACFARLANE, DUNCAN, servant to William and Hugh Stirling, possibly emigrated from Leith on the snow Hope of Leith, Captain Greig, arrived in Georgia on 1 August 1734. [ESG#87]

MCFARLANE, J., a tailor arrived in Georgia from London on 29 November 1764. [Ga.Gaz.#86]; a tailor in Savannah, pro.21 September 1867 Georgia.

MCFARLANE, JAMES, born in Glasgow 1780, a bookbinder in Georgia, died on 28 July 1814. [Savannah Republican: 10.11.1814]; born 1776, to US 1802, a bookseller in Savannah 1812, [1812]

MACFRARY, JAMES, land grant in Ebenezer, Georgia, on 7 June 1757, [CRG#28/1.109]

MCGEE, WILLIAM, a house roofer, born in Scotland during 1817, wife Lavinia born in Massachusetts, infant born in Mississippi, settled in Warren County, Mississippi. [C]

MCGHIE, FRANCIS ALEXANDER, born on 20 November 1806 in Toull, died in Tuscaloosa, Alabama, on 20 August 1856. [Buittle g/s]

MCGILLIVRAY, ALEXANDER, land grant in St George parish, and in Augusta, Georgia, 3 February 1762. [PRO.CO.5.648.E68] [CRG#28/1.417]; Colonel Alexander McGillivray, born in Inverness, Chief of the Creek Indians, died in 1792. [SM#54.310][GM.62.577]

MCGILLVRAY, Mr ...., from Drumnaglass, Inverness-shire, Chief of the Creeks, died in Pensacola, West Florida, on 17 February 1793. [GM.63.767][SM#55.413]

MCGILLIVRAY, ARCHIBALD, born in 1726, granted 50 acres in Georgia on 3 September 1735. [PRO.CO.5.668][ESG#83]

MCGILLVRAY, DUNCAN, born in 1717, an indentured servant, emigrated from Inverness on the Two Brothers, Captain William Thomson, for Georgia in July 1737, arrived there on 20 January 1737. [ESG#32]

MCGILLVRAY, FARQUHAR, born in 1711, servant to John Cuthbert of Drakies, Inverness, emigrated from Inverness on the Prince of Wales, Captain George Dunbar, on 20 October 1735, arrived in Georgia on 10 January 1736. [ESG#83]

MCGILLIVRAY, JAMES, late of Savannah, Georgia, then in Inverness, brother of Lachlan McGillivray, [refers to his brother Lachlan McGillivray; Andrew McCudie; William Mein; Robert Mackay; James MacIntosh] pro November 1806 PCC

MCGILLIVRAY, JAMES, late of Georgia, deceased, eldest son of Archibald McGillivray, 1809. [NAS.GD176.895]

MCGILVRAY, JOHN, will subscribed in Georgia on 24 February 1748. [Ga. Loose Collection]

MCGILLVRAY, Lieutenant Colonel JOHN, in Georgia, in 1789. [NAS.RS.Ross & Cromarty#74]

MCGILLVRAY, JOHN, late in West Florida, now in Jamaica, 1787. [NAS.CS17.1.6/164, 246]

MCGILLIVRAY, LACHLAN, of Drumnaglass, born in 1725, servant to John Mackintosh, emigrated from Inverness to Georgia on the Prince of Wales, Captain George Dunbar, on 20 October 1735, arrived on 10 January 1736. [SHCG#50][ESG#84]

MCGILLIVRAY, LAUCHLAN, land grant on the Little Ogeechee River, Georgia, on 15 May 1756, [Grant book A, #125]; land grant of 1000 acres in St George parish, Georgia, on 7 July 1761, a town lot in Savannah on 27 November 1761, a town lot in Augusta on 3 February 1762, [PRO.CO.5.648.E46/68] [CRG#28/1.361, 371, 435][Grant book C, #351; Grant book D, #188/189/387]; Grant book E, #153; Grant book F, #354; Grant book H, #12; in Georgia 9.1763, [Ga.Gaz.#26]; in Vale Royal Plantation on 28 September 1764, [Ga.Gaz.#78, 86]; President of the St Andrew's Society of Savannah 1769-1770, [SSS#88]; a planter in Vale Royal, Savannah, Georgia,[deed refers to William Struthers in Chatham County, Georgia, and to John Henderson]; 1781.[NAS.RD2.239/2.129]

MCGILVERAY, MARTHA, granted 400 acres on the Savannah River 12.8.1737. [SPC.43.317]

MCGOWAN, ROBERT, born 1787, emigrated to USA in 1807, a blacksmith in New Orleans. [1812]

MCGOWRAN, PETER, servant of the Trustees, arrived in Georgia 10.1.1734. [ESG#84]

MCGREGOR, DUNCAN, born in Scotland 1784, emigrated via North Carolina to Georgia, a farmer in Montgomery County, Georgia. [C]

MACGREGOR, GREGORY, born 1723, a five year indentured servant, embarked for Georgia 19 November 1737, arrived 14 January 1738. [ESG#32]

MACGREGOR, JANE, servant of William and Hugh Stirling, arrived in Georgia on 1 August 1734. [ESG#84]

MCGREGOR, JOHN, sr., soldier of the Black Watch, imprisoned in the Tower of London on a charge of mutiny, transferred to Oglethorpe's Regiment in Georgia 1743, transferred to an Independent Company in 1749. [GHS, Cate Colln. 45/3172]

MCGREGOR, JOHN, jr., soldier of the Black Watch, imprisoned in the Tower of London on a charge of mutiny, transferred to Oglethorpe's Regiment in Georgia 1743. [GHS, Cate Colln. 45/3172]

MCGREGOR, JOHN, born 1 December 1797, son of Thomas McGregor and Margaret McLaren in parish of Dull, Perthshire, emigrated via Oban, Argyll, to Charlottetown, Prince Edward Island, on 6 October 1808, a piper, settled in Nacagdoches, Texas, sergeant and cannoneer, fought at the Battle of Bexar in December 1835, died at the Alamo, Texas, 6 March 1836. [SGen.39.2.84][DRTL][Dull OPR]

MCGREGOR, JOHN, a gardener, born in Scotland 1790, settled in Adams County, Mississippi. [C]

MACGREGOR, WILLIAM, (?), settler in New Hanover, south of the Altamaha River, Georgia, 1759. [CRG#28/1.189]

MCGRUER, ALEXANDER, born 1711, an indentured servant, emigrated from Inverness on the Two Brothers, Captain William Thomson, for Georgia in July 1737, arrived on 20 January 1737. [ESG#32]

MCGRUER, ANNE, born 1733, a twenty year indentured servant, embarked for Georgia 19 November 1737, arrived 14 January 1738. [ESG#32]

MCGRUER, or FRASER, JOHN, born 1719, an indentured servant, emigrated from Inverness on the Two Brothers, Captain William Thomson, in July 1737 to Georgia, arrived on 20 January 1737. [ESG#32]

MCGUIRE, EDWARD, land grant in St John's parish, Georgia, 7 August 1759, [CRG#28/1.326]

MCGUIRE, JOSEPH, land grant in Newport, Georgia, 7 February 1760, [CRG#28/1.327]; in Sapelo, Georgia, 1763. [Ga.Gaz.#34]

MCHARDY, WILLIAM, born 1797, eldest son of Mr Charles McHardy, {1745-1815}, schoolmaster of Fetteresso, Kincardineshire, and Henrietta Murray {1767-1819}, died in Savannah 22 September 1820. [AJ#3800][Fetteresso g/s]

MCHARLEY, Mrs CECILIA, born in Scotland 1798, husband Thomas a laborer born in Ireland 1800, daughter Bridget born in Ireland, children Mary Ann and Thomas born in Alabama, settled in Alabama. [C]

MCHENRY, JAMES, granted 150 acres in St George parish, Georgia, 1 July 1760. granted a town lot in Savannah 7.9.1762, [PRO.CO.5.648.E30/E71][CRG#28/1.323, 436][Grant book D, #195]; died in Savannah 20 April 1768. [GaGaz#3/2]

MCHENRY, JAMES, born in Forres, Morayshire, during 1788, settled in America during 1806, partner in firm of Andrew Low and Company in Savannah, died in Lexington, Oglethorpe County, Georgia, on 22 September 1826. [Georgia Republican, 10.10.1826]; born 1788, to US 1806, a merchant in Savannah 1812, [1812]

MCHENRY, Mrs MARION, born in Edinburgh 1795, married James McHenry in Savannah, Georgia, died in Lexington, Oglethorpe County, Georgia, on 22 October 1822. [Georgia Journal, 5.11.1822]

MCHENRY, MATTHEW, a minister in Pensacola, on 1 February 1768. [JCTP#75.107]

MCHENRY, ROBERT, born in Glasgow, died in Darien, Georgia, on 7 September 1822. [Georgia for the Country, Savannah, 10.9.1822]

MACINTOSH, ADAM, born in 1719, a laborer in Lange, a servant, emigrated from Inverness to Georgia on the Prince of Wales, Captain George Dunbar, on 20 October 1735, landed on 10 January 1736. [ESG#33]

MACINTOSH, AENEAS, Ranger Captain at Fort St George and later at Palachocolas, on 20 April 1738. [CRG.3.427], brother of the laird of Macintosh, signed a treaty with the Creek Indians in Georgia on 11 August 1739, returned to Scotland on 27 February 1740. [ESG#85]

MCINTOSH, ANGUS, soldier of the Black Watch, imprisoned in the Tower of London on a charge of mutiny, transferred to Oglethorpe's Regiment in Georgia during 1743, settled in Georgia. [GHS, Cate Colln. 45/3172]

MACINTOSH, ANN, land grant in St Andrew's parish, Georgia, on 4 December 1759, [CRG#28/1.318]

MCINTOSH, ARCHIBALD (?), born in Scotland during 1815, a clerk, settled in Mobile, Alabama. [C]

MACINTOSH, BENJAMIN, born in 1691, a farmer in Dorres, Inverness-shire, emigrated from Inverness on the Prince of Wales, Captain George Dunbar, on 20 October 1735, arrived in Georgia on 10 January 1736, settled in Darien, husband of Catherine, father of Elizabeth, Janet, and Lachlan. [ESG#85]

MACINTOSH, CATHERINE MUNRO, born in 1716, emigrated from Inverness on the Prince of Wales, Captain George Dunbar, to Georgia on 20 October 1735, landed there on 10 January 1736. [ESG#33]

MCINTOSH, DANIEL, born in 1778, a storekeeper, died on 20 October 1807. [Savannah Death Register]

MACINTOSH, DONALD, born in Inverness during 1726, servant of Alexander Macintosh, emigrated from Inverness to Georgia on the Prince of Wales, master George Dunbar, on 20 October 1735, arrived at Tybee Bar, on 10 January 1736, settled in Darien on the River Altahama during February 1736, later moved to Sapelo River in 1746, died there during 1801. [Colonial Museum and Savannah Advertiser 3.7.1801]; land grant of 100 acres in St Andrew's parish, Georgia, on 21 May 1762. [PRO.CO.5.648.E68][CRG#28/1.426][ESG#85]

MACINTOSH, DONALD, born 1721, a 5 year indentured servant, emigrated to Georgia 19 November 1737, landed 4.1.1737. [ESG#33]

MACINTOSH, DONALD, granted 500 acres in Newport, St John's parish, Georgia, 5.4.1757. [Grant Book A.377][CRG#28/1.115]; 1763. [Ga.Gaz.#34]

MACINTOSH, DONALD, servant of John Macintosh of Inverness, a servant in Darien, Georgia, 6 May 1741. [ESG#85]

MACINTOSH, GEORGE, granted 500 acres in Darien on 11 February 1757, [CRG#28/1/50]; in 1763, [Ga.Gaz.#34]; granted 400 acres in St John's and St Andrew's parishes, Georgia, on 6 September 1774. [Grant Book M.350]

MACINTOSH, ISABEL, born 1726, a 4 year indentured servant, emigrated to Georgia 19 November 1737, landed 14 January 1738, at Darien on 6 May 1741. [ESG#33]

MACINTOSH, JAMES, formerly of Mobile, West Florida, late of the Chicksaw Nation, pro. April 1787 PCC

MACINTOSH, JOHN, born on 24 March 1700 son of Lachlan Macintosh and Mary Lockhart in Badenoch, married Margory Fraser in Dores on 4 March 1725, with children William, Lachlan, and John, emigrated from Inverness to Georgia on The Prince of Wales, master George Dunbar, on 20 October 1735, arrived in Georgia on 10 January 1736, settled at Darien in February 1736, imported 3 male and 1 female indentured servants from Inverness to Georgia on the Two Brothers, Captain Thomson, 1738, Captain of the Highland Company 1736- , petitioned Oglethorpe re slavery on 3 January 1739, at the Siege of St Augustine, captured on 10 June 1740, prisoner of the Spanish 1740-1748, imprisoned in Havanna, Cuba, and later in St Sebastian, Spain, appointed Conservator of the Peace for the District of Midway River and Great Ogeeche and at Darien on 10 July 1751, granted 150 acres in Darien, Georgia, on 11 February 1757, died at Essich on the Sapelo River, near Darien, in September 1761. [CRG#3.427] [GHQ.LVII.1] [Caledonian Mercury#3365][PRO.CO.5.669.77; CO.5.646.C10] [AGA#65][CRG#28/1.50][CRG#30.7][GaGaz#36][ESG#86]

MACINTOSH, JOHN, son of John MacIntosh of Holme, born 1711, emigrated from Inverness on the Prince of Wales, Captain George Dunbar, to Georgia on 20 October 1735, arrived there on 10 January 1736. [SHCG#50]

MACINTOSH, JOHN, born 1720, a laborer in Inverness, a servant, emigrated from Inverness on the Prince of Wales, Captain George Dunbar, to Georgia on 20 October 1735, arrived on 10 January 1736, possibly killed at Fort Moosa in June 1741 leaving a widow and 3 children. [ESG#34]

MACINTOSH, JOHN, emigrated 1737, settled at Leniwilg on the Altamaha River, Georgia. [SPC.1737.454]; at New Inverness 1739. [Ga.Col.Rec.3.427]; petitioned Oglethorpe re slavery on 3 January 1739. [AGA#65]

MACINTOSH, JOHN, land grant of 500 acres in St Andrew parish, Georgia, on 3 December 1760. [PRO.CO.5.648.E68][CRG#28/1.419]

MACINTOSH, JOHN, granted 300 acres in Newport, St John's parish, Georgia, on 1 May 1759. [Grant Book B.101]

MACINTOSH, JOHN, born 1743, a ropemaker, emigrated via Newcastle to Georgia on the Georgia Packet in September 1775, settled in Friendsborough, Georgia. [PRO.T47.9/11]

MCINTOSH, JOHN, an Indian trader in Mobile in 1764. [NLS#MS119]

MCINTOSH, JOHN, a merchant in Savannah, died in Columbia County on 17 June 1810. [Colonial Museum and Savannah Advertiser: 4.7.1810]

MACINTOSH, LACHLAN, husband of Margaret, servants of Benjamin Macintosh in Darien, Georgia, around 1740. [ESG#86]

MACINTOSH, LACHLAN, a Ranger at Fort Argyle lying between Darien and Savannah, Georgia, around 1740. [ESG#86]

MACINTOSH, LACHLAN, born on 17 March 1725 in Raits, Badenoch, Inverness-shire, son of John Mohr Macintosh and Margaret Fraser, emigrated from Inverness to America on the Prince of Wales Captain George Dunbar, on 20 October 1735, arrived in Georgia on 10 January 1736, settled in St Andrew's parish, Georgia, planter and Revolutionary General, died in Savannah on 19 February 1806, buried in the Colonial Cemetery. [Savannah Death Register][WWWA#418]

MACINTOSH, LACHLAN, Indian trader in Augusta, Georgia, on 20 November 1756, [PRO.CO5/646, C17]; land grant in Augusta on 7 February 1758, [CRG#28/1.234]

MACINTOSH, LACHLAN, granted 500 acres in Newport, St John's parish, Georgia, on 11 February 1757, and an island in the Altamaha River on 4 July 1758. [Grant Book A.311][CRG#28/1/50, 243]

MACINTOSH, LACHLAN, {of Darien}, granted 500 acres in St John's parish on 4 October 1774. [Grant Book M.577]

MACINTOSH, LACHLAN, President of the St Andrew's Society of Savannah 1791-1792. [SSS#88]

MACINTOSH, MARY, born 1721, a 4 year indentured servant, emigrated to Georgia 19 November 1737, landed 14 January 1738. [ESG#34]

MCINTOSH, Mrs MARY, born in Scotland 1770, emigrated via North Carolina to Georgia, settled in Montgomery County, Georgia. [C]

MACINTOSH, ROBERT, from Moy, servant to James MacQueen, emigrated from Inverness on the Prince of Wales, Captain George Dunbar, to Georgia, on 20 October 1735, arrived there on 10 January 1736; possibly a servant of Edward Davison, employed in the Scout boat, Georgia, during 1738. [ESG#86]

MACINTOSH, RODERICK, born 1722, a farmer, emigrated from Inverness on the Prince of Wales, Captain George Dunbar, to Georgia on 20 October 1735, arrived there on 10 January 1736, of the Highland Company of Rangers in 1741. [ESG#86]

MACINTOSH, RODERICK, granted 500 acres in St John's parish, Georgia, on 4 December 1759. [Grant Book B.287][CRG#28/1.312]

MACINTOSH, SARAH, a servant of David Douglas in Georgia around 1740. [ESG#86]

MACINTOSH, WILLIAM, born on 27 January 1726 in Borlum, Inverness-shire, son of John Macintosh and Margery Fraser, emigrated to Georgia on the The Prince of Wales, master George Dunbar, on 20 October 1735, arrived there on 10 February 1736, imported 1 male indentured servant from Inverness to Georgia on the Two Brothers, Captain Thomson, 1738; at the Siege of St Augustine 1740, escaped from the Spanish, settled at Darien, granted 500 acres in Newport District, Georgia, on 11 February 1757, married Jane Mackay, father of John, Lachlan, Margery, and Barbara. [GHQ.LVII.1][PRO.CO.5.646.E10][CRG#30.8] [Grant Book A.310][Caledonian Mercury#337.][CRG#28/1/50]

MCINTOSH, WILLIAM, (?), settler in New Hanover south of the
Altamaha River, Georgia, 1759. [CRG#28/1.189]

MCINTOSH, ...Lieutenant of the Highlanders, killed in Georgia on 20
October 1763. [GaGaz#29]

MACINTOSH, ..., daughter of Benjamin MacIntosh, from Inverness to
Georgia on the Two Brothers, Captain Thomson, in 1738,
[CRG#30.7]

MCINVER, MURDO, servant to John Cuthbert of Drakies, emigrated
from Inverness on the Prince of Wales, Captain George Dunbar, on
20 October 1735, arrived in Georgia on 10 January 1736.
[ESG#84]

MCINTYRE, A.C., born 1792, emigrated to US 1807, a printer's
apprentice in Savannah 1812.[1812]

MCINTYRE, DANIEL, born in Scotland 1802, a planter, wife Betsy born
in Mississippi 1813, children Janet born 1835, Duncan born 1836,
daniel born 1838, A. (male) born 1840, Nancy born 1842, and John
born 1844, all born in Mississippi, settled in Jefferson County,
Mississippi. [C]

MCINTYRE, DUNCAN, Sr., soldier of the Black Watch, imprisoned in
the Tower of London on a charge of mutiny, transferred to
Oglethorpe's Regiment in Georgia 1743, transferred to an
Independent Company in 1749. [GHS, Cate Colln. 45/3172]

MCINTYRE, HUGH, born 1726, a 7 year indentured servant, emigrated
to Georgia 19 November 1737, landed 14 January 1738. [ESG#34]

MCINTYRE, JANE, born in Scotland 1788, Hugh McIntyre, a farmer,
born in South Carolina 1788, Daniel McIntyre, born in Telfair
County, Georgia, 1827, Elizabeth McIntyre, born in Telfair
County, Georgia, 1825, and Susannah McIntyre, born in Telfair
County, Georgia, 1848, resident there. [C]

MCINTYRE, JOHN, born in Scotland 1808, a ships carpenter, wife Euphemia born in Scotland 1810, settled in Alabama. [C]

MCINTYRE, Mrs LUCY, born in Scotland 1821, a farmer's wife in Montgomery County, Georgia. [C]

MCINTYRE, WILLIAM, servant of William and Hugh Stirling, probably emigrated from Leith on the snow Hope of Leith, Captain Greig, arrived in Georgia on 1 August 1734. [ESG#86]

MCINTYRE, ..., a Ranger Captain at Fort Prince George, Georgia, during 1738. [CRG, 10.5.1738]

MCIVER, ALEXANDER, planter in Liberty County, Georgia, nephew and heir of Dr Alexander Munro, 1824. [NAS.GD128.52/5]; pro. September 1837 PCC

MCIVER, DONALD, Augusta, Georgia, died at St Bartholemew's Island, West Indies, pro February 1817 PCC

MCIVER, JOHN, formerly in Georgia, then in New York City, admin. November 1821 PCC; cnf 1824 Edinburgh. [NAS.SC70.1.31]

MCIVER, JOHN, a farmer, born in Scotland 1780, John McIver, a blacksmith, born in North Carolina 1815, Florida McIver born in Scotland 1780, settled in Walton County, Florida. [C]

MCIVER, JOHN, born in Greenock, settled in Columbia, South Carolina, around 1820, died in Alabama on 25 May 1833. [Telescope, 18.6.1833]

MCIVER, RODERICK, planter on the Welsh Tract, Peedee River, Georgia, in September 1763. [Ga.Gaz.#23]

MACKANY, RODERICK, born 1723, an indentured servant, emigrated from Inverness on the Two Brothers, Captain William Thomson, in July 1737 to Georgia, arrived on 20 January 1738. [ESG#32]

MACKAY, ALEXANDER, of Lange, born 1715, an indentured servant, a labourer, emigrated from Inverness on the Prince of Wales, Captain George Dunbar, to Georgia on 20 October 1735, arrived on 10 January 1736. [ESG#32]

MACKAY, ANGUS, born 1722, a labourer in Tongue, Sutherland, an indentured servant, emigrated from Inverness on the Prince of Wales, Captain George Dunbar, to Georgia on 20 October 1735, landed on 10 January 1736. [ESG#32]

MACKAY, ANGUS, born 1726, a tailor, an indentured servant, embarked on the Loyal Judith for Georgia on 21 September 1741, arrived on 2 December 1741. [PRO.CO.5.668] [ESG#32] [CRG.30.197/199]

MACKAY, ANGUS, born 1713, from Andratichlis, an indentured servant, emigrated from Inverness on the Prince of Wales, master George Dunbar, to Georgia on 20 October 1735, landed on 10 January 1736. [ESG#32]

MACKAY, ANGUS, granted 150 acres in Newport, St John's parish, on 6 December 1757. [Grant Book A.505][CRG#28/1.118]; in South Newport 1763. [Ga.Gaz.#34]

MACKAY, CATHERINE, daughter of Christian Lossley or Mackay a widow, an indentured servant, emigrated to Georgia on 21 September 1741, landed on 2 December 1741. [ESG#32]

MACKAY, CHARLES, born 1724, emigrated from Inverness on the Prince of Wales, Captain George Dunbar, to Georgia on 20 October 1735, arrived there on 10 January 1736, Ensign of an Independent Highland Company there, received land grants in Georgia ca1743, in Darien and Fredericia, Georgia, 1747. [SGen.XLI.1][PRO.CO5.668.130/1][PCCol.6.498][ESG#84]

MACKAY, DANIEL, land grant in Darien, Georgia, on 7 February 1758, [CRG#28/1.234]

MACKAY, DANIEL, (?), settler in New Hanover south of the Altamaha River, Georgia, 1759. [CRG#28/1.189]

MACKAY, DANIEL, granted 200 acres in St John's parish, Georgia, in 1761. [Grant Book C.403]

MACKAY, DONALD, born 1715, a labourer, an indentured servant, son James born 1733, and daughter Margaret born 1729, embarked on the Loyal Judith for Georgia on 21 September 1741, landed on 2 December 1741. [PRO.CO.5.668][ESG#32] [CRG.30.197/199]

MACKAY, DONALD, born 1726, a labourer, an indentured servant, embarked on the Loyal Judith for Georgia on 21 September 1741, landed on 2 December 1741. [PRO.CO.5.668][ESG#33][CRG.30.197/199]

MACKAY, DONALD, granted 250 acres in Newport, Georgia, on 11 February 1757. [PRO.CO.5.646.C10]

MACKAY, DONALD, partner in Donald Mackay and Company and in MacKay and Spalding, dissolved 22 June 1768 on the death of Mackay. [Ga.Gaz.#247]

MACKAY, DONALD BAIN, born 1708, from Tar, a labourer, an indentured servant, emigrated to Georgia on 21 September 1741, landed on 2 December 1741. [ESG#32]

MACKAY, DONALD, granted 250 acres in Newport, St John's parish, Georgia, on 11 February 1757. [Grant Book A.308][CRG#28/1/50]

MACKAY, DONALD, of Fredericia, Georgia, died on the plantation of Hon. James Mackay at Strathy Hall on the Ogychee in February 1768. [Ga.Gaz.#229]

MACKAY, ELIZABETH, born 1727, single, an indentured servant, embarked on the Loyal Judith on 21 September 1741 for Georgia, landed on 2 December 1741. [PRO.CO.5.668][ESG#33]

MACKAY, ELIZABETH ANN, granted 177 acres in St John's parish, Georgia, on 7 February 1775. [Grant Book M.1025]

MACKAY, GEORGE, born 1727, a cowherd, an indentured servant, embarked on the Loyal Judith for Georgia on 21 September 1741, landed on 2 December 1741. [PRO.CO.5.668][ESG#33][CRG.30.197/199]

MACKAY, HUGH, third son of Charles Mackay of Sandwood, in Georgia 1735-1740, recruited 170 emigrants from Sutherland for the Altahama River settlement in 1735. [SGen.XLI.1]

MACKAY, HUGH, son of Roderick Mackay and Isobel Gray in Clashneach of Durness, Sutherland, granted 500 acres in Georgia on 24 July 1735; arrived in Georgia during January 1736, an officer of Oglethorpe's Regiment and later Captain of the Highland troop of Rangers, died in 1743, husband of Helen who emigrated on 14 October 1735, arrived in Georgia in February 1736. [SGen.XLI.1][PRO.CO.5.668][ESG#84]

MACKAY, HUGH, in Riarchar, son of Charles Mackay and Elizabeth Mackay, formerly Major of General Oglethorpe's Regiment of Foot in Georgia 1742, tack of Riarchar near Dornoch, Sutherland, and later the wadset of Farr, married (1) Margaret Gunn, eldest daughter of Alexander Gunn of Badinloch, chief of the Gunns, parents of Elizabeth, married (2) Mary Ross, parents of Hugh, Donald and Alexander. [NAS.RS37.IX.516; X.140; XI.41] [BM#329]

MACKAY, ISOBEL, born 1729, an indentured servant, embarked on the Loyal Judith for Georgia on 21 September 1741, landed on 2 December 1741. [PRO.CO.5.668][ESG#33][CRG.XXX.197/199]

MACKAY, JAMES, settled in New Inverness by 1739. [Ga.Col.Rec.3.427]; petitioned Oglethorpe re slavery on 3 January 1739. [AGA#65]

MACKAY, JAMES, emigrated to Georgia 1735, officer in Oglethorpe's Regiment and later Commander of an Independent Company of

Foot in South Carolina 1736-1755, land grant of 300 acres in St
George's parish, Georgia, on 21 May 1762, and a town lot in
Savannah, on 7 September 1762, [PRO.CO.5.648.E68]
[CRG#28/1.435]; died in Alexandria, Georgia, 178-. [SGen.XLI.1]

MACKAY, JAMES, granted 650 acres on the Newport River and on an
island in the St Catherine River on 8 September 1756, also on 5
April 1757. [Grant Book A.314] [CRG#28/1/51.58]; 1763.
[Ga.Gaz. #34]

MACKAY, JAMES, of Tar, born 1724, emigrated from Inverness on the
Prince of Wales, Captain George Dunbar, on 20 October 1735,
arrived in Georgia on 10 January 1736, settled in Darien, killed at
the Siege of St Augustine in June 1740. [ESG#84]

MACKAY, JAMES, born in 1701, a farmer from Durness, Sutherland,
emigrated from Inverness on the Prince of Wales, Captain George
Dunbar, on 20 October 1735, arrived in Georgia on 10 January
1736, settled in Darien, killed or made prisoner at Fort Moosa in
June 1740, left a wife Barbara McLeod and children, Barbara
{died 6 May 1741 at Darien}, Donald, and Jeanne. [ESG#84]

MACKAY, JOHN, born in 1686, a farmer in Durness, Sutherland,
emigrated from Inverness on the Prince of Wales, Captain George
Dunbar, on 20 October 1735 with wife Janet born 1703, children
Elizabeth, Hugh, John, Mary, and William, arrived in Georgia on
10 January 1736. [ESG#84]

MACKAY, JOHN, born 1725, labourer in Tongue, Sutherland,
indentured servant emigrated from Inverness on the Prince of
Wales, Captain George Dunbar, to Georgia on 20 October 1735,
arrived on 10 January 1736. [ESG#33]

MACKAY, JOHN, born 1716, servant to Joseph Stanley, an indentured
servant, emigrated from Gravesend to Georgia on the Anne,
Captain Thomas Shubrick, on 16 November 1732, landed on 1
February 1733, died on 25 July 1733. [ESG#33/110]

MACKAY, JOHN, gentleman from Sutherland, arrived in Georgia on 1 February 1733, received a 500 acre grant in Georgia on 3 September 1735, settled in Josephstown, died on 25 July 1736. [PRO.CO5.670.220][ESG#84]

MACKAY, JOHN, born in 1697, from Lairg, Sutherland, emigrated from Inverness on the Prince of Wales, Captain George Dunbar, on 20 October 1735, arrived in Georgia on 10 January 1736, husband of Janet Macintosh, father of Donald, Jeanne, and Patrick. [ESG#84]

MACKAY, JOHN, possible land grant in Little Ogeechee, Georgia, 1753. [Plat book c, #49]

MACKAY, JOHN, granted 50 acres in St Andrew parish, Georgia, on 13 April 1761. [PRO.CO.5.648.E46] [CRG#28/1.361]

MACKAY, MARIAN, born 1731, an indentured servant, embarked on the Loyal Judith, Captain John Lemon, for Georgia on 21 September 1741, landed on 2 December 1741. [PRO.CO.5.668] [ESG33][CRG.30.197/199]

MACKAY, MURDOCH, emigrated from Caithness on the Marlborough, Captain Thomas Walker, to Savannah, Georgia, in September 1775, an indentured servant of Thomas Brown there. [PRO.AO13.34.123-5]

MACKAY, NEIL, from Tar, indentured servant emigrated from Inverness on the Prince of Wales, Captain George Dunbar, to Georgia on 20 October 1735, landed on 10 January 1736, possibly settled in Darien, Georgia. [ESG#33]

MACKAY, PATRICK, of Sidera and Scoury, Sutherland, second son of Captain Hugh Mackay of Borley and Jane Dunbar, married Helen Mackay 1716, father of Jane and Catherine, emigrated to Georgia "with a large body of people from Eddrachillis" in 1732, Captain of an Independent Company there 1734-1735, a merchant in Josephstown, Georgia, granted 500 acres in Georgia on 3 September 1735, granted 600 acres and a town lot in Savannah on 9 December 1756, settled in South Carolina, member of the King's

Council of South Carolina 1756, Judge of the General Court 1757, founder and first president of the St Andrews Society of Charleston. pro.1777 South Carolina. [SGen.XLI.1] [PRO.CO.5.646.C9; CO5.640.45; CO5.670.220] [BM#294][Grant book A, #293/294/295; Grant book B, #31/75] [PRO.CO.5.668][CRG#28/1/32.47][ESG#84]

MACKAY, PATRICK, owner of the sloop Isabella, master Isaac Martin, built in New England 1748, registered in Georgia on 30 December 1755, arrived in Savannah from Jamaica with a cargo of 4 negroes on 18 May 1755. [PRO.CO5.709]

MACKAY, PATRICK, President of the St Andrew's Society of Savannah 1764-1768. [SSS#88]

MACKAY, PATRICK, land grant in Savannah, Georgia, on 11 October 1764. [Ga.Gaz.#80]

MACKAY, or MORRISON, ROBERT, born 1718, an indentured servant emigrated from Inverness on the Two Brothers, Captain William Thomson, to Georgia in July 1737, landed on 20 January 1737. [ESG#33]

MCKAY, ROBERT, born in Cromarty 1801, died in Milledgeville, Georgia, 10 August 1833. [Southern Recorder, 14.8.1833]

MACKAY, SAMUEL, born 1728, to Georgia, officer of Oglethorpe's Regiment 1742-1749, officer of Independent Companies 1749-1761. [SGen.XLI.1]

MACKAY, WILLIAM, son of Patrick Mackay, arrived in Georgia on 1 February 1733, settled in Savannah. [ESG#84]

MACKAY, WILLIAM, born 1726, a cowherd, an indentured servant, embarked on the Loyal Judith for Georgia on 21 September 1741, landed on 2 December 1741.
[PRO.CO.5.668][ESG33][CRG.30.197/199]

MACKAY, WILLIAM, born 1717, from Tar, an indentured servant emigrated from Inverness on the Prince of Wales, Captain George Dunbar, to Georgia on 20 October 1735, landed on 10 January 1736. [ESG#33]

MACKAY, WILLIAM, born 1723, a cooper from Tar, an indentured servant emigrated from Inverness on the Prince of Wales, Captain George Dunbar, to Georgia on 20 October 1735, landed on 10 January 1736. [ESG#33]

MACKAY, WILLIAM, of Lavig, servant to Mackay of Scourie, soldier of an Independent Company of Highlanders in 1741. [ESG#85]

MACKAY, WILLIAM, born in 1724, an indentured servant emigrated from Inverness on the Two Brothers, Captain William Thomson, to Georgia in July 1737, landed on 20 January 1737. [ESG#33]

MACKAY, PAUL, born in Scotland during 1822, settled in Alabama. [C]

MACKAY, WILLIAM, born around 1724, servant to Mackay of Strothie, settled in Georgia around 1740. [ESG#85]

MACKAY, ..., of Scourie, a gentleman, emigrated from Inverness on the Prince of Wales, Captain George Dunbar, on 20 October 1735, arrived in Georgia on 10 January 1736. [ESG#84]

MACKAY, ... of Strothie, a gentleman, emigrated from Inverness on the Prince of Wales, Captain George Dunbar, on 20 October 1735, arrived in Georgia on 10 January 1736. [ESG#84]

MACKAY, WILLIAM, subscribed to a will in 1762. [Cuyler Colln., UGA Library]

MCKELLAR, JOHN, born in Argyll 1776, member of the firm of McKellar and Ainsley in Augusta, Georgia, resident in Cambridge, South Carolina, died on 23 November 1802. [Augusta Chronicle: 22.2.1817]

MCKENZIE, ALEXANDER, born 1719, an indentured servant, emigrated from Inverness on the Two Brothers, Captain William Thomson, to Georgia on 24 June 1737, landed on 20 January 1737. [ESG#33]

MCKENZIE, ALEXANDER, land grant of 150 acres in St Andrew's parish, Georgia, on 7 December 1762. [PRO.CO.5.648.E48][CRG#28/1.442]

MACKENZIE, ANDREW, born 1725, a 5 year indentured servant, emigrated to Georgia 19 November 1737, landed 14 January 1738, died in June 1738. [ESG#33]

MACKENZIE, CATHERINE, servant to Noble James in Georgia around 1740. [ESG#85]

MACKENZIE, CHRISTINA, born in Scotland 1790, settled in Dallas County, Alabama. [C]

MACKENZIE, DONALD, born 1727, an indentured servant, emigrated from Inverness on the Two Brothers, Captain William Thomson, to Georgia on 24 June 1737, landed there on 20 January 1738. [ESG#33]

MCKENZIE, DUNCAN, born in Scotland 1794, a merchant, arrived in Savannah late 1821 on the ship Pallas, Captain Land. [USNA/par]

MACKENZIE, JOHN, born 1714, an indentured servant, emigrated from Inverness on the Two Brothers, Captain William Thomson, to Georgia in July 1737, landed there on 20 January 1737. [ESG#33]

MCKENZIE, JOHN, born 1786, emigrated to US 1806, a merchant in Augusta, Georgia, 1812. [1812]

MCKENZIE, JOHN, born in Scotland 1781, a merchant, arrived in Savannah late 1821 on the ship Pallas, Captain Land. [USNA/par]

MCKENZIE, JOHN, born in Scotland 1798, a merchant, Cyder Alley born 1831 and Isabella born 1836, both in Alabama, settled in Coosa District, Coosa County, Alabama. [C]

MCKENZIE, KENNETH, in Georgia, cnf 1868 Edinburgh. [NAS.SC70.1.137]; c.f. born 1789, to US 1811, a clerk in Augusta 1812, [1812]

MCKENZIE, PETER, granted 10,000 acres in East Florida 1767. [PCCol.V.590]

MACKENZIE, THOMAS, born 1726, an indentured servant, emigrated from Inverness on the Two Brothers, Captain William Thomson, to Georgia in July 1737, landed on 20 January 1737, at Darien on 6 May 1741. [ESG#33]

MACKENZIE, THOMAS, born 1798, settled in Savannah 1817, member of the firm Mackenzie and Hernandez, died on 21 September 1823 in Purrysburg, South Carolina. [GR:1.9.1823]

MACKENZIE, WILLIAM, born 1732, an indentured servant, emigrated from Inverness to Georgia on the Two Brothers, Captain William Thomson, in July 1737, landed on 20 January 1737, at Darien 6 May 1741. [ESG#33]

MCKENZIE, Captain W. M., from Cromarty, H.M. Collector of Customs at Sunbury, Georgia, during 1771, father of John, Christina [married ... Yonge], Anna Jean [married John Simpson jr, Chief Justice of Georgia, Loyalist. [SGen#44.3.131]

MACKEY, JOHN, born 1790, settled in Augusta during 1810, died on 1 October 1812. [Augusta Chronicle: 9.10.1812]

MACKEY, WILLIAM, sailor, son of Robert Mackey in Woodhaven, died in Savannah, Georgia, before 1781. [Pro. 1781 PCC]

MACKIE, DAVID, born in 1764, son of Thomas Mackie and Margaret Louden, died in Savannah during 1794. [Colvend g/s]

MCKIE, JOHN, born 1790, emigrated to US 1810, a merchant's clerk in Augusta 1812. [1812]

MCKIE, PETER, settled in Augusta, died on 27 September 1811. [Augusta Chronicle: 4.10.1811]

MCKIMMIE, ALEXANDER, born 1691, a laborer, emigrated from Inverness on the Prince of Wales, Captain George Dunbar, on 20 October 1735, arrived in Georgia on 10 January 1736. [ESG#85]

MCKINNON, ARCHIBALD, born 1735, a farmer in Mull, Argyll, emigrated with wife Janet, from Greenock, Renfrewshire, to Georgia on the Georgia in July 1775. [PRO.T47.12]

MCKINNON, CATHERINE, born in Scotland 1768, settled in Walton County, Florida. [C]

MCKINNON, CHARLES WILLIAM, granted 5,000 acres of land in Georgia 1771, appointed to the Council of Georgia on 21 August 1776. [PC.Col.V.595]; in St Augustine, Florida, in 1776. [NAS.NRAS#0631, GDB 1776/1] [JCTP#83.41]

MCKINNON, CHRISTIAN, born in Scotland 1760, settled in Walton County, Florida. [C]

MCKINNON, JOHN, born 1747, a farmer in Mull, Argyll, emigrated from Greenock, Renfrewshire, to Georgia on the Georgia in July 1775. [PRO.T47.12]

MCKINNON, JOHN, born in Skye, Inverness-shire, 1768, died in Savannah, Georgia, on 5 November 1825. [Augusta Herald: 17.7.1821]

MCKINNON, JOHN, a farmer, born in Scotland 1790, Catherine McKinnon born in Scotland 1801, Angus McKinnon born in North Carolina 1827, Neil McKinnon born 1829, Bell Ann McKinnon born 1832, Ann born 1834, Charles born 1836, Janet McKinnon born 1838, John McKinnon born 1840, Alexander McKinnon born 1842, Daniel McKinnon born 1844, Catherine McKinnon born

1846, Elizabeth McKinnon born 1842, John McKinnon born 1844, all born in Florida, settled in Walton County, Florida. [C]

MCKINNEN, ROBERT, of the 35th Regiment, died at Pensacola, West Florida, pro. June 1767 PCC

MCKOW, WILLIAM, born in Scotland during 1817, a laborer, wife Margaret born in Scotland 1821, sons William and Robert (both born in Scotland), settled in Alabama. [C]

MCLACHLAN, DANIEL, offered to recruit 100 Highlanders for Georgia during 1737. [SPC.43.112/187/281][PRO.CO5.690#80]

MCLACHLAN, LACHLAN, proposed to recruit 100 Highlanders for Georgia during 1737. [SPC.43.189/204/256]

MCLAIN, A., born in Scotland 1804, a laborer, settled in Alabama. [C]

MCLATCHIE, CHARLES, agent for Spalding and Kelsall on the Suwanee River, East Florida, in 1774; partner in Panton, Leslie and Company, Indian traders in Florida, Loyalist, settled in St Marks during 1783, died there on 14 October 1787. [Mowat#25][IT#48]

MCLATCHIE, ELIZABETH, daughter of Charles McLatchie in East Florida, married Andrew Campbell a merchant in Glasgow, in Ayr on 30 November 1801. [SM#63.886]

MCLATCHIE, ROBERT, a schoolmaster, died in Savannah on 10 December 1766. [GaGaz#3/1]; pro.17 December 1766 Georgia

MCLAUCHLIN, DANIEL, a farmer, born in Scotland 1784, Margaret McLauchlin, born in Scotland 1795, John McLauchlin, a teacher, born in North Carolina 1825, Duncan McLauchlin, born in North Carolina 1831, Alexander McLauchlin, born in North Carolina 1836, settled in Telfair County, Georgia. [C]

MCLAUCHLIN, MARGARET, born in Scotland 1790, settled in Telfair County, Georgia. [C]

MCLAUGHLIN, Mrs MARGARET, born 1780, settled in Georgia around 1800, died in Lumber City, Telfair County, on 6 July 1855. [Southern Recorder]

MCLEA, ARCHIBALD, New York, died in New Orleans on 26 August 1819. [EA#5838.303]

MCLEA, WILLIAM, merchant in the firm McLea and Mackie in Augusta, died in Sandhills, Georgia, on 16 July 1821. [Augusta Herald: 17.7.1821]; born 1789, to USA 1811, a merchant's clerk in Augusta 1812, [1812]

MACLEAN, ALEXANDER, born 1708, an indentured servant, emigrated from Inverness on the Two Brothers, Captain William Thomson, to Georgia in July 1737, landed on 20 January 1737; imported 1 female indentured servant from Inverness on the Two Brothers, Captain Thomson, 1738. [ESG#34][CRG#30.7]

MACLEAN, ALEXANDER, born 1709, a farmer in Inverness, emigrated from Inverness on the Prince of Wales, Captain George Dunbar, to Georgia on 20 October 1735, arrived there on 10 January 1736, died in March 1736. [ESG#86]

MACLEAN, ALLAN, born 1720, a farmer in Inverness, emigrated from Inverness on the Prince of Wales, Captain George Dunbar, to Georgia on 20 October 1735, arrived there on 10 January 1736. [ESG#86]

MCLEAN, DANIEL, a farmer, born in Scotland 1768, Florida McLean born in Scotland 1775, Daniel McLean, a farmer, born in North Carolina 1811, and John McLean born in Florida 1830, settled in Walton County, Florida. [C]

MCLEAN, DONALD, late of the Montgomery's Highlanders, an overseer for James Penman in East Florida in 1769. [NAS.NRAS.771, bundle 491]

MACLEAN, DONALD, from Argyll, a planter and merchant in St Augustine, East Florida, died there in 1778, [his testament refers to his brothers and executors Allan MacLean, Lauchlan MacLean, and James Maclean, tenant farmers in Gerradh, in the barony of Ardgour, Argyll; James Penman late of St Augustine, now a merchant in London; Reverend John Forbes, chaplain to Fort St Augustine; John Campbell jr., WS.] cnf 25 January 1786 Edinburgh [NAS.CC8.8.127]; 1785, [NAS.CS17.1.4/195]

MCLEAN, DONAL, a farmer, born in Scotland 1769, settled in Walton County, Florida. [C]

MACLEAN, GEORGE, born 1711, a farmer in Ardelack, emigrated from Inverness on the Prince of Wales, Captain George Dunbar, to Georgia on 20 October 1735, arrived there on 10 January 1736. [ESG#86]

MCLEAN, JAMES, a farmer, born in Scotland 1808, Catherine McLean born in North Carolina 1816, Daniel G. McLean born 1839, James McLean born 1843, and John McLean born 1849, all children born in Florida, settled in Walton County, Florida. [C]

MACLEAN, JOHN, from Inverness, of the Highland Company of Rangers in Georgia during 1741. [ESG#86]

MACLEAN, JOHN, born 1721, servant to Robert MacPherson of Alvie, emigrated from Inverness on the Prince of Wales, Captain George Dunbar, to Georgia, on 20 October 1735, arrived there on 10 January 1736. [ESG#86]

MACLEAN, JOHN, born 1713, a 4 year indentured servant, emigrated to Georgia 19 November 1737, landed 14 January 1738. [ESG34]; settled in New Inverness by 1739. [CRG#3.427]; petitioned Oglethorpe re slavery on 3 January 1739. [AGA#65]

MCLEAN, JOHN, soldier of the Black Watch, imprisoned in the Tower of London on a charge of mutiny, transferred to Oglethorpe's Regiment in Georgia during 1743. [GHS, Cate Colln. 45/3172]

MCLEAN, JOHN, a planter, died in Georgia in January 1774. [GaGaz#2/2]

MCLEAN, R. born in Scotland 1818, a clerk, settled in Alabama. [C]

MACLEAN, SIMON, servant to Allan MacLean in Georgia around 1740. [ESG#86]

MCLEAN, T., land grant in St Matthew's parish, Georgia, on 11 September 1764. [Ga.Gaz.#78]

MCLEISH, Mrs AGNES, born in Scotland, died in Savannah, Georgia, during 1817. [S.42.17]

MCLEISH, JOHN, soldier of the Black Watch, imprisoned in the Tower of London on a charge of mutiny, transferred to Oglethorpe's Regiment in Georgia during 1743. [GHS, Cate Colln. 45/3172]

MACLELLAN, ..., in West Florida, during 1769. [JCTP#76.248]?

MCLEOD, ALEXANDER, born 1726, an indentured servant, emigrated from Inverness to Georgia on the Two Brothers, Captain William Thomson, in July 1737, landed on 20 November 1738. [ESG#34]

MCLEOD, ANGUS, born 1724, a labourer from Apint, an indentured servant, emigrated from Inverness on the Prince of Wales, Captain George Dunbar, to Georgia on 20 October 1735, landed on 10 January 1736, soldier in Oglethorpe's Independent Highland Company on 6 May 1741. [ESG#34]

MCLEOD, ANGUS, born 1724, a weaver from Hawnick, a servant of Mackay of Strothie, emigrated from Inverness on the Prince of Wales, Captain George Dunbar, to Georgia, on 20 October 1735, arrived there on 10 January 1736. [ESG#86]

MCLEOD, CATHERINE, born 1724, a 4 year indentured servant, emigrated to Georgia 19 November 1737, landed 14 January 1738. [ESG#34]

MCLEOD, DONALD, born 1723, from Tar, a servant of Mackay of Strothie, emigrated from Inverness on the Prince of Wales, Captain

George Dunbar, to Georgia, on 20 October 1735, arrived there on 10 January 1736, of the Highland Independent Company 1741. [ESG#86]

MCLEOD, Dr DONALD, born in Skye, Inverness-shire, 1754, settled in Georgia 1779, died in Savannah, Georgia, on 20 June 1802. [Colonial Museum and Savannah Advertiser, 22.6.1802]

MCLEOD, EVAN, born 1727, an indentured servant, emigrated from Inverness on the Two Brothers, Captain William Thomson, to Georgia in July 1737, landed on 20 January 1737. [ESG#34]

MCLEOD, GEORGE, born 1724, a laborer, servant to Mackay of Strothie, emigrated from Inverness on the Prince of Wales, Captain George Dunbar, to Georgia on 20 October 1735, arrived there on 10 January 1736. [ESG#86]

MCLEOD, HUGH, born 1723, a laborer, a servant to Mackay of Strothie, emigrated from Inverness on the Prince of Wales, Captain George Dunbar, to Georgia on 20 October 1735, arrived there on 10 January 1736, soldier of the Highland Independent Company in Georgia 1741. [ESG#87]

MCLEOD, JOHN, an indentured servant, emigrated from Inverness on the Two Brothers, Captain William Thomson, on 24 June 1737, landed in Georgia on 20 January 1737. [ESG]

MACLEOD, JOHN, born 1723, a laborer, servant of Mackay of Strothie, emigrated from Inverness on the Prince of Wales, Captain George Dunbar, to Georgia on 20 October 1735, arrived there on 10 January 1736, soldier of the Highland Company of Rangers during 1741. [ESG#87]

MCLEOD, JOHN, born in Skye, Inverness-shire, ordained on 15 October 1735 by the Presbytery of Edinburgh as a minister of the Church of Scotland, emigrated from Inverness on the Prince of Wales, Captain George Dunbar, to Georgia on 20 October 1735 as a missionary of the Society in Scotland for Propagating Christian Knowledge, arrived in Georgia on 10 January 1736, received a 300 acre land grant at New Inverness, Darien, Georgia, on 10 October 1739, moved to Edisto Island, South Carolina, during 1741. [SSPCK pp, Edinburgh] [F.7.664][PRO.CO.5.668; CO5.670.421] [ESG#87]

MACLEOD, JOHN, born 1712, a fisherman, an indentured servant, emigrated from Inverness on the Loyal Judith for Georgia on 21 September 1741. [PRO.CO.5.668] [CRG#30.197/199][ESG.34]

MCLEOD, JOHN, land grant in St Philip's parish, Georgia, on 1 July 1760, [CRG#28/1.325]

MACLEOD, MARY, servant to Thomas Causton in Georgia around 1740. [ESG#87]

MCLEOD, MARY, born in Scotland 1765, Alexander McLeod, a farmer, born in Scotland 1800, Sarah McLeod born in Scotland 1808, Daniel born 1831, Alexander McLeod born 1833, John McLeod born 1837, Duncan McLeod born 1840, Florida McLeod born 1842, and Mary McLeod born 1844, all children born in Florida, settled in Walton County, Florida. [C]

MCLEOD, MARY, born in Scotland 1782, Allen McLeod, a farmer, born in North Carolina 1818, Catherine McLeod, born in Telfair County, Georgia, 1826, and Catherine McLeod, born in Telfair County, Georgia, 1845, settled there. [C]

MCLEOD, MURDOCH, land grant in Darien, Georgia, on 7 February 1758, [CRG#28/1.234]; land grant of 150 acres in St Andrews parish, Georgia, on 7 July 1761.[CRG#28/1.420] [PRO.CO.5.648.E68]

MCLEOD, MURDOCH, born in 1773, died in Savannah on 26 August 1823. [Daily Georgian: 26.8.1823]

MCLEOD, RODERICK, born 1719, an indentured servant, emigrated from Inverness on the Two Brothers, Captain William Thomson to Georgia in July 1737, landed on 20 January 1737, a soldier in Oglethorpe's Highland Company on 6 May 1741. [ESG#34]

MCLEOD, RODERICK, born 1717, an indentured servant emigrated from Inverness on the Two Brothers, Captain William Thomson, on 24 June 1737, landed in Georgia on 20 January 1737. [ESG#34]

MCLEOD, RODERICK, granted 200 acres in Newport, St John's parish, Georgia, on 3 February 1767. [Grant Book F.70]

MCLEOD, RODERICK, born 1788, emigrated to USA in 1807, a merchant in Savannah during 1812. [1812]

MCLEOD, RODERICK, a farmer, born in Scotland 1788, Mary McLeod born in South Carolina 1793, Gabriel McLeod born 1824, John McLeod born 1828, Jenny McLeod born 1830, William McLeod born 1831, Ann McLeod born 1836, Mary McLeod born 1838, Robert McLeod born 1840, Thomas McLeod born 1842, Frances McLeod born 1844, and Francis McLeod born 1846, all children born in Alabama, settled in Walton County, Florida. [C]

MCLEOD, WILLIAM, a farmer, born in Scotland 1792, Sarah McLeod born in South Carolina 1801, Neil McLeod born in South Carolina 1824, Mary McLeod born 1833, Nancy McLeod born 1835, Jane McLeod born 1837, Alexander McLeod born 1837, William McLeod born 1843, and Norman McLeod born 1845, all born in Florida, settled in Walton County, Florida. [C]

MCLINZEY, MURRAY, born 1746, a cartwright, emigrated via London to Pensacola, West Florida, on the Success's Increase on 14 August 1774. [PRO.T47.9/11]

MCMASTER, SAMUEL, born 1786, emigrated to USA in 1807, a merchant in New Orleans. [1812]

MCMASTERS, WILLIAM, born in Galloway, settled in McIntosh County, Georgia, married Jane Carnochan also from Galloway, on 9 April 1826. [Daily Georgian, 11.4.1826]

MCMILLAN, A. P., a merchant tailor, born in Scotland 1818, wife Jane born in England, son William born in Mississippi 1846, settled in Adams County, Mississippi, before 1850. [C]

MCMILLAN, DAVID, born 1795, son of Robert McMillan {1757-1844}, died in Alabama on 10 August 1842. [Monigaff g/s]

MCMILLAN, JOHN, soldier of the Black Watch, imprisoned in the Tower of London on a charge of mutiny, transferred to Oglethorpe's Regiment in Georgia during 1743. [GHS, Cate Colln. 45/3172]

MCMILLAN, MARY, born in Scotland 1779, settled in Montgomery County, Georgia. [C]

MCMILLAN, N., born in Scotland 1815, a sailor, settled in Alabama. [C]

MCMILLAN, THOMAS, born in Scotland 1804, a merchant, wife L.R. born in South Carolina 1812, children Mary and Thomas (born in South Carolina) and children Ina, Martha, Louisa, Robert, Emma, Ellen, and William (born in Alabama), settled in Mobile, Alabama. [C]

MCMULLEN, ISOBEL, born 1744, resident of St Augustine, East Florida, in 1786. [1786 Census of St Augustine]

MCMULLIN, WILLIAM, a trader among the Chickesaws during 1735. [SPAWI.1735.157.xii]?; land grant of 200 acres on the Savannah River on 14 August 1737, [SPC.43.317]

MACMURRWICK, ALEXANDER, born 1721, servant to Colin Campbell, emigrated from Inverness on the Prince of Wales, Captain George Dunbar, to Georgia on 20 October 1735, arrived there on 10 January 1736. [ESG#87]

MCNAB, ..., in Mobile, 1767. [NLS#MS119]

MCNAIR, HUGH, baptised on 5 March 1810 in Paisley Abbey, son of Robert McNair and Agnes Walker, in Paisley, Renfrewshire, a

waiter in New Orleans, died in February 1844, cnf 1852
Edinburgh. [NAS.SC70.1.74][Paisley Abbey OPR]

MCNAIR, JAMES, second son of Reverend James McNair in
Slamannan, Lanarkshire, died in Moone, New Orleans, on 3
October 1824. [BM#15.131] (?died in Mobile 3 October 1823, see
F.1.229, MAGU#223)

MCNAIR, JAMES, [probably baptised on 27 December 1807 in Paisley
Abbey, son of Robert McNair and Agnes Walker, {OPR}], a baker
from Paisley, Renfrewshire, settled in New Orleans, died August
1843, cnf. 1852. [NAS.SC70.1.74]

MCNEIL, ARCHIBALD, formerly in Colonsay, sometime Lieutenant
Colonel of the Aberdeenshire Fencibles, then HM Consul in
Leghorn, late in Louisiana, 1809. [NAS.CS17.1.29/104]; HM
Consul in New Orleans, Louisiana, died on way from Canada to
New York on 25 September 1808.
[SM#71.78][EA#4607][NAS.NRAS#GD51.6/1657; 1/580]

MCNEIL, HUGH, born 1799, a merchant in Macon, died in Savannah on
24 June 1826. [Daily Georgian: 11.7.1826]

MCNEIL, JOHN, born in Scotland 1831, a laborer settled in Mobile,
Alabama. [C]

MCNICOL, NICOL, soldier of the Black Watch, imprisoned in the
Tower of London on a charge of mutiny, transferred to
Oglethorpe's Regiment in Georgia during 1743. [GHS, Cate Colln.
45/3172]

MCNISH, JOHN, born in Galloway, a merchant in Savannah, Georgia,
died in Georgia on 19 December 1826. [Georgia Republican,
20.12.1826]; born 1782, to USA 1803, a merchant in Savannah
1812, [1812][possibly the John McNish baptised on 21 December
1780 in the parish of Girthon, son of William McNish and Mary
Minzies, {Girthon OPR}]

MACNIVEN, ALLAN, born 1777, a shopkeeper, died on 13 October 1805. [Savannah Death Register]

MCOMISH, JOHN, settled in New Orleans, on died 19 August 1830. [NAS.SH]

MCPHERSON, ALEXANDER, sr., soldier of the Black Watch, imprisoned in the Tower of London on a charge of mutiny, transferred to Oglethorpe's Regiment in Georgia during 1743. [GHS, Cate Colln. 45/3172]

MACPHERSON, ALEXANDER, pronotary in West Florida during 1771. [PRO.CO5.613.141]

MCPHERSON, ANGUS, jr., soldier of the Black Watch, imprisoned in the Tower of London on a charge of mutiny, transferred to Oglethorpe's Regiment in Georgia during 1743. [GHS, Cate Colln. 45/3172]

MACPHERSON, DONALD, son of John MacPherson an Inverness merchant, apprenticed to Alexander MacPherson, in Pensacola, pronotary of the General Council of Pleas in West Florida on 22 May 1771. [PRO.CO5.613.141]

MCPHERSON, GEORGE, a jeweller, born in Scotland, wife Isabella born 1820, children John born 1848 and George born 1849 both in Mississippi, settled in Adams County, Mississippi. [C]

MACPHERSON, JAMES, a minor, son of Captain Patrick MacPherson, arrived in Georgia on 1 February 1733, settled in Savannah, moved to Carolina by 29 February 1737. [ESG#87]

MCPHERSON, JAMES, soldier of the Black Watch, imprisoned in the Tower of London on a charge of mutiny, transferred to Oglethorpe's Regiment in Georgia during 1743. [GHS, Cate Colln. 45/3172]

MACPHERSON, JAMES "OSSIAN", in New Orleans, secretary to the Governor of West Florida during 1764. [NAS.NRAS#0631]

MACPHERSON, JOHN, born 1723, an indentured servant, emigrated from Inverness on the Two Brothers, Captain William Thomson, to Georgia in July 1737, landed on 20 January 1737. [ESG#34]

MCPHERSON, JOHN, soldier of the Black Watch, imprisoned in the Tower of London on a charge of mutiny, transferred to Oglethorpe's Regiment in Georgia during 1743. [GHS, Cate Colln. 45/3172]

MACPHERSON, JOHN, granted 250 acres in St John's parish, Georgia, in 1759? [Grant Book C.401]; land grant in St John's parish on 11 September 1764. [Ga.Gaz.#78]

MACPHERSON, NORMAN, born 1717, a laborer, emigrated from Inverness on the Prince of Wales, Captain George Dunbar, to Georgia on 20 October 1735, arrived there on 10 January 1736. [ESG#87]

MCPHERSON, PAUL, soldier of the Black Watch, imprisoned in the Tower of London on a charge of mutiny, transferred to Oglethorpe's Regiment in Georgia during 1743. [GHS, Cate Colln. 45/3172]

MACPHERSON, ROBERT, born 1717, a farmer from Alvie, Inverness-shire, emigrated from Inverness on the Prince of Wales, Captain George Dunbar, to Georgia, on 20 October 1735, arrived there on 10 January 1736. [ESG#87]

MACPHERSON, ROBERT, second son of Alexander MacPherson of Elzy, Caithness, died in Nashville, Tennessee, on 11 August 1838. [AJ#4745]

MACPHERSON, WILLIAM, granted 200 acres in St John's parish, Georgia, on 2 September 1766. [Grant Book E.350]

MCPHERSON, ..., Ranger captain at Fort Argyle during 1738. [Ga.Council Records, 10.5.1738]

MCQUAIG, JOHN, born in Scotland 1780, emigrated to North Carolina, later a farmer in Montgomery County, Georgia. [C]

MCQUEEN, Mrs ANNE, died during 1809. [Colonial Cemetery, Savannah, g/s]

MACQUEEN, JAMES, born 1722, from Inverness, emigrated from Inverness on the <u>Prince of Wales</u>, Captain George Dunbar, to Georgia on 20 October 1735, arrived there on 10 January 1736. [ESG#87]

MACQUEEN, JAMES, born 1722, servant to James MacQueen in Inverness (above), emigrated from Inverness on the <u>Prince of Wales</u>, Captain George Dunbar, to Georgia on 20 October 1735, arrived there on 10 January 1736. [ESG#87]

MCQUEEN, JAMES, son of James McQueen of Corrieburgh, signed a treaty with the Creek Indians in Georgia on 11 August 1739, an Ensign of a Troop of Rangers, at the Siege of St Augustine in 1740, captured by the Spanish on 10 June 1740, imprisoned in Havanna, Cuba, and in St Sebastian, Spain. [Caledonian Mercury#3365]

MCQUEEN, JOHN, born in 1773, died during 1822. [Colonial Cemetery, Savannah, g/s]

MCQUEEN, JOHN, born in Scotland 1773, emigrated via North Carolina to Georgia, settled in Georgia 1821, a farmer in Montgomery County, Georgia. [C]

MCQUIN, JOHN, born 1789, settled in USA 1804, a merchant in Augusta 1812. [1812]

MCRAE, CATHERINE, daughter of Hugh McRae in Kintail, Ross and Cromarty, emigrated to Wilmington, North Carolina, 1770, married Donald MacRae, settled in Georgia. [CMR]

MCRAE, CATHERINE, born in Scotland 1766, Duncan McRae jr., a farmer, born in South Carolina 1806, Jane McRae, born 1813, Caroline McRae, born 1836, Marion McRae, born 1837, Charles

McRae, born 1839, Henry McRae, born 1841, George McRae, born 1843, William McRae, Margaret McRae, born 1847, and Thomas McRae, born 1848, also Anna McLeod born 1837, all born in Telfair County, Georgia, resident there. [C]

MCRAE, CHRISTOPHER, born 1774, emigrated to America, settled in Montgomery County, Georgia, before 1821. [C]

MCRAE, DANIEL, born in Scotland 1766, settled in Montgomery County, Georgia. [C]

MACRAE, DUNCAN, born on 16 April 1796, son of Reverend John MacRae and Madeline MacRae in Glen Shiel, died in Florida. [F.7.151]

MCREA, HUGH, born 1761, settled in Carroll County, Georgia, before 1850. [C]

MCRAE, KENNETH, born 1802, a planter, arrived in Charleston, South Carolina, in November 1826 from Glasgow on the brig Andromeda, to settle in Florida. [USNA.par]

MCRAY, SARAH, born in Scotland 1790, Hugh McRay, a farmer, born in 1810, Christian McRay born 1812, Laughlin McRay, a laborer, born 1822, Charles McRay, a laborer, born 1822, and William, a laborer, born 1824, all born in North Carolina, settled in Walton County, Florida. [C]

MCSVEIN, MALCOLM, a farmer, born in Scotland 1775, Sarah McSvein born in North Carolina 1790, settled in Walton County, Florida. [C]

MCVAIN, Reverend JOHN, died at Fourteen Mile House, Georgia, on 8 December 1828. [Statesman and Patriot: 27.12.1828]

MCVICARS, CHRISTIE, born 1741, died on 11 December 1804. [Savannah Death Register]

MCWHAN, THOMAS, son of James McWhan and Jane Haining, settled as a merchant in New Orleans before 1848. [NAS.SH]

MACER, ALEXANDER, servant of Hugh Anderson in Georgia around 1740. [ESG#83]

MACK, M., born in Scotland 1810, a laborer, settled in Mobile, Alabama. [C]

MAHAN, JANE, born in Scotland 1805, settled in Alabama. [C]

MAIN, GEORGE, born 1718, a servant to Donald Stewart, emigrated from Inverness on the Prince of Wales, Captain George Dunbar, to Georgia on 20 October 1735, arrived there on 10 January 1736. [ESG#87]

MAIN, Mrs MARIA, born in Scotland 1822, husband John R. Main born in Mississippi 1815, children all born in Mississippi after 1839, settled in Warren County, Mississippi. [C]

MALCOLM, FARQUHAR, formerly in Georgia, late in London. pro.May 1791 PCC

MALCOLM, JANE, a servant of A. Grant, possibly emigrated from Leith on the snow Hope of Leith, Captain Greig, arrived in Georgia during 1734. [ESG#87]

MALLOCH, EDWARD, born in Scotland in 1819, settled in Gonzales, Texas. [C]

MANGLE, Mrs MARIA, born in Scotland 1812, husband M. born in Ireland, settled in Alabama. [C]

MANN, WILLIAM, formerly in Jamaica, late in Pensacola, West Florida, pro.12.1781 PCC

MANSON, ANDREW, born 1786, emigrated to USA 1809, a merchant in Brunswick 1812. [1812]

MANSON, BARBARA, born 1752, a spinster, emigrated from Newcastle to Georgia on the Georgia Merchant in September 1775, settled in Friendsborough, Georgia. [PRO.T47.9/11]

MANSON, ELIZABETH, born in Kirkwall, Orkney, on 20 December 1748, daughter of William Manson and Marion Blaw, emigrated from Newcastle to Georgia on the Georgia Merchant in September 1775, settled in Friendsborough, Georgia. [PRO.T47.9/11]

MANSON, ELIZABETH, born 1766, emigrated from Newcastle to Georgia on the Georgia Merchant in September 1775, settled in Friendsborough, Georgia. [PRO.T47.9/11]

MANSON, JANET, born 1756, a servant in Dunnet, Caithness, emigrated from Caithness via Kirkwall, Orkney, to Savannah, Georgia, on the Marlborough, Captain Thomas Walker, in September 1775, settled in Richmond County, Georgia, as an indentured servant of Thomas Brown. [PRO.T47.12][PRO.AO13.34.123-5]

MANSON, MARGARET, born in Kirkwall, Orkney, on 24 July 1751, daughter of William Manson and Marion Blaw, a spinner, emigrated from Newcastle to Georgia on the Georgia Merchant in September 1775, settled in Richmond County, Georgia. [PRO.T47.9/11]

MANSON, THOMAS, born in Kirkwall, Orkney, on 3 May 1759, son of William Manson and Marion Blaw, a yeoman, emigrated from Newcastle to Georgia on the Georgia Packet in September 1775, settled in Richmond County, Georgia. [PRO.T47.9/11]; a Quaker and a Loyalist in 1776, returned home in 1781.

MANSON, WILLIAM, born on 24 July 1751, a weaver in Dunnet, Caithness, with wife Elizabeth Sinclair, emigrated from Kirkwall to Savannah, Georgia, on the Marlborough in September 1775, settled in Richmond County, Georgia. [PRO.T47.12]

MANSON, Captain WILLIAM, from Orkney, settled in Georgia, a Loyalist, merchant in Augusta 1780. [NAS.NRAS.0627][NAS.NRAS.1015.15]

MARSHALL, GEORGE, a wright in Dunshalt, Fife, then in New Orleans, dead by 1843. [NAS.SH]

MARSHALL, WILLIAM, baptised in Dundee on 7 September 1740, son of William Marshall {died 1781} a merchant in Dundee and Christian Pilmore {1720-1751}, died in New Orleans on 23 December 1803. [Dundee OPR] [Dundee, Howff, g/s]

MARSHALL, WILLIAM, a settler in Mississippi and West Florida, 1794. [NAS.CS17.1.13/303]

MARTIN, ISAAC, (?), master of the sloop Isabella, in Georgia during 1755. [PRO.CO5.709]

MARTIN, DANIEL, born in 1760, a seaman, died on 15 July 1823. [Georgia Republican: 24.7.1823]

MARTIN, GEORGE, born in Scotland 1815, a merchant, wife Mary born in Pennsylvania 1822, daughter Anna born in Pennsylvania, and son George born in Alabama, settled in Mobile, Alabama. [C]

MARTIN, JAMES, born in Dundee, emigrated to Charleston, South Carolina, in 1771, settled as a baker and merchant in Savannah, Georgia, Loyalist - returned to Britain from Savannah on the Unity, Captain Wardell, in May 1776, arrived in Dundee during July 1776. [PRO.AO13.36.697/705]

MARTIN, JOHN, born 1740, a 4 year indentured servant, emigrated to Georgia 19 November 1737, landed 14 January 1738. [ESG34]

MARTIN, POLLY, born in Scotland 1760, settled in Lowndes County, Georgia. [C]

MARTIN, ROBERT, born 1749, a yeoman, emigrated from Newcastle to Georgia on the Georgia Merchant in September 1775, settled in Friendsborough, Georgia. [PRO.T47.9/11]

MASTERSON, THOMAS, servant to Hugh Anderson in Georgia around 1740. [ESG#88]

MATHESON, DUNCAN, born 1784 in Ross-shire, died in Georgia on 30 September 1812, buried in St Paul's, Augusta, Georgia. [Augusta g/s]; born 1784, to USA 1806, a merchant in Augusta 1812, [1812]

MATHESON, MURDOCH, born 1790, emigrated to USA 1809, a merchant in Augusta 1812. [1812]

MAXTON, ANDREW, settler in New Hanover, south of the Altamaha, in 1759. [CRG#28/1.188]

MAXWELL, AUDLEY, granted 350 acres in Medway, St John's parish, 5 March 1756, and 500 acres there on 8 September 1756, also 150 acres there 30 September 1757, plus 350 acres in St John's parish 7 July 1761. [Grant Books A.191/196; A.443; C.333] [Ga.Gaz.#80][CRG#28/1.3701]

MAXWELL, AUDLEY, jr., granted 200 acres in Medway on 8 September 1756. [Grant Book A.197]; land grant in Midway 30 September 1757, [CRG#28/1.112]

MAXWELL, JAMES, in St Philip's parish, Chatham County, Georgia, around 1767. [CRG]

MAXWELL, JAMES, jr., granted 690 acres in St John's parish, Georgia, on 5 July 1768. [Grant Book G.138]

MAXWELL, JOHN, in Georgia in September 1763. [Ga.Gaz.#23]

MAXWELL, JOHN, a planter in St Phillip's parish, Chatham County, Georgia, husband of Mary ..., pro. 1767 Georgia

MAXWELL, JOSEPH WILLIAM, eldest son of James Maxwell a gentleman in Medway, Liberty County, Georgia, matriculated at Glasgow University 1797, graduated MD at Edinburgh University 1803. [MAGU#183]

MAXWELL, PRIMROSE, settled in Frederica, Georgia, by 1741. [ESG#88]

MAXWELL, ROBERT, born in Scotland 1831, a seaman in Harrison County, Mississippi. [C]

MAXWELL, THOMAS, granted 850 acres in St John's parish, Georgia, on 3 August 1762. [Grant Book D.157][CRG#28/1.432]

MAXWELL, WILLIAM, born in 1742, a yeoman, emigrated from Newcastle to Georgia on the Georgia Packet in September 1775, settled in Friendsborough, Georgia. [PRO.T47.9/11]

MAXWELL, WILLIAM, in St Philips parish, Chatham County, Georgia, around 1767. [CRG]

MEARNS, ANDREW, born in Aberdeen during 1800, a merchant in Savannah, died on 24 February 1820. [Colonial Museum and Savannah Advertiser: 25.2.1820]

MELDRUM, Miss ...., married James Oliver of Georgia, in Berwick-on-Tweed in November 1804. [SM#66.971]

MELLIS, WILLIAM, born in Perthshire, a merchant in Savannah, Georgia, died in Darien, Georgia, on 7 August 1811. [Colonial Museum and Savannah Advertiser, 5.9.1811]

MELLORD, DAVID, from Roa, Orkney, emigrated from Caithness via Kirkwall, Orkney, on the Marlborough, Captain Thomas Walker, to Georgia in September 1775, a servant to Thomas Brown in Richmond County, Georgia, 1783. [PRO.AO13.34]

MELLORD, ISABELLA, from Roa, Orkney, emigrated from Caithness via Kirkwall, Orkney, on the Marlborough, Captain Thomas Walker, in September 1775, a servant to Thomas Brown in Richmond County, Georgia, 1783. [PRO.AO.13.34]

MELVILLE, WILLIAM, son of Alexander Melville of Hallfield, Fife, {1784-1842} and Grace Babington {1779-1823}, died in Austin, Texas, aged 25. [Dumfries g/s]

MELVIN, JAMES, born 1776, a mariner, died on 31 August 1808. [Savannah Death Register]

MERCER, JOHN, born 1753, a gentleman, died on 9 August 1810. [Savannah Death Register]

MERCER, SAMUEL, a settler in Georgia, on 9 December 1738. [AGA#59]; husband of Elizabeth ...., land grant in Hardwick on 8 September 1756. [CRG#28/1/47][Grant book A, #284/292]

MERRYLEES, JAMES, in Savannah, Georgia, 1790. [NAS.CS17.1.9/8]

MILBURN, ELIZABETH, born during 1755, a spinner, emigrated from Newcastle to Georgia on the Georgia Packet in September 1775, settled in Friendsborough, Georgia. [PRO.T47.9/11]

MILLEN, JOHN, born in Aberdeen, settled in Savannah, Georgia, 1783, died on 28 October 1811. [Savannah Republican, 29.10.1811]

MILLEN, ROBERT, born in Scotland during 1755, a spinner, emigrated from Newcastle to Georgia on the Georgia Packet in September 1775. [PRO.T47.9/11]

MILLEN, STEPHEN, land grant in St Matthew's parish, Georgia, on 27 November 1761, [CRG#28/1.370]

MILLER, DAVID, born during 1715, servant to Mackay of Strothie, emigrated from Inverness on 20 October 1735 on the Prince of Wales, Captain George Dunbar, arrived in Georgia on 10 January 1736, soldier of the Highland Independent Company on 6 May 1741. [ESG#88]

MILLER, ELIZABETH, born in 1747, a servant in Bower, Caithness, emigrated from Kirkwall, Orkney, to Savannah, Georgia, on the Marlborough in September 1775. [PRO.T47.12]

MILLER, GEORGE, son of George Miller and Janet Morrison, died in Savannah on 28 September 1839. [Tulliallan, Clackmannan, g/s]

MILLER, JAMES, baptised on 27 May 1714 in Inverness, son of William Miller, shoemaker, and Elspet Geddes, a squarewright in Georgia. Brother of David Miller, a squarewright in Inverness, Scotland. [GSA.Ga.Misc.Bonds Y-2.321]; ? land grant in Little Ogeechee, Georgia, on 7 November 1755, [Grant book A, #22]

MILLER, JAMES, born during 1723, servant of James Anderson, emigrated from Inverness on 20 October 1735 on the Prince of Wales, Captain George Dunbar, arrived in Georgia on 10 January 1736. [ESG#88]

MILLER, JAMES, born in 1778, a waggoneer, died on 21 October 1807. [Savannah Death Register]

MILLER, JOHN, born in 1764, died on 16 October 1807. [Savannah Death Register]

MILLER, NEIL, a tinman, born in Scotland during 1801, settled in Harrison County, Mississippi. [C]

MILLER, PETER, born in Scotland during 1787, a laborer, wife Lucy born in North Carolina during 1787, settled in Cocke County, Tennessee. [C]

MILLAR, ROBERT, born during 1768 in Thurso, Caithness, a merchant, died in Georgia on 26 March 1808. [Savannah Death Register] [Colonial Museum and Savannah Advertiser, 29.3.1808]

MILLER, ROBERT, born during 1817, son of David Miller {1776-1824} a brewer and Isabella Gilchrist {1767-1849}, died in New Orleans on 6 December 1850. [Howff g/s, Dundee]

MILLER, WILLIAM, born during 1736, a farmer in Evie, Orkney, emigrated from Kirkwall, Orkney, to Savannah, Georgia, with his wife Margaret Irvine, and children Isobel, Hugh, William, and

John, on the Marlborough, Captain Thomas Walker, in September 1775, settled in Richmond County, Georgia. [PRO.T47.12][PRO.AO13.34.123-5]

MILLER, WILLIAM, born in Scotland during 1796, a butcher, daughter Jeanette born in New York 1830 and daughter Margaret born in Scotland 1827, settled in Mobile, Alabama. [C]

MILLIGAN, WILLIAM, in Mobile, died on 3 April 1844, cnf 1845. [NAS.SC70.1.66]

MILLS, ANDREW, born in 1771, a mariner, died on 6 January 1811. [Savannah Death Register]

MILLS, WILLIAM, born in 1778, a stonemason, died on 24 December 1805. [Savannah Death Register]

MILNE, ALEXANDER, born in Fochabers, Morayshire, died in New Orleans during 1838. [Inverness Courier, 26.12.1838]

MILNE, ANDREW, born 1789, emigrated to USA in 1806, a merchant in New Orleans, [1812]

MILNE, JOHN, born in Aberdeen, settled in Savannah, Georgia, 1783, died there on 28 October 1811. [Savannah Republican: 29.10.1811]

MINTY, WILLIAM, from Ellon, Aberdeenshire, then of Ascension parish, Louisiana, married Eliza Gordon, youngest daughter of William Gordon in Belhelvie, at Ellon on 28 July 1849. [AJ#5299]

MITCHELL, ALEXANDER, a merchant in Savannah, died on 3 October 1798. [Colonial Museum and Savannah Advertiser: 9.10.1798]

MITCHELL, ANDREW, arrived in Georgia before February 1739, moved to Carolina in December 1740. [ESG#89]

MITCHELL, DAVID BRYDIE, born on 22 October 1766 son of John Mitchell in Muthill, Perthshire, emigrated to America in 1783, inherited property from his uncle David Brydie in Savannah, Georgia, politician, militiaman, Solicitor General of Georgia, Governor of Georgia, died in Milledgeville, Georgia, on 22 April 1837. [Duke University, DBMitchell pp]

MITCHELL, JAMES ALEXANDER, born in 1821, only son of James Mitchell, Lieutenant of the 68th Infantry, died in New Orleans on 12 December 1845. [AJ#5115]

MITCHELL, JOHN, land grant in St John's parish, Georgia, on 13 April 1761, [CRG#28/1.415]

MITCHELL, JOHN, a merchant in St Augustine, East Florida, trading to the Mississippi on 31 October 1776. [NAS.NRAS.0159.C4]; a Scottish Loyalist from Virginia, petitioned the Council of West Florida for land on the Pearl River, West Florida, on 26 December 1776. [PRO.CO5.34]

MITCHELL, ROBERT, born on 1 July 1776 in Perth, a merchant in Savannah, Georgia, died on 26 December 1830, buried in the Old Colonial Cemetery, Savannah, pro. October 1846 PCC. [Savannah g/s]

MITCHELL, THOMAS REEVES, in Mississippi, 1846. [NAS.SH]

MOAT, ALEXANDER, born 1757, a carpenter in Kirkwall, Orkney, emigrated from Kirkwall to Savannah, Georgia, on the Marlborough in September 1775. [PRO.T47.12]

MOFFATT, Mrs B., a governess, born in Scotland, settled in Adams County, Mississippi. [C]

MOFFATT, R.D., born in Scotland 1816, a merchant, wife Elizabeth born 1822, children William and Robert born in South Carolina, settled in Mobile, Alabama. [C]

MONCRIEFF, ISABELLA, died in St Augustine, East Florida, pro. October 1779 PCC

MONCRIEFF, JAMES, military engineer in St Augustine, East Florida, 1763-. [Mowat#166]

MONEYEY, WILLIAM, born in Edinburgh 1752, a merchant in Charleston, died in Savannah on 30 September 1819. [Savannah Republican: 30.9.1819]

MONNOX, INGRAM M., born 1772, a merchant, died on 23 November 1804. [Savannah Death Register]

MONRO, ALEXANDER, born 1711, a farmer in Inverness, emigrated from Inverness, with his wife Margaret (?), on the Prince of Wales, Captain George Dunbar, on 20 October 1735, arrived in Georgia on 10 January 1736, died 1740. [ESG#89]

MONRO, ALEXANDER, born 1716, from Dornoch, a laborer, emigrated from Inverness on the Prince of Wales, Captain George Dunbar, on 20 October 1735, arrived in Georgia on 10 January 1736, died 1740. [ESG#89]

MONRO, DONALD, born 1696, a laborer from Alnit Rossit(?), emigrated from Inverness on the Prince of Wales, Captain George Dunbar, on 20 October 1735, arrived in Georgia on 10 January 1736. [ESG#89]

MONRO, DONALD, born 1721, a 7 year indentured servant, emigrated to Georgia 19 November 1737, landed 14 January 1738, died 6.1738? [ESG#36]

MONROE, DONALD, land grant of 100 acres in St Andrew parish, Georgia, 2 October 1759. [PRO.CO.5.648.E46][CRG#28/1.365]

MONRO, HECTOR, born 1716, a labourer in Tongue, Sutherland, an indentured servant, emigrated from Inverness on the Prince of Wales, Captain George Dunbar, to Georgia on 20 October 1735, arrived there in January 1736. [ESG#36]

MONRO, JAMES, land grant in St Andrew's parish, Georgia, on 4 December 1759, [CRG#28/1.320]

MONRO, JOHN, born 1725, a laborer from Alnit Rossit(?), {Alness, Ross-shire,?} emigrated from Inverness on the Prince of Wales, Captain George Dunbar, on 20 October 1735, arrived in Georgia on 10 January 1736. [ESG#89]

MONRO, JOHN, born 1720, a 7 year indentured servant, emigrated to Georgia 19 November 1737, landed 14 January 1738. [ESG#36]; land grant in St Andrew's parish 1 July 1760, [CRG#28/1.30]

MONRO, JOHN, born 1720, a laborer from Kiltairn, emigrated from Inverness on the Prince of Wales, Captain George Dunbar, on 20 October 1735, arrived in Georgia on 10 January 1736. [ESG#89]

MONRO, ROBERT, born 1724, a laborer from Dornoch, Sutherland, emigrated from Inverness on the Prince of Wales, Captain George Dunbar, on 20 October 1735, arrived in Georgia on 10 January 1736. [ESG#89]

MONRO, WILLIAM, born 1728, a laborer from Dornoch, Sutherland, emigrated from Inverness on the Prince of Wales, Captain George Dunbar, on 20 October 1735, arrived in Georgia on 10 January 1736. [ESG#89]

MONRO, WILLIAM, born 1701, a farmer from Durness, Sutherland, emigrated from Inverness on the Prince of Wales, Captain George Dunbar, on 20 October 1735, arrived in Georgia on 10 January 1736, soldier of the Highland Company of Rangers 1741, father of Elizabeth born 1724 and Margaret born 1727. [ESG#89]

MONTGOMERY, ALEXANDER, granted 10,000 acres in East Florida 1766. [PCCol.V.590]

MONTGOMERY, J. T., born in Scotland 1840, settled in Mobile, Alabama. [C]

MONTGOMERY, Sir ROBERT, of Skermorlie, Ayrshire, "leased all that tract of land which lies between the rivers Altamaha and Savannah" 18 June 1717, [SPAWI#1717/608]; "Sir Robert covenants that he shall immediately transport thither at his own proper cost and charges a considerable number of families with all necessaries for making a new settlement." 19 June 1717, [SPAWI#1717/609]

MONTGOMERY, R. H., born in Scotland 1814, wife Alison born in Scotland 1816, son George born in Scotland 1833, daughter Margaret born in New York 1838, settled in Harrison County, Mississippi. [C]

MONTGOMERY, SAMUEL, sr., Savannah, Georgia, father of Samuel, William and Jane, pro. June 1797 PCC

MOODIE, ANN, born 1749 in Scotland, daughter of Thomas Moodie and Jean Mackenzie, married George Houstoun in Christchurch, Georgia, 14 December 1774, died at White Bluff, Georgia, in February 1821; granddaughter of John McKenzie, a shipmaster in North Berwick, East Lothian, 1818. [NAS.SH] [GaGaz, 21.12.1774][Savannah Death Register][Bonadventure g/s]

MOODIE, THOMAS, Cocklaw, Beith, Fife, and wife Ann McKenzie, settled in Georgia around 1750, Secretary to the Governor. [Houstouns of Georgia, p134]; land grant in Savannah on 6 October 1767, [Grant book F, #386]

MOODY, ..., born 1797, a ships carpenter, died in Savannah on 31 August 1823. [Daily Georgian: 4.9.1823]

MOORE, WILLIAM, born in Scotland 1822, a carpenter, settled in Alabama. [C]

MORE, ALEXANDER, born on 13 April 1756 in Kirkwall, Orkney, son of Alexander More and Isobel Spence, a housecarpenter, emigrated from Kirkwall, Orkney, to Georgia on the <u>Marlborough</u>, Captain Thomas Walker, in September 1775, settled in Richmond County, Georgia, as an indentured servant of Thomas Walker. [PRO.T47.12][PRO.AO13.34.123-5]

MORE, SARAH, born in Scotland 1810, William More, a farmer, born in South Carolina 1792, Margaret More born 1837, William More born 1838, David More born 1841, Nancy More born 1843, and John born 1845, all children were born in Florida, settled in Walton County, Florida. [C]

MORGAN, DANIEL, born 1839, a mason from Crossdykes, Fife, son of .... Morgan, Castlebrae Cottage, Burntisland, died in Macon, USA, on 1 July 1866. [Fife Herald]

MORN, JOHN, born 1763, Birsay, Orkney, emigrated from Kirkwall, Orkney, to Savannah, Georgia, in September 1775 on the Marlborough. [PRO.T47.12]

MORRINE, WILLIAM, baptised in parish of Dunscore, Dumfries-shire, on 30 April 1780, son of John Morrine, a storekeeper, died in Savannah, Georgia, on 10 August 1805. [Dunscore OPR][Savannah Courier, 4.9.1805] [Savannah Death Register]

MORRIS, Mrs ELIZABETH, born in Scotland 1797, settled in Alabama, mother of Martha, Mary and Georgiana, (all born in Alabama). [C]

MORRIS, Mrs ISABELLA, born in Scotland 1820, settled in Alabama before 1838, daughter (?) Catherine born in Alabama 1838. [C]

MORRISON, CATHERINE, born 1719, from Durness, Sutherland, a servant of William Monro, emigrated from Inverness on the Prince of Wales, Captain George Dunbar, on 20 October 1735, arrived in Georgia on 10 January 1736. [ESG#90]

MORRISON, DAVID, a merchant and shipowner in Montrose, Angus, emigrated with his wife Elizabeth Mitchell, to America, settled in New Orleans in 1790, died there in 1808. [ANY#2/202]

MORRISON, HUGH, born 1713, a labourer in Tongue, Sutherland, an indentured servant, emigrated from Inverness on the Prince of Wales, Captain George Dunbar, to Georgia on 20 October 1735, landed on 10 January 1736, soldier in Oglethorpe's Independent Highland Company on 6 May 1741. [ESG36]; settled at New

SCOTS IN GEORGIA AND THE DEEP SOUTH, 1735-1845

Inverness by 1739. [CRG.3.427]; petitoned Oglethorpe re slavery on 3 January 1739. [AGA#65]; land grant in St Andrew's parish, Georgia, on 4 July 1758, [CRG#28/1.328]

MORRISON, HUGH, born 1718, a farmer, emigrated from Inverness on the Prince of Wales, Captain George Dunbar, on 20 October 1735, arrived in Georgia on 10 January 1736, a Ranger of the Highland Company on 6 May 1741. [ESG#90]

MORRISON, JOHN, soldier of the Black Watch, imprisoned in the Tower of London on a charge of mutiny, transferred to Oglethorpe's Regiment in Georgia during 1743, settled in Georgia. [GHS, Cate Colln. 45/3172]

MORRISON, Dr RODERICK, a physician in Bridgeport, Mississippi, from around 1838. [NAS.GD403.68.7]

MORTON, JOHN, born in Scotland 1828, a gardener, settled in Mobile, Alabama. [C]

MOULTRIE, CECILIA, a widow in St Augustine, East Florida, pro. March 1781 PCC

MOULTRIE, JAMES, appointed as Chief Justice of East Florida, in November 1763. [AJ#827]

MOWAT, ELIZABETH, born 1755, a farm servant in the Shetland Islands, emigrated from Kirkwall, Orkney, to Savannah, Georgia, on the Marlborough, Captain George Prissick, in September 1774, settled in Richmond County, Georgia, as an indentured servant of Thomas Brown. [PRO.T47.12][PRO.AO13.34.123-5]

MOWAT, JAMES, born 1761, a farm servant in St Andrews parish, Orkney, emigrated from Kirkwall, Orkney, to Savannah, Georgia, on the Marlborough, Captain George Prissick, in September 1774, settled in Richmond County, Georgia, as an indentured servant of Thomas Brown. [PRO.T47.12][PRO.AO13.34.123-5]

MOWAT, JOHN, born 1758, a farm servant in Deerness, Orkney, emigrated from Kirkwall, Orkney, to Savannah, Georgia, on the Marlborough Captain George Prissick, in September 1774, an indentured servant of Thomas Brown in Georgia. [PRO.T47.12][PRO.AO13.34.123-5]

MUIR, JAMES, born 1694, a perukemaker, with wife Ellen born 1694, and sons John born 1730 and George, emigrated via Gravesend to Georgia on the Anne, Captain Thomas, on 16 January 1732, he died in Carolina in September 1739. [ESG#36/109]; reference to on 9 December 1738, [AGA#59]

MUIR, JOHN, land grant in Savannah on 4 December 1759, [Grant book B, #526]

MUNRO, ALEXANDER, settled at New Inverness by 1739. [CRG.3.427]; petitioned Oglethorpe re slavery on 3 January 1739. [AGA#65]

MUNRO, DAVID, a planter in Natchez, pro.15 January 1792 Natchez [refers to nephew George Gunn Munro in Braemore parish, Caithness; executors David Ross, John Bisland and George Cochrane]

MUNRO, JAMES, born 1708, a cowherd, an indentured servant, embarked on the Loyal Judith for Georgia on 21 September 1741, with wife Janet McLeod born 1715, landed on 2 December 1741. [PRO.CO.5.668][ESG#37][CRG.30.197/199]

MUNRO, SIMON, in Georgia, in December 1763, [Ga.Gaz.#38]

MUNROE, THOMAS, born in Scotland 1803, a farmer, Sarah E. Munroe born in Virginia 1815, settled in Gadsden County, Florida. [C]

MUNRO, WILLIAM, settled at New Inverness, Georgia, by 1739. [CRG.3.427]; petitioned Oglethorpe re slavery on 3 January 1739. [AGA#65]

SCOTS IN GEORGIA AND THE DEEP SOUTH, 1735-1845

MUNROE, WILLIAM, born in Scotland in 1819, a farmer, Cornelia M. Munroe born in Alabama in 1828, Thomas Munroe born in Florida in 1845, William Munroe born in Florida in 1847, Henrietta J. Munroe born in Virginia in 1834, Sarah B. Munroe born in Florida in 1849, Benjamin Munroe a clerk born in Virginia in 1832, settled in Gadsden County, Florida. [C]

MURCHISON, DONALD, born in Bochearron, Ross-shire, emigrated to America 1816, a merchant at Fort Clairborne, Mobile, and Wilmington, North Carolina, died at Line Creek, Alabama, 13 November 1819. [Camden Gazette, 30.12.1819]

MURCHISON, JOHN, born 1705, a labourer in Kildruth, emigrated from Inverness on the Prince of Wales, Captain George Dunbar, to Georgia on 20 October 1735, landed on 10 January 1736. [ESG#36]

MURE, JOHN, a merchant in New Orleans, married Fanny Elizabeth Carter, in London on 15 July 1856. [CM#20844]

MURE, ..., son of William Mure, HM Consul, born in New Orleans on 4 April 1850. [W#1109]

MURRAY, ALEXANDER, born 1710, a labourer in Rogart, Sutherland, an indentured servant, emigrated from Inverness on the Prince of Wales, Captain George Dunbar, to Georgia on 20 October 1735, landed on 10 January 1736. [ESG#37]

MURRAY, ALEXANDER, born 1724, a laborer, emigrated from Inverness on the Prince of Wales, Captain George Dunbar, on 20 October 1735, arrived in Georgia on 10 January 1736. [ESG#90]

MURRAY, ALEXANDER, soldier of the Black Watch, imprisoned in the Tower of London on a charge of mutiny, transferred to Oglethorpe's Regiment in Georgia 1743. [GHS, Cate Colln. 45/3172]

MURRAY, ALEXANDER, born in 1814, son of Hector Murray and Catherine Brown, died in New Orleans 1854.[Pollockshaws g/s]

MURRAY, ANDREW, a partner in the firm of McMahan and Gilbert, merchants in Galveston, Texas, son of Thomas Murray LL.D. in Edinburgh, died in Galveston, Texas, on 6 December 1858. [EEC#23311][CM#21623]

MURRAY, ANN, born 1723, single, an indentured servant, embarked on the Loyal Judith for Georgia on 21 September 1741, landed on 2 December 1741. [PRO.CO.5.668][ESG37][CRG.30.197/199]

MURRAY, CHARLES, baptised on 7 September 1811, son of Reverend Andrew Murray {1754-1844} and Janet Mackay in Auchterderran, Fife, settled in Louisiana, died 1853. [Auchterderran OPR] [Auchterderran g/s]

MURRAY, CHRISTIAN, born 1719, a 4 year indentured servant, emigrated to Georgia 19 October 1737, landed on 14 January 1738, at Darien on 6 May 1741. [ESG38]

MURRAY, DAVID, son of John Murray of Philipshaugh, Selkirkshire, settled in Christchurch parish, Georgia, married Lucia ..., father of Charles, died 29 April 1771 in Savannah, Georgia, pro. 21 May 1771 Georgia, (will refers to his wife Lucia, his brother John Murray of Philiphaugh, Charles Murray late of Madeira, John Graham in Savannah, William Telfair and Edward Telfair merchants in Savannah), pro.17 February 1770 South Carolina. [AJ#1226]

MURRAY, DAVID, born 1755, a housecarpenter in Kirkwall, Orkney, emigrated from Kirkwall to Savannah, Georgia, on the Marlborough, Captain Thomas Walker, in September 1775, settled in Richmond County, Georgia, as an indentured servant of Thomas Brown. [PRO.T47.12][PRO.AO13.34.123-5]

MURRAY, GABRIEL, born 1799 son of John Murray and Margaret Gairdner in Woodlaw, Lauder, Berwickshire, a merchant in Augusta, Georgia, died 3 January 1832, [Lauder g/s]; cnf 1863 Edinburgh. [NAS.SC70.1.47]

MURRAY, GEORGE, born in 1777, emigrated to US 1802, a planter in Richmond County 1812. [1812]

MURRAY, GEORGE, born in Scotland 1809, a baker, wife Catherine born in Scotland 1809, daughter Catherine born in Scotland 1838, settled in Mobile, Alabama. [C]

MURRAY, JOHN, born 1716, a servant of Mackay of Scourie, emigrated from Inverness on the Prince of Wales, Captain George Dunbar, on 20 October 1735, arrived in Georgia on 10 January 1736. [ESG#90]

MURRAY, JOHN, granted 10,000 acres in East Florida during 1766, and another 10,000 acres there in 1767. [PCCol.V.590]

MURRAY, Mrs, wife of John Murray late of Glasgow, died in Augusta, Georgia, in 1807. [AJ#3092]

MURRAY, ..., son of Andrew Murray, late of Blandfield House, Edinburgh, then a merchant in Galveston,Texas, born in Corpus Christi on 2 January 1859. [CM#21657]

MUTTER, JAMES, land grant in Savannah 1 May 1759, 27 November 1761, [Grant book B, #111, Grant book C, #357]; land grant in Christ Church parish 6 November 1764, [Grant book E, #63]; land grant in Christchurch 27 November 1761, [CRG#28/1.371]

NEALE, THOMAS, a settler in Georgia, on 9 December 1738. [AGA#59]

NELSON, JANE, servant to Hugh Anderson around 1740. [ESG#91]

NELSON, MALCOLM, a planter in Savannah, son of Jane Nelson, pro.3 April 1778 Georgia.

NETHERLAND, JOHN, a carpenter, born in Scotland 1804, wife Mary born in Kentucky, infant son William born in Mississippi, settled in Warren County, Mississippi. [C]

NEVILLE, U., born in Scotland 1812, a laborer, settled in Alabama. [C]

NEWALL, CUNNINGHAM, born 1769, a merchant, died on 24 July 1807. [Savannah Death Register][Colonial Museum and Savannah Advertiser: 28.7.1807]

NICHOLSON, ALEXANDER, born in Scotland 1798, a farmer, Martha born in Tennesee 1798, Susan born in North Carolina 1832, settled in Coosa District, Coosa County, Alabama. [C]

NICHOLSON, DUNCAN, born 1776, emigrated to North Carolina before 1809, married Mary Black, settled in Stewart County, Georgia. [SG]

NICHOLSON, MALCOLM, of the firm of S.J.Hobson of New Orleans, died in New Orleans on 11 June 1833. [AJ#4464][SG#164]

NICOL, ALEXANDER, "under indenture to go to Georgia but having revolted was now absconding" on 19 July 1738. [Elgin Kirk Session Records, Morayshire]

NICOL, WALTER, emigrated from Scotland to Louisiana, settled in St Helen's parish; married Jane Harvey in Springfield, Livingston parish 1821, a timber executive in New Orleans, died 1861. [University of North Carolina, Walter Nicol's Diary]

NICOL, ..., son of James Nicol, born in Baton Rouge, Louisiana, on 24 September 1841. [AJ#4896]

NISBET, ALEXANDER, born 1778, emigrated to US 1809, a saddler in Augusta 1812. [1812]

NICOL, ALEXANDER, an indentured servant for Georgia who attempted to avoid shipment, on 19 July 1738. [Elgin Kirk Session Records, Morayshire]

NOBLE, DUNCAN, born 1761, a Catholic, a tailor in St Augustine, East Florida, during 1786. [FHR#18][1786 Census of St Augustine]

NOBLE, JOHN, soldier of the Black Watch, imprisoned in the Tower of London on a charge of mutiny, transferred to Oglethorpe's Regiment in Georgia 1743, transferred to an Independent Company in Georgia 1749. [GHS, Cate Colln. 45/3172]

NORN, JOHN, born 29 November 1761 in Orphir, Orkney, son of William Norn and Marjory Spence, emigrated from Kirkwall, Orkney, to Savannah, Georgia, on the Marlborough in September 1775, settled in Richmond County, Georgia. [PRO.T47.12]

O'DWYER, MICHAEL, born in Scotland 1795, a teacher, arrived in Savannah late 1821 on the ship Georgia, Captain Varnum. [USNA/par]

OGILVIE, GEORGE, born in Galloway during 1762, died in Georgia on 7 December 1794. [Georgia Gazette, 15.12.1797]

OGILVIE, HENRY, baptised in Dundee on 31 August 1736, son of Henry Ogilvie and Catherine Robertson, [Dundee OPR]; from Dundee, died in Pensacola, West Florida, admin. February 1785 PCC; a shipmaster in Charleston, South Carolina, who died in Pensacola, West Florida, 1779, son of Henry Ogilvy of Templehall, [refers to his widow and executrix Hannah Meadows (later wife of David Scott); their infant daughter Harriet; Catherine Robertson, widow of Henry Ogilvy of Templehall; Alexander Ogilvy, eldest son of Henry Ogilvy of Templehall; John Gordon WS] cnf 27 May 1784 Edinburgh. [NAS.CC8.8.126/1][NAS.SH]

OGILVIE, JAMES, from Leith, Midlothian, died in Georgia 1790. [Georgia Gazette, 19.8.1790]

OGLETHORPE, JAMES, trustee for the Colony of Georgia was admitted as a burgess and guildsbrother of Inverness via his proxy Captain George Dunbar, master of the Prince of Wales, on 22 September 1735. [Inverness Burgess Roll]

OLIPHANT, JAMES, born 1741, a yeoman, emigrated from Newcastle to Georgia on the Georgia Packet in September 1775, settled in Friendsborough, Georgia. [PRO.T47.9/11]

OLIPHANT, W., born in Scotland 1822, a laborer, settled in Mobile, Alabama. [C]

OLIVER, JAMES, born in Berwick on Tweed during 1774, a planter, married ... Meldrum in   Berwick on Tweed in November 1804, died in Savannah, Georgia, 26 May 1808. [SM.66.971; 70.719] [Savannah Republican, 28.5.1808] [Savannah Death Register]

OLIVER, THOMAS, born in 1745, (possibly son of Thomas Oliver a nailer in Denholm, Roxburghshire), a blacksmith and an indentured servant, with his wife and 2 children, emigrated from Whitby to Savannah on the Marlborough in August 1774. [PRO.T47.9/11]

ORD, WALTER, servant to Andrew Grant, arrived in Georgia on 1 August 1734. [ESG#91]

ORMISTON, THOMAS, land grant of 200 acres in Georgia on 21 March 1736, died in Carolina during August 1742. [ESG#91]

ORMOND, HELEN, [possibly the Helen baptised in parish of South Leith on 14 January 1820, daughter of James Ormond and Isabell Christie, {South Leith OPR}], daughter of John Ormond in Leith, died in Verdura, Florida, on 27August 1841. [EEC#20273]

ORMOND, RUSSELL, [probably the Russel baptised in the parish of South Leith on 28 June 1818, daughter of James Ormond and Isabell Christie, [South Leith OPR}]; daughter of John Ormond in Leith, wife of Joseph Chaires in Tallahassee, died in Verdura, Florida, 29 August 1841. [EEC#20273]

ORMISTON, THOMAS, a merchant in Edinburgh, emigrated to Savannah, Georgia, 1736, granted 200 acres in Georgia on 31 March 1736. [PRO.CO.5.668/CO.5.670.283/308][SPC.143.148]

ORR, CHARLES, born in Scotland 1833, son of John and Elizabeth Orr, a waterman, settled in Alabama. [C]

ORRY, WILLIAM, with John and Jane, emigrated from Kirkwall, Orkney, to Georgia in September 1774 on the Marlborough, Captain George Prissick, indentured servants of Thomas Brown in Georgia. [PRO.AO13.34.123-5]

OSWALD RICHARD, a Scots merchant in London, granted 500 acres in October 1751. [PRO.CO5/669]

OSWELL, WILLIAM, a ginwright, born in Scotland 1810, settled in Warren County, Mississippi. [C]

PALE, SUSAN, born in Scotland 1830, settled in Alabama. [C]

PANTON, WILLIAM, born 1742 son of John Panton and Barbara Wemyss in the Mains of Aberdour, Aberdeenshire, emigrated after 1765, Indian trader in Savannah, partner in firm of Panton, Leslie and Company; later in Pensacola, West Florida, died on 26 February 1801at sea, pro. December 1804 PCC [IT#18]

PARKER, GEORGE, in Savannah, Georgia, 1799. [NAS.CS17.1.18/183]

PATTERSON, JAMES, born 1791, emigrated to US 1809, a clerk in St Simon's 1812. [1812]

PATTERSON, SIMON, jr., a merchant in Georgia, 1801. [NAS.CS17.1.9/201]

PATTERSON, WILLIAM, land grant in Savannah on 7 September 1762, [CRG#28/1.436][Grant book D, #196]

PENDRICH, WILLIAM, servant to Andrew Grant, arrived in Georgia on 1 August 1734. [ESG#92]

PENMAN, ARCHIBALD, a merchant in Florida, son of George Penman a shoemaker in Edinburgh, 1785. [NAS.CS17.1.4/193]

PENMAN, JAMES, formerly a clerk to Peter Taylor an army contractor in Germany, then an estate manager in East Florida 1766, in St Augustine, East Florida, 1772, resident of South Carolina who was

admitted as a burgess of Glasgow on 2 September 1784, a
merchant in St Augustine.
[NAS.AC.7.59/27.8.1788][NAS.NRAS.771, bundle
29/491][NAS.NRAS#0181;11][Glasgow Burgess Roll]

PETERS, JANET, born in Scotland 1809, settled in Mobile, Alabama.
[C]

PETRIE, PETER, born 1764, a farm servant in St Andrews parish,
Orkney, emigrated from Kirkwall, Orkney, to Savannah, Georgia,
on the Marlborough, Captain George Prissick, in September 1774,
settled in Richmond County, Georgia, as an indentured servant of
Thomas Brown. [PRO.T47.12][PRO.AO13.34.123-5]

PETTIGREW, JOHN, Indian trader in Augusta 15 June 1756,
[PRO.CO5.646, C15]; land grant of 200 acres in Augusta District,
Georgia, on 5 April 1757, [PRO.CO.5.646.C10][CRG#28/1.62];
land grant in Augusta on 5 June 1759, [CRG#28/1.332]; in
Sunbury, St Joseph's parish, Georgia, pro. 8 October 1775 Georgia.
[refers to Pettigrew and Paterson {Pettigrew in Georgia. and Simon
Paterson sr & jr, in Glasgow}, mother Janet, eldest sister Janet,
Robert Baillie in St Andrews parish, Roderick McIntosh in St
Andrews parish, Walter Wilson in Glasgow, David Fleming,
Donald Fraser collector, James Beverley schoolmaster in Sunbury,
William Wallace 'my clerk', sisters Janet, Grizel, Elizabeth,
Margaret, Mary, and Agnes; his estate in Green, Barony, Glasgow;
executors Robert Baillie in St Andrews parish, Simon Paterson sr
& jr in Glasgow, David Fleming and Donald Fraser in Sunbury]

PHILLIPS, JOHN CAMERON, born 1825 probably in Glasgow, a
stevadore in New Orleans, married Maria Kelly there in 1848,
settled in Brownsville, Texas, died 1848. [C]

PIRRIE, ALEXANDER, settled in Augusta during 1797, died on 22
October 1801. [GaGaz#31, 5.11.1801]

PLAINE, JAMES, son of Francis Plaine, sometime merchant in Paris,
who died in Savannah, Georgia, in September 1798, [refers to his
executors Rose Marguerite Plaine his sister, John Francis Plaine his

brother, and James Hutton of the Post Office in London; John
Wilson in London; David Thomson WS in Edinburgh; Robert
Oliphant of Rossie Square {Edinburgh?}; Dr Thomas Young, a
physician, and his wife Barbara Gibson in Edinburgh; Dr James
Hutton physician in Edinburgh; Samuel Mitchelson WS; Sir James
Hay of Hayston; Robert Young, upholsterer in Edinburgh; John
Hay and Samuel Anderson bankers in Edinburgh; William Wilson
writer in Edinburgh] cnf 23 February 1807 Edinburgh

POLSON, JOHN, Navidale, Sutherland, emigrated via Stromness and
Carolina to Georgia in April 1761. [NLS:Delvine PP.MS1487]
[SGen.XLI.2]

POLWART, JOHN, servant to William and Hugh Stirling, arrived in
Georgia on 1 August 1734, boatman to John Latter, died in
Fredericia during 1738. [ESG#93]

PORTEOUS, GEORGE, born in Scotland 1811, a clerk, settled in
Alabama. [C]

PORTEOUS, SIMON, born 1726, a mason, emigrated from Newcastle to
Georgia on the Georgia Packet in September 1775, settled in
Friendsborough, Georgia. [PRO.T47.12]

POW, DAVID, born 1774, a mariner, died on 19 September 1804.
[Savannah Death Register]

POWRIE,? ("Pouvroy"), JOHN, servant to James Houstoun, arrived in
Georgia on 1 August 1734. [ESG#93]

POWRIE, ? ("Pouvroy"), MARTHA, servant to James Houstoun, arrived
in Georgia on 1 August 1734. [ESG#93]

PRATT, JOHN, born in Scotland 1812, wife Elizabeth born in
Pennsylvania 1825, settled in Gonzales, Texas. [C]

PRESTON, GEORGE, jr., of Valleyfield, granted 500 acres in Georgia
25 November 1737 and on 15 March 1738, sent over 10 servants.
[PRO.CO.5.668; CO.5.670.335.][SPAWI.1738#109] [ESG#93]

PRIMROSE, EDWARD, died in Augusta on 4 October 1808. [Colonial Museum and Savannah Advertiser: 14.10.1808]

PRINGLE, HENRY TIMBRAL, late of Aberdeen, died in Savannah, USA, on 10 October 1867. [AJ#6257]

PRINGLE, R., appointed member of the Council of Georgia, 2 March 1752. [SCGaz#927]

PROFIT, CHARLES, from Dundee, in New Orleans, Louisiana, 1805. [NAS.CS17.1.24/161]

PROVAN, Dr MATTHEW, son of John Provan a manufacturer in Kilsyth, Stirlingshire, educated at Glasgow University ca.1802, died in Natchez, Mississippi, on 4 October 1823. [BM#15.131][MAGU#201]

PURDIE, JOHN, servant to A. Grant, arrived in Georgia on 1 August 1734. [ESG#93]

PURVES, Mrs ANN, born in Scotland 1812, wife of John Purves born 1802, settled in Warren County, Mississippi. [C]

PURVES, BURRIDGE, baptised on 17 December 1808 in Kirkcaldy, Fife, son of Burridge Purves and Mary Brown, {Kirkcaldy OPR}]; son of Burridge Purves of Glassmount, Fife, died at his plantation on the Yazoo on 1 September 1837. [DPCA#1839]

PURVES, JOHN HOME, baptised on 25 January 1784 in Hutton parish, Berwickshire, eldest son of Sir Alexander Purves of Purves Hall, Berwickshire, HM Consul in Pensacola, West Florida, died there on 30 September 1827. [Hutton OPR] [GM#97.573][BM#23.270] [AJ#4172][EEC#18146]

PURVES, JOHN, Warren, Mississippi, eldest son of Beveridge Purves of Glassmount, Fife, died at Oakland Plantation, near Vicksburg, Mississippi, on 19 October 1850, [FJ]; cnf. 1864. [NAS.SC70.1.122]

PURVES, ROBERT, born in Scotland 1800, a merchant, wife Mary born in S.C. 1810, daughter Elizabeth born in S.C., children Sarah, Cornelia, Frances, Robert, John, Carolina, and William, (all born in Alabama), and daughter Mary born in Scotland 1838, emigrated to South Carolina by 1833, later settled in Alabama. [C]

PURVES, WILLIAM, baptised on 8 October 1810 in parish of Kinghorn, Fife, youngest son of Beveridge Purves of Glassmount, and Mary Brown, died at Oakland Plantation, near Vicksburg, Mississippi, on 23 January 1842. [Kinghorn OPR] [FJ,10.3.1842]

PURVES, ..., daughter of Robert Purves, born in Springhill, Mobile, on 4 November 1840. [EEC#20145]

RAE, JAMES, master of the Minerva of Dundee, arrived in Charleston, South Carolina, from Dundee with passengers some of whom were bound for Florida on 26 August 1765. [SCGaz]

RAE, JAMES, died in Richmond County, Georgia, in March 1789. [GaGaz#3/1]

RAE, JOHN, a settler in Georgia on 9 December 1738, [AGA#59]; in Augusta 1750. [PRO.CO.5.668.46]; granted 450 acres in Christ Church parish, Georgia, 2 November 1762. [PRO.CO.5.648.E68] [Grant book D, #218; Grant book H, #26] [CRG#28/1.439]; at Rae's Hall Plantation, near Augusta, in September 1763. [Ga.Gaz.#24, 274]

RAILLIE, JOHN, died in McIntosh County, Georgia, on 22 April 1820. [BM#7.705]

RALSTON, GEORGE, born 1766, emigrated to US 1794, a merchant in Savannah 1812. [1812]

RAMSAY, ALEXANDER, Lieutenant of the Royal Artillery, third son of Captain Ramsay of the Royal Navy, died in New Orleans on 1 January 1815. [Inveresk g/s]

RAMSAY, DAVID, died on 21 September 1799. [Augusta Chronicle: 28.9.1799]

RAMSAY, JAMES, born 1779, emigrated to USA in 1802, a merchant in Charleston and later New Orleans. [1812]

RAMSAY, JAMES, born in Scotland during 1813, wife Elizabeth born in Scotland 1814, settled in Gonzales, Texas. [C]

RAMSAY, THOMAS, born 1776, a baker, died on 13 January 1805. [Savannah Death Register]

RANKIN, ROBERT, a merchant and grocer in Edinburgh 1821-1834, absconded to New York, later in Savannah. [NAS.CS46.1835]

RATTRAY, ALEXANDER, servant to Patrick Houstoun, arrived in Georgia on 1 August 1734. [ESG#95]

RAY, ISABEL, born in Scotland 1804, Daniel Ray born in North Carolina 1804, Colin Ray born in Florida 1838, Isabel Ray born in Florida 1840, and Mary Ray born in Florida 1842, settled in Walton County, Florida.[C]

READY, THOMAS, servant to Patrick Houstoun, arrived in Georgia on 1 August 1734, died on 1 September 1738. [ESG#93]

REDFORD, ROBERT, servant to Joseph Wardrope, arrived in Georgia on 1 August 1734, land grant in Savannah in April 1737, died in June 1738, his widow Sarah married John Goldwyre and moved to Carolina in August 1742. [ESG#94]

REED, JAMES, baptised on 4 May 1800 in Kilmarnock, Ayrshire, eldest son of James Reed MD and Elizabeth Brown, died in New Orleans on 18 September 1839. [Kilmarnock OPR][SG#821]

REID, D., born in Scotland 1813, a merchant, wife Jane born in Ireland 1814, settled in Mobile, Alabama. [C]

REID, GEORGE, born 1782, emigrated to US 1807, a merchant's clerk in Savannah 1812. [1812]

REID, JAMES, land grants 11 February 1757, 30 September 1757, in Christchurch 3 November 1761, in Savannah 7 December 1762, [CRG#28/1.49, 232, 367, 442]; member of the Council of Georgia 1759, [CRG#28/1.180]

REID, JAMES HOPE, third son of ... Reid a farmer in Parbroath, Fife, a merchant in Savannah, died in New York on 16 September 1848. [FH]

REID, JOHN, born in Scotland, deserted from Captain Massey's Independent Company in Georgia in July 1736. [SCGaz#131]

REID, ROBERT, born in Scotland 1817, a merchant, settled in Alabama. [C]

REID, THOMAS, born in Scotland 1822, a baker, wife Sarah born in Ohio 1822, son J. born in Ohio 1846, settled in Alabama. [C]

REID, WILLIAM, servant to Patrick Tailfer around 1740. [ESG#93]

REYNOLDS, ALEXANDER, servant to William Wardrope around 1740. [ESG#94]

RHENOH, JANET, from Wick, Caithness, emigrated from Caithness via Kirkwall, Orkney, on the Marlborough, Captain Thomas Walker, to Savannah, Georgia, in September 1775, an indentured servant of Thomas Brown in Georgia. [PRO.AO13.34.123-5]

RIDOUT, JOSEPH, born in Berwick 1774, a mariner, died in Savannah, Georgia, in February 1811. [Savannah Death Register]

RINTOUL, ("Rantowl"), ALEXANDER, land grant in Savannah 1736, moved to Charleston, South Carolina, in February 1737. [ESG#93]

RITCHIE, STEWART, born 1770, emigrated to US 1805, a planter in Camden County 1812. [1812]

ROAN, Mrs JANE, born in Scotland 1810, emigrated to America before 1836, husband John Roan a laborer born in Georgia 1802, son James born in Tennessee 1836, settled in Alabama. [C]

ROBERTS, JOHN, born 1745, a merchant, with his wife Margaret born 1752, emigrated from London to Georgia on the Georgia Diana in March 1775. [PRO.T47.9/11]

ROBERTSON, ANDREW, a recruit for the independent company, emigrated from Gravesend on the Mary Ann, Captain Thomas Shubrick, for Georgia 13 August 1737. [SPC.43#459]

ROBERTSON, ANGUS, soldier of the Black Watch, imprisoned in the Tower of London on a charge of mutiny, transferred to Oglethorpe's Regiment in Georgia 1743. [GHS, Cate Colln. 45/3172]

ROBERTSON, A., partner in G. Baillie and Company in Savannah, dissolved 11 May 1768. [Ga.Gaz.#242]

ROBERTSON, CHRISTINA, baptised on 19 April 1812, second daughter of William Robertson a merchant in Dalkeith, Midlothian, and Allison Jamieson, married Andrew Aitchison of Jackson, Louisiana, in New Orleans on 27 November 1833. [Dalkeith OPR] [AJ#4493]

ROBERTSON, DAVID DUNCAN, son of Samuel Robertson in Ednam, Berwickshire, died in Savannah, Georgia, 1817. [S#31.17]

ROBERTSON, DUNCAN ENEAS, born in Rochine(?), Scotland, son of Charles Robertson and Jean Rose, and Maria Badon, born in New Orleans, daughter of Jose Badon and Catalina Montelimar, were married in Louisiana 7 March 1797.[LGS]

ROBERTSON, JAMES, born 1739, a farm servant in Evie, Orkney, emigrated with his wife Christian Linay from Kirkwall to Savannah, Georgia, on the Marlborough, Captain Thomas Walker, in September 1775, settled in Richmond County, Georgia, as an

indentured servant to Thomas Brown. [PRO.T47.12]
[PRO.AO13.34.123-5]

ROBERTSON, Colonel JAMES, served in America from 1756 to 1783,
barrack master general in America 1765-1776, Governor of New
York 1779-1783, granted 10,000 acres in East Florida 1766.
[PCCol.V.590][NAS.GD172, box 48]

ROBERTSON, JAMES, possibly from Elgin, Morayshire, settled in
Georgia later in Jamaica, 1787, [deed refers to James Milne in
Elgin; William Gillan; Alexander Watson; John Cunningham].
[NAS.RD3.247.402]

ROBERTSON, JAMES, born in Scotland in 1816, a sailor, settled in
Mobile, Alabama. [C]

ROBERTSON, JOHN, born in Edinburgh during 1787, a carpenter, died
in Savannah, Georgia, on 6 September 1809. [Savannah Death
Register]

ROBERTSON, MICHAEL, born 1755, a farm servant in Harray, Orkney,
emigrated from Kirkwall to Savannah, Georgia, on the
Marlborough, Captain Thomas Walker, in September 1775, settled
in Richmond County, Georgia, as an indentured servant of Thomas
Brown. [PRO.T47.12][PRO.AO13.34.123-5]

ROBERTSON, THOMAS, born in Aberdeen during 1768, customs
officer and city surveyor, died in Savannah, Georgia, on 27
December 1810. [Savannah Death Register]

ROBERTSON, WILLIAM, born in 1720, a cowherd, embarked on the
Loyal Judith for Georgia on 21 September 1741, landed on 2
December 1741. [PRO.CO.5.668][ESG44][CRG.XXX.197/199]

ROBINSON, ISAAC, born in Scotland during 1808, died at the Alamo 6
March 1836. [DRTL]

ROBINSON, Mrs ELIZABETH, born in Scotland 1822, wife of
Christopher Robinson born in Denmark 1818, daughter Elizabeth

B. born in Scotland 1847, settled in Harrison County, Mississippi. [C]

ROBINSON, ISAAC, born in Scotland 1803, emigrated to New Orleans, settled in Refugio, Texas, died at the Alamo on 6 March 1836. [DRTL]

ROBINSON, JAMES, a baker, born in Scotland 1804, wife Margaret born in Scotland 1809, son George born in Mississippi 1845, settled in Adams County, Mississippi. [C]

ROBINSTONE, A., born in Scotland 1825, a carpenter, settled in Mobile, Alabama. [C]

ROBSON, ROBERT, born 1747, a yeoman, emigrated with his wife Jane ..., and children Eleanor born 1769, James born 1771, and Mary born 1774, from Newcastle to Georgia on the Georgia Packet in September 1775, settled in Richmond County, Georgia. [PRO.T47.9/11]

ROSE, ALEXANDER, granted 250 acres in Newport, St John's parish, 6 December 1757. [Grant Book A.586]

ROSE, ALEXANDER, son of William Rose in Dornoch, Ross and Cromarty, died in Darien, Georgia, on 20 May 1819. [S.3.131][EA#5805]

ROSE, DONALD, born 1712, a servant, emigrated from Inverness on the Two Brothers, Captain William Thomson, to Georgia in July 1737, landed on 20 January 1737, soldier in Oglethorpe's Independent Highland Company 6 May 1741. [ESG44]

ROSE, DONALD, born 1731, a 17 year indentured servant, emigrated to Georgia 19 November 1737, landed 14 January 1738. [ESG44]

ROSS, ALEXANDER, arrived in Georgia as an indentured servant 28 December 1734, [ESG#94]; a sawyer and laborer in Savannah 1745. [PRO.CO.5.668.190]; land grants in Newport 6 December 1757, and in St Philip's parish 4 July 1758, [CRG#28/1.237, 244]

ROSS, ALEXANDER, born 1792 in Golspie, Sutherland, died at The Thicket, McIntosh County, Georgia, in 1819. [Darien Gazette, 24.5.1819]

ROSS, ANDREW, born 1784, a merchant, died on 19 September 1804. [Savannah Death Register]

ROSS, DANIEL, born 1721, 6 year indentured servant, emigrated to Georgia 19 November 1737, landed 14 January 1738, died at Darien 1738. [ESG#45]

ROSS, DAVID, a merchant in Baton Rouge, Mississippi, 1783, 1785. [NAS.CS17.1.2; 6/15]

ROSS, GEORGE, a merchant in Baton Rouge, Mississippi, 1783. [NAS.CS17.1.2]

ROSS, GILBERT, granted 10,000 acres in East Florida 1767. [PC.Col.V.590]

ROSS, HUGH, servant to William and Hugh Stirling, arrived in Georgia on 1 August 1734, a carpenter and a laborer. [ESG#94]

ROSS, HUGH, born 1705, from Drenach, servant to Mackay of Scourie, emigrated from Inverness on the Prince of Wales, Captain George Dunbar, on 20 October 1735, arrived in Georgia on 10 January 1736, settled in Darien, there 1741. [ESG#94]

ROSS, HUGH, land grants in Darien, Abercorn and Savannah on 7 February 1758, [CRG#28/1.239]; land grant in Savannah on 6 December 1758, [Grant book A, #611]; land grant of 300 acres in St George's parish, and also 50 acres in St Andrew's parish, Georgia, on 21 May 1762. [PRO.CO.5.648.E68][CRG#28/1.422]

ROSS, HUGH, shopkeeper in Savannah, wife Ann - daughter of late Daniel Stewart shipmaster in Inverness, Scotland, son John, executor wife Ann, subscribed 1 November 1762. Pro. 27 April 1775 Chatham County, Georgia.[Will Book A]; 29 March 1764,

[Ga.Gaz.#52];died in Savannah during December 1774.
[GaGaz#3/1]

ROSS, HUGH, land grant in St Andrew's parish, Georgia, on 11 October
1764. [Ga.Gaz.#34,80,89]

ROSS, JAMES, servant to Patrick Houstoun, arrived in Georgia on 1
August 1734. [ESG#95]

ROSS, JAMES, a miller from Waffin, emigrated from Inverness on the
Prince of Wales, Captain George Dunbar, on 20 October 1735,
arrived in Georgia on 10 January 1736. [ESG#94]

ROSS, JOHN, pro.25 August 1760 Georgia

ROSS, JOHN, son of the laird of Arnage in Aberdeenshire, an Indian
trader at Fort Pitt, then a planter and merchant in East Florida,
manager of William Elliot's estate in East Florida before 1775,
elected member of the East Florida Assembly 1781, land grant in
Indiantown Creek there, a Loyalist, moved to Dominica 1785.
[NAS.GD186]

ROSS, JOHN, born in Scotland during 1820, a clerk, settled in Mobile,
Alabama. [C]

ROSS, ROBERT, born in Aberdeen, a merchant in Pensacola, West
Florida, 1764-1772, a planter and a merchant in Mississippi 1772-
1778, a Loyalist, settled in Shelbourne, Nova Scotia, before 1785.
[PRO.AO13.26.414/423][NAS.CS17.1.2]

ROSS, THOMAS, an Indian trader in Georgia before 1766, pro.16
October 1766 Georgia

ROSS, WILLIAM, born in 1705, an indentured servant, emigrated from
Inverness on the Two Brothers, Captain William Thomson, to
Georgia in July 1737, landed on 20 January 1737. [ESG45]

ROSS, WILLIAM, born in 1712, an indentured servant, emigrated from Inverness on the Two Brothers, Captain William Thomson, to Georgia in July 1737, landed on 20 January 1737. [ESG45]

ROY, JAMES, born in Fife, died in Augusta, Georgia, on 25 July 1818. [Colonial Museum and Savannah Advertiser, 4.8.1818]

RUSSELL, JAMES, a saddler in Augusta, Georgia, 1819- [NAS.NRAS#1267]

RUSSELL, WILLIAM, born 28 April 1798, son of Alexander Russell in Glasgow, educated at Glasgow University around 1811, emigrated to Savannah, Georgia, in 1819, a schoolteacher, died in Massachusetts on 17 May 1873. [MAGU#259]

RUTHERFORD, JAMES, land grant of 250 acres in Ogeechee district, Georgia, on 6 December 1757. [PRO.CO.5.648.E46][CRG#28/1.365][Grant book C, #229]

RUTHERFORD, JOHN, servant to Andrew Grant, arrived in Georgia on 1 August 1734. [ESG#95]

RUTHERFORD, JOHN, born in Scotland 1827, a clerk, settled in Alabama. [C]

RUTHERFORD, WILLIAM, emigrated to America 1816, an overseer who settled in Rapides, Louisiana, before 1850. [LGS#XII/16]

RUTHERFORD, W.E., born in Scotland 1826, a merchant, settled in Alabama. [C]

SAGE, J., born 1832, son of William Sage and Susan Sage in Perth, a physician, settled in Jefferson County, Georgia, died during 1852. [Perth Greyfriars g/s]

SALISBURY, CHARLES, born in Scotland 1745, a yeoman, emigrated from Newcastle to Georgia on the Georgia Packet in September 1775, settled in Friendsborough, Georgia. [PRO.T47.9/11]

SALTER, JAMES, born in Scotland 1820, a merchant, wife Mary born 1828, and daughter Elizabeth born 1848, (both in Alabama), settled in Alabama. [C]

SAWERS, WILLIAM, born 1779 youngest son of Robert Sawers of Drumteach, East Monklands, Lanarkshire, died on Sullivan's Island 30 August 1800. [GC#1426]

SCENTERS, JAMES, born in Scotland 1831, a barber, settled in Alabama. [C]

SCOTT, ALISON ERSKINE, baptised on 25 January 1808, youngest daughter of Ebenezer Scott a surgeon in Dalkeith, Midlothian, and Christian Mutter, married W.G.Adams a merchant in Memphis, Tennessee, there on 18 January 1839. [Dalkeith OPR] [EEC#19874]

SCOTT, FRANCIS, born 1692, a reduced military officer, emigrated from Gravesend on the Anne, Captain Thomas Shubrick, to Georgia on 16 November 1732, died on 2 January 1734. [ESG#47/110]; Francis Scott in Savannah subscribed to a will 25 December 1730, [University of Georgia, K. Read MS]

SCOTT, GAVIN, born 1766, Glasgow, a hairdresser in Chatham County, Georgia, died on 5 November 1812, [Colonial Cemetery, Savannah, g/s]; pro. 3 February 1812 Chatham County, Georgia, (his will refers to sister Jane and brother in Glasgow, executors Robert Fair a shoemaker and Thomas Williams a mariner).

SCOTT, Lieutenant Colonel GEORGE, granted 20,000 acres in East Florida 1766. [PC.Col.V.590]

SCOTT, JAMES, servant to Andrew Grant, arrived in Georgia on 1 August 1734. [ESG#95]

SCOTT, JAMES, born 1750, a carpenter, emigrated from Newcastle to Georgia on the Georgia Packet in September 1775, settled in Friendsborough, Georgia. [PRO.T47.9/11]

SCOTT, JAMES, born in Scotland 1804, a sailor, settled in Alabama. [C]

SCOTT, JOHN, servant to Andrew Grant, arrived in Georgia on 1 August 1734. [ESG#95], possibly John Scott the blacksmith, father of Thomas and William. [ESG#95]

SCOTT, JOHN, born 1745, a yeoman, emigrated with his wife Margaret ... born 1740, and children William born 1762, John born 1765, Mary born 1767, Agnes born 1771, and Margaret born 1773, from Newcastle to Georgia on the Georgia Packet in September 1775, settled in Friendsborough, Georgia. [PRO.T47.9/11]

SCOTT, JOHN, granted 20,000 acres in East Florida 1767. [PC.Col.V.591]

SCOTT, WILLIAM, in Savannah, Georgia, died in Liverpool on 14 July 1830, cnf 1831. [NAS.SC70.1.45]

SCOTT, WILLIAM, second son of Lieutenant Scott of the Fife Militia, died in Mobile, Alabama, on 11 July 1860. [FH]

SCRIMGEOUR, CHARLES, born 1748, a millwright, died on 28 September 1804. [Savannah Death Register]

SENIOR, GEORGE, (?), land grant in St Andrew's parish, Georgia, on 5 February 1760, [CRG#28/1.320]

SEYMOUR, Reverend JAMES, educated at King's College, Aberdeen, 1766, emigrated to Georgia 1771, an Anglican minister in Augusta, Georgia, 1773-1782. [SPCK pp, London][FPA#300][Mowat#166]; together with Alexander Findlay granted 300 acres in Christ Church parish, Georgia, on 1 August 1769. [Grant book G, #387] he died on passage from St Augustine to Nassau in August 1784. [Gaz.State Ga#2/3]

SHADFORTH, WHITAKER, born 1754, a watchmaker, emigrated from Newcastle to Georgia on the Georgia Packet in September 1775, settled in Friendsborough, Georgia. [PRO.T47.9/11]

SHAND, GEORGE, born in Huntly, Aberdeenshire, died in New Orleans on 2 September 1839. [AJ#4803]

SHARP, JAMES, baptised on 4 April 1790 in Dundee, son of William Sharp and Isabella Kinnear, a tanner, died in New Orleans on 13 August 1829. [Dundee OPR][Dundee, Howff, g/s]

SHAW, ANNA, born in Scotland 1796, John Shaw a farmer born in Florida in 1828, Ann Shaw born in North Carolina in 1832, settled in Gadsden County, Florida. [C]

SHAW, JAMES, died on Cumberland Island, Georgia, on 8 January 1820. [EA#5872.151][EEC#16971]

SHAW, R.D., born in Scotland 1799, a farmer, Mary J. born 1812 in Louisiana, sons Horatis N. born 1831 in Amite County, a farmer, George W. born 1836 in Amite County, Henry C. born 1844 in Amite County, William H.H. born 1841 in Louisiana, John S. born 1848 in Amite County, and Richard J. born 1849, in Amite County, settled in Amite County, Mississippi. [C]

SHAW, WILLIAM, a merchant in Clarke County, died on 20 September 1809. [Georgia Express: 7.10.1809]

SHAW, WILLIAM, born in Scotland in 1798, a gardener, children Margaret, John, Mary, William, James, and Dolly, (all born in Alabama), settled in Alabama. [C]

SHEARER, DONALD, 16, a labourer in Tonge, a servant, emigrated to Georgia on 20 October 1735, landed on 10 January 1736. [ESG47]

SHEPHERD, ABRAM, born in Scotland in 1805, a laborer, settled in Mobile, Alabama. [C]

SHEPHERD, DAVID, son of William Shepherd {1792-1832}, settled in New Orleans, Louisiana, before 1847. [Dunfermline g/s]

SHEPHERD, HELEN, born in Scotland in 1815, settled in Mobile, Alabama, daughter E.W. Shepherd born in Alabama in 1841. [C]

SHERROT, HELEN, born in Ayr in 1800, grandniece of William Shaw a
shopkeeper, died in White Bluff, Georgia, on 21 October 1814.
[Savannah Republican, 27.10.1814]

SHIELDS, JAMES, died in Darien, Georgia, on 14 September 1821.
[Darien Gazette: 15.9.1821]

SIBBALD, GEORGE, a merchant in St Mary's, Georgia, 1807.
[NAS.CS17.1.26/474]

SIMMONS, JACK, a sailor, born in Scotland in 1820, resident in
Harrison County, Mississippi. [C]

SIMPSON, ADAM, a cabinetmaker, born in Scotland in 1815, wife
Margaret born in Louisiana in 1823, settled in Warren County,
Mississippi. [C]

SIMPSON, Mrs ANNA JEAN, wife of John Simpson in Savannah,
disposed of 500 acres in Christchurch parish, Georgia, to John
Bowman in Savannah, in 1774. [NAS.GD77.167]

SIMPSON, JOHN, land grant in Savannah, Georgia, on 25 September
1760, [CRG#28/1.327] [Grant book B, #451]; land grant in Christ
Church parish on 7 March 1769, [Grant book G, #288]; granted
600 acres in St John's parish on 5 June 1771. [Grant Book I, #352]

SIMPSON, JOHN, of Grueldykes, a merchant in Sunbury, Georgia, in
1774. [NAS.CS16.1.157, 165]

SIMPSON, J., in Sunbury, subscribed towards a Presbyterian Meeting
House in Savannah during 1768. [Ga.Gaz.#291]

SIMPSON, JOHN, of Savannah, husband of Jean Simpson, died in
Edinburgh, pro. December 1788 PCC

SIMPSON, JOHN, baptised in Kirkcaldy, Fife, on 3 September 1809, son
of James Simpson {1770-1852} and Christine Whyte {1777-1841}
died in New Orleans 16 October 1843.[Kirkcaldy OPR: g/s]

SIMPSON, WILLIAM, from Edinburgh, appointed Chief Justice of
Georgia, in November 1763; pro.21 December 1768 Georgia.
[AJ#827]; in 1766, [NAS.NRAS#0771]; married Anna Jean,
daughter of Captain W.M.MacKenzie the Customs Collector at
Sunbury. [SGen.44.3.131]

SIMPSON, WILLIAM, granted 300 acres in St John's parish, Georgia, on
2 June 1772. [Grant Book I.630]

SINCLAIR, ALEXANDER, born in Caithness in 1789, died in Savannah,
Georgia, on 30 October 1813. [Savannah Republican, 2.11.1813];
born in 1787, to USA during 1809, a merchant's clerk in Savannah
in 1812, [1812]

SINCLAIR, ARCHIBALD, servant to Patrick Houstoun, arrived in
Georgia on 1 August 1734, possibly granted a lot in Fredericia and
a tythingman there 1738-1739, husband of Isabel, parents of James,
and Margaret. [ESG#96]

SINCLAIR, ARCHIBALD, servant to Mr Houstoun in Savannah,
emigrated in 1737, settled in Fredericia, Georgia. [SPC.1737.596]

SINCLAIR, BENJAMIN W., third son of Alexander Sinclair a merchant
in Thurso, Caithness, married Susan C. Faries, second daughter of
Major Faries of Savannah, in Savannah, North America, on 24
November 1842. [AJ#4965]

SINCLAIR, JAMES, born in 1755, a farm servant in Holm, Orkney,
emigrated from Kirkwall, Orkney, to Savannah, Georgia, on the
Marlborough, Captain Thomas Walker, in September 1775, settled
in Richmond County, Georgia, as an indentured servant of Thomas
Walker. [PRO.T47.12][PRO.AO13.34.123-5]

SINCLAIR, JOHN, servant to John Macintosh of Dores, Inverness-shire,
emigrated from Inverness on the Prince of Wales, Captain George
Dunbar, on 20 October 1735, arrived in Georgia on 10 January
1736. [ESG#96]

SINCLAIR, JOHN, son of Sir William Sinclair, granted 5,000 acres in East Florida in 1767. [PRO.CO5.542]

SINCLAIR, MARGARET, born 1755, a servant in Bower, Caithness, emigrated from Caithness via Kirkwall, Orkney, to Savannah, Georgia, on the <u>Marlborough</u>, Captain Thomas Walker, in September 1775. [PRO.T47.12][PRO.AO13.34.123-5]

SINCLAIR, WILLIAM, son of George Sinclair, to Georgia as an indentured servant of William Bradley in January 1735. [PRO.CO.5.668.16][ESG#96]

SINCLAIR, Sir WILLIAM, granted 10,000 acres in East Florida in 1767. [PRO.CO5.542][PC.Col.V.591]

SINCLAIR, ..., a former indentured servant of Sir Patrick Houston, in Savannah on 28 November 1737. [CRG.XXII.1/16]

SKINNER, ALEXANDER, in St Augustine, East Florida, Superintendent of Indian Affairs in the Southern District of North America, Admin.February 1800 PCC

SLOANE, ALEXANDER, baptised in Whithorn parish, Kirkcudbright, on 31 December 1794, son of Anthony Sloane and Jane Lowrie, settled in New Orleans, died in Whithorn, Kirkcudbrightshire, on 13 December 1835. [Whithorn OPR] [NAS.SH]

SLOANE, ANTHONY, baptised in Whithorn parish, Kirkcudbrightshire, on 21 September 1803, son of Anthony Sloane and Jane Lowrie, died in New Orleans on 3 January 1844. [Whithorn OPR] [NAS.SH]

SLOAN, GEORGE, born in Scotland in 1820, a blacksmith, settled in Alabama. [C]

SLOANE, PETER, from Kirkcudbrightshire, died in New Orleans on 18 May 1849. [NAS.SH]

SMALL, MARY, born in Scotland 1783, settled in Autauga County, Alabama. [C]

SMELLIE, PATRICK, emigrated to Savannah, Georgia, on the snow Kinnoull, Captain Alexander Alexander, and was granted 100 acres between the Savannah and the Saludy Rivers on 30 May 1768. [Ga.Co.Journal#34.148/151]

SMITH, Captain ALEXANDER, master of the Charlotte of Belfast, late of Aberdeen, born 1807, son of Alexander Smith a shoemaker in Aberdeen and Isabella Main {1779-1827}, died in New Orleans on 10 March 1848. [AJ#5233][Banchory-Tiernan g/s]

SMITH, ALEXINA, born in Scotland in 1832, settled in Alabama. [C]

SMITH, ANN, born in Scotland in 1818, settled in Mobile. [C]

SMITH, DAVID, late merchant in the Bahamas, died on his plantation in Louisiana on 24 April 1813. [EA#5218.423]

SMITH, DAVID, died in Attacapas, Louisiana, 14 February 1829. [EEC#18318]

SMITH, DUNCAN, born in Scotland 1816, wife Margaret born in Georgia 1823, children all born in Georgia, William in 1843, Susan in 1845, Euphemia in 1846, and Robert in 1849, settled in Lowndes County, Georgia. [C]

SMITH, JAMES, arrived in Georgia on 27 January 1734, granted a lot in Savannah, married the widow Close on 8 February 1734, left the colony to settle in Scotland in May 1740. [ESG#96]

SMITH, JAMES, a minister, grandson of Peter Smith in Doune, Perthshire, settled in Nashville, Tennessee, before 1835. [NAS.SH]

SMITH, JAMES, second son of John Smith in Largo, Fife, died in Savannah, Georgia, on 25 October 1817. [S.2.52]

SMITH, JESSIE, born in Scotland in 1828, settled in Alabama. [C]

SMITH, Dr JOHN, born in Scotland, settled in Charles County, Maryland, moved to Mississippi, returned to Norfolk, Virginia, imprisoned in Frederick Town, Maryland, 23 November 1775. [AJ#1469]

SMITH, JOSEPH HARRIS, [possibly baptised in Paisley Abbey on 12 January 1812, son of Joseph Smith and Mary McIntosh, {Paisley Abbey OPR}]; from Paisley, Renfrewshire, died in New Orleans in September 1850. [W#1205]

SMITH, MARY, born in Scotland 1844, settled in Alabama. [C]

SMITH, MICHAEL, born in Stirling, son of Hugh Smith and Mary Robertson, and Maria Antonia Rillieux, born in New Orleans, daughter of Vincent Rillieux and Maria Tronquet, were married in Louisiana 13 April 1801.[LGS]

SMITH, WALTER, born in Ayrshire 1784, died in Georgia 13 May 1840. [Georgia g/s]

SMITH, ..., son of James Smith in Mississippi, born at 23 Upper Gray Street, Edinburgh, on 19 March 1856. [CM#20744]

SMYLIE, JAMES, husband of Jane Watson, in Upper Barr, Killean and Kilkenzie parish, Kintyre, Argyllshire, emigrated to North Carolina 1776, settled in Scotland County, North Carolina, later in Amite County, Mississippi 1810. [NCSA.2.26]

SNEDDON, JAMES, a civil engineer in Macon, Georgia, married Agnes Bryson Whyte, third daughter of Robert Whyte a merchant in Edinburgh, in New York on 14 December 1851. [W#1279]

SNEDDON, WILLIAM, born in Scotland 1824, a clerk, wife Jane born in Scotland 1827, settled in Alabama before 1848, father of Jesse and William. [C]

SOMERVILLE, ALEXANDER, son of Reverend Simon Somerville in Elgin, died in Tuscombea, Alabama, 11August 1838.[AJ#4737]

SOMERVILLE, EDWARD, land grants in Christchurch and in Savannah 3 December 1760, [CRG#28/1.363][Grant book C, #192/193]; deceased by April 1763, executors John Rae and Thomas Eatton. [Ga.Gaz.#3]

SOUTHWARD, ALEXANDER, born 1778, a seaman, died on 14 November 1805. [Savannah Death Register]

SPALDING, JAMES, son of Thomas Spalding and Anna Learmonth, born Ashentilly, Perthshire, 1735, emigrated to Georgia 1760, settled on St Simon's Island, married Margery McIntosh 1772, father of Thomas born 1774, politician, died 1794. [Georgia g/s]

SPALDING, JAMES, a merchant in Florida 1769, [NAS.CS16.1.138]; a merchant in Bonnington Mills, Edinburgh, son of James Spalding, emigrated to America before 1772, settled in East Florida and in St Simon's Island, Georgia; merchant in East Florida and Georgia 20 October 1772; partner in firm of Spalding and Kelsall; in Savannah 20 July 1780, [deed refers to sister Grizel Cuthbert; David Spalding of Ashintully; Walter Brown and Robert Kelsall merchants in Georgia]; [NAS.GD174.][NAS.RD4.259.758][NAS.RS27.201.215]

SPENCE, DAVID, in Augusta, Georgia, 9 November 1827. [NAS.RD5.339.492/501]

SPENCE, JAMES, born on 30 October 1732 son of John Spence and Ann Petrie, a farmer in St Andrew's parish, Orkney, emigrated from Kirkwall with his wife Mary Gorne and children Barbara, James, and Helen, to Savannah, Georgia, on the Marlborough, Captain George Prissick, in September 1774, settled in Richmond County, Georgia, as an indentured servant of Thomas Brown. [PRO.T47.12][PRO.AO13.34.123-5]

SPENCE, JOHN, born 1705, servant to John Cuthbert of Drakies, emigrated from Inverness on the Prince of Wales, Captain George Dunbar, on 20 October 1735, arrived in Georgia on 10 January 1736. [ESG#97]

SPENCE, JOHN, born 29 December 1728 in Kirkwall, Orkney, son of
Gilbert and Elizabeth Spence, a sailor in Kirkwall, emigrated from
Kirkwall to Savannah, Georgia, on the <u>Marlborough</u> during
September 1774, settled in Richmond County, Georgia.
[PRO.T47.12]

SPENCE, JOHN, born in Scotland 1810, a slater, wife Mary born in
Scotland 1810, settled in Alabama. [C]

SPENCE, WILLIAM, born in Scotland 1806, a bricklayer, wife Jane born
in Scotland 1817, children Jane, Mary, and William, (all born in
Scotland), children Margaret, Matilda, Sarah and Frances, (all born
in Alabama), settled in Alabama around 1840. [C]

SPINK, JAMES, born in Arbroath, Angus, during 1800, settled in Darien,
Georgia, died in Savannah, Georgia, on 16 November 1822. [Daily
Georgia, 21.11.1822] [Darien Gazette: 21.11.1822]

STANLEY, WILLIAM, born in Scotland 1800, resident of a hotel in
Harrison County, Mississippi. [C]

STARK, JAMES, born 1763, a tailor, died in Georgia on 1 September
1806. [Savannah Death Register][Colonial Museum and Savannah
Advertiser: 3.9.1806]

STEDMAN, JAMES, emigrated to Savannah, Georgia, on the snow
<u>Kinnoull</u>, Captain Alexander Alexander, and was granted 100
acres between the Savannah and the Saludy Rivers on 30 May
1768.[Ga.Co.Journal#34.148/151]

STEDMAN, WILLIAM, land grant on Skidaway Island, Christ Church
parish, 7 February 1758, and on May Island and Gannet Island,
Christ Church parish, 2 May 1769, [Grant book A, #626; Grant
book G, #320]?

STEELE, GEORGE, born in Scotland 1810, a tin manufacturer, settled in
Alabama. [C]

STEEL, J.D., born in Scotland 1814, a merchant, wife Elizabeth born in South Carolina, settled in Alabama. [C]

STEELE, WILLIAM, born in Scotland 1826, a tin manufacturer, settled in Alabama. [C]

STEPHENS, DONALD, born 1688, a laborer from Lange, settled in Georgia around 1741. [ESG#97]

STEPHEN, WILLIAM, born 1751, a carpenter, emigrated via London to Pensacola, West Florida, on the Success's Increase on 14 August 1774. [PRO.T47.9/11]

STEVENSON, JOHN, a merchant in Glasgow, granted 500 acres in October 1751. [PRO.CO5/669]

STEVENSON, WILLIAM, formerly in Glasgow, died in Georgia 1811. [Edinburgh Advertiser #4971]

STEWART, ALEXANDER, Lieutenant of General James Oglethorpe's Regiment, died in Fredericia, Georgia. [Pro. April 1748 PCC]

STEWART, ANDREW, to leave Georgia in January 1764. [Ga.Gaz.#42]

STEWART, ANNE, in Darien on 6 May 1741. [ESG#97]

STEWART, ANN, land grant in Savannah on 1 May 1759, [Grant book B, #70]; daughter of Daniel Stewart shipmaster in Inverness, wife of Hugh Ross a shopkeeper in Savannah, mother of John, [Pro. 27 April 1775 Chatham County, Georgia.]

STEWART, CHARLES, servant to Andrew Grant, arrived in Georgia on 1 August 1734. [ESG#97]

STEWART, CHARLES, born in Perth, resident of New York, died in Georgia on 12 August 1800. [Georgia g/s][Colonial Museum and Savannah Advertiser, 15.8.1800]

STEWARD, CHARLES, born in Scotland 1815, a farmer, Margaret Steward, born 1815, Rebecca Steward, born 1842, John Steward, born 1844, Minerva Steward, born 1846, Elizabeth Steward, born 1848, and Daniel Steward, born 1849, all born in Telfair County, Georgia, with Margaret McLauchlin, born in Scotland 1790, settled in Telfair County, Georgia. [C]

STEWART, CHRISTOPHER, born 1780, emigrated to USA in 1804, a painter in New Orleans. [1812]

STEWART, DAVID, born 1718, a surgeon from Cromdale, Morayshire, emigrated from Inverness on the <u>Prince of Wales</u>, Captain George Dunbar, on 20 October 1735, arrived in Georgia on 10 January 1736. [ESG#97]

STEWART, DONALD, born 1693, a mariner from Inverness, emigrated from Inverness, with his wife Jeanne born 1706, on the <u>Prince of Wales</u>, Captain George Dunbar, on 20 October 1735, arrived in Georgia on 10 January 1736, granted a lot in Savannah, master of a sloop, drowned in Port Royal Sound during 1740. [ESG#97]

STEWART, DONALD, born 1718, servant to Donald Stewart of Inverness, in Georgia around 1740. [ESG#97]

STEWART, DONALD, a settler in Georgia, reference to on 9 December 1738, [AGA#59]

STEWART, DONALD, born 1713, an indentured servant, emigrated from Inverness on the <u>Two Brothers</u>, Captain William Thomson, to Georgia in July 1737, landed on 20 January 1737, drowned 1741. [ESG#50]

STEWART, DONALD, born 1707, a 4 year indentured servant, emigrated to Georgia 19 November 1737, landed 14 January 1738, died 6 August 1741. [ESG#50]

STEWART, DONALD, born in Scotland 1756, a husbandman and indentured servant, emigrated from London to Georgia on the <u>Mary</u> in February 1774. [PRO.T47.9/11]

STEWART, GEORGE, granted 10,000 acres of land in West Florida during 1767. [PC.Col.V.593]

STEWART, GILBERT, in Edinburgh, wrote of 4 young gentlemen, each with 10 servants, going from Edinburgh to Georgia, on 20 October 1733. [NAS.GD38.2.4.96]

STEWART, JAMES, born 1710, an indentured servant, emigrated from Inverness on the Two Brothers, Captain William Thomson, to Georgia in July 1737, landed on 20 January 1737, soldier of Oglethorpe's Independent Highland Company on 6 May 1741. [ESG#50]

STEWART, JAMES, born in Kilmarnock, Ayrshire, settled in Darien, Georgia, 1818, died at Lower Bluff, Georgia, on 20 August 1822. [Darien Gazette, 24.8.1822]

STEWART, JAMES, in Georgia during 1763. [Ga.Gaz.#34]

STEWART, JAMES, born during 1782, a silversmith in Savannah, died on 28 September 1811. [Colonial Museum and Savannah Advertiser: 30.9.1811]

STEWART, JOHN, born in Argyll during 1766, a merchant, died in Georgia on 24 April 1806. [Savannah Death Register]

STEWART, JOHN, sr., granted 500 acres in Newport, St John's parish, Georgia, on 7 February 1758; land grant in Savannah on 1 July 1760. [Grant Book A.637] [CRG#28/1.242, 322]

STEWART, JOHN, granted 300 acres 1 July 1760, 178 acres 7 September 1762, 142 acres 1 November 1768, and 400 acres 4 July 1769 all in St John's parish, Georgia. [Grant Books B.421, D.192, and G221/369] [CRG#28/1.325]

STEWART, JOHN, jr., granted 500 acres on the South Branch of the Newport River on 5 March 1756; land grants in Newport, Georgia, on 5 February 1757. [Grant Book A.77] [CRG#28/1.109]

STEWART, JOHN, a planter in St John's parish, Georgia, pro. 30 October 1765 Georgia.

STEWART, JOHN, Lieutenant in the Carolina Highlanders Regiment, died in Woodville, New Orleans, brother of Alexander Stewart, Admin. October 1827 PCC

STEWART, JOHN, born in Scotland during 1827, a laborer, wife Elizabeth born in Ireland during 1831, settled in Alabama. [C]

STEWART, JOHN, born in Scotland during 1824, settled in Adams County, Mississippi. [C]

STEWART, MATHEW W., born during 1791, emigrated to USA in 1801, a planter on Whitmarsh Island 1812. [1812]

STEWART, RANDALL, born in Callander, Perthshire, during 1756, married Margaret Smith, to America 1806, settled in Buncombe County, North Carolina, later in Bibb County, Georgia, died there in 1844. [NCSA.2.103]

STEWART, ROBERT, land grant in Darien, Georgia, on 6 December 1757, [CRG#28/1.118]

STEWART, ROBERT, in St Andrew's parish, Georgia, 1763. [Ga.Gaz.#34]

STEWART, ROBERT, co-owner of the brigantine Betsey which was registered in Savannah on 11 October 1762. [PRO.CO5.709]

STEWART, ROBERT, born in Scotland during 1807, a farmer, wife Elizabeth born 1807, daughters Adeline born 1834, L. born 1839, Elizabeth born 1842, and sons A.W. born 1836, James born 1843, Elam born 1845, and Robert born 1847, all born in Amite County, Mississippi, settled there. [C]

STEWART, ROGER, born in Scotland 1822, son of Roger Stewart {1744-1822} a merchant, and Jean .....{1758-1822}, a merchant, died in Springhill, Mobile, Alabama, on 25 May 1858, [Inverkip Street g/s, Greenock]; settled in Georgia by 1844 and in Alabama by 1847, wife Isabel born in Georgia 1825, children William and Andrew, (born in Georgia), Anne and Roger (born in Alabama). [C]

STEWART, THOMAS, born in Dumfries during 1777, an architect in Augusta, Georgia, died in Camp Hope, Milledgeville, Georgia, in September 1826. [Georgia Republican, 30.9.1826]

STEWART, Mrs SARAH, born in Scotland during 1785, husband James born in North Carolina during 1780, a teacher, settled in Coosa District, Coosa County, Alabama. [C]

STEWART, WILLIAM, born in 1751, a mason, emigrated via Newcastle to Georgia on the Georgia Packet in September 1775, settled in Friendsborough, Georgia. [PRO.T47.9/11]

STIRK, BENJAMIN, land grant in Christ Church parish on 13 April 1761, [Grant book C, #123]

STIRK, Mrs JOHN WILLIAMSON, born 1795, daughter of Captain John Baugh of the 58th Regiment of Foot, died in Savannah, Georgia, on 25 August 1819. [BM#6.359]

STIRLING, ALEXANDER, a planter near St Francisville, Louisiana. [1812]

STIRLING, GEORGE, from Edinburgh, son of John Stirling in Glasgow, a Lieutenant of General Oglethorpe's Regiment, died in Georgia, Admin. January 1749 PCC

STIRLING, HUGH, granted 500 acres in Georgia on 14 November 1733. [PRO.CO5.668; CO5.670.127]; merchant in Glasgow, emigrated to Georgia in March 1734, possibly on the snow Hope, master Greig, from Leith, arrived in Georgia on 1 August 1734, [ESG#97] [SCGaz.11.5.1734]; settled at Stirling's Bluff on the Ogychee, Georgia, died during 1740. [PRO.CO5.670.127][ESG#97]

STIRLING, Sir JAMES, land grant of 550 acres in St Philip parish, Georgia, on 23 April 1761.[PRO.CO.5.648.E46][CRG#28/1.361]

STIRLING, WILLIAM, granted 500 acres in Georgia on 14 November 1733. [PRO.CO.5.668; CO5.670.128]; merchant in Glasgow, emigrated to Georgia in 1734, {possibly on the snow Hope, Captain Greig, from Leith}, settled at Stirling's Bluff on the Ogychee, Georgia. [PRO.CO5.670.128]; reference to on 9 December 1738, [AGA#59]; petition re Wilmington Island, Georgia, on 5 May 1740. [PRO.CO.5.667.327]; moved to Carolina on 30 August 1743. [ESG#97]

STODART, A., born in Scotland 1808, a merchant, settled in Alabama. [C]

STODART, D., born in Scotland 1806, a merchant, settled in Alabama. [C]

STRACHAN, CHARLES, in Georgia during October 1763. [Ga.Gaz.#29]

STRACHAN, CHARLES, from Savannah via New Providence to Mobile on the sloop Adventurea, Captain Robert Stapleton, on 24 December 1763, an Indian trader in Mobile from 1763 to 1768, returned to Scotland in July 1768 on the death of his grandfather, settled in Kinnaber, Montrose. [NLS#MS119]

STRACHAN, JOHN, born in Scotland 1808, a farmer, settled in Dallas County, Alabama. [C]

STRACHAN, JOHN, born in Scotland 1817, a gardener, wife Martha born in England 1817, son George born in Louisiana 1837, children John, Joseph, Margaret, Cochran, and George (all born in Alabama), settled in Alabama by 1837. [C]

STRONACH, JOHN, born 1709, a 3 year indentured servant, emigrated to Georgia with wife Catherine born 1702, a 3 year indentured servant, {alive at Darien on 6 May 1741} under Captain Thomson 19 November 1737, landed 24 January 1738, an invalid at Darien on 6 May 1741, father of William born 1737, and Priscilla born 1741. [ESG#51]

STRONACH, MICHAEL, born 1721, an indentured servant, emigrated from Inverness on the Two Brothers, Captain William Thomson, to Georgia in July 1737, landed on 20 January 1738. [ESG#51]

STROTHERS, A., a merchant in Pensacola, 1781. [NAS.NRAS#0174]

STRUTHERS, JOHN, from Glasgow, died on the ship Planter in the Savannah River, Georgia, 3 March 1790. [SM#52.205][GaGaz: 4.3.1790]; born in Glasgow in January 1764, son of John Struthers, maltman burgess, and Hannah Stiven, a brewer, died in Savannah, Georgia, on 24 February 1790. [Colonial Cemetery g/s, Savannah]

STRUTHERS, WILLIAM, baptised on 27 May 1733 in Alva parish, Stirlingshire, son of John Struthers and Mary Harrower, [Alva OPR]; granted 500 acres in St Paul's parish, Georgia, on 7 December 1762, [PRO.CO.5.648.E68][CRG#28/1.441]; in Chatham County, Georgia, 1781.[NAS.RD2.239/2.129]; Indian trader in Augusta, Georgia, pro. 5 March 1761 Georgia. [power of attorney to brother John a schoolmaster in Alva, Scotland, 14 November 1760]

STUART, CHARLES, in Mobile, West Florida, 1767, [NLS#MS119]; pro. September 1781 PCC

STUART, CHARLES, died in Georgia on 12 August 1800. [Colonial Museum and Savannah Advertiser: 15.8.1800]

STUART, DAVID KNOX, a physician in New Orleans, son of John Stuart of East Kilbride, Lanarkshire, died in New Orleans on 10 April 1851, [W#1248]; cnf 1853. [NAS.SC70.1.81]

STUART, JAMES, granted 200 acres on 1 November 1774 and 300 acres on 7 February 1775 both in St John's parish, Georgia. [Grant Book M.730/1051]

STUART, JOHN, land grant in Savannah on 1 July 1760, [Grant book B, #395]; land grant in St John's parish, Georgia, on 7 September 1762, [CRG#28/1.436]

STUART, JOHN, born ca.1700, son of baillie John Stewart a merchant in Inverness, settled in Charleston, South Carolina, during 1748, Superintendent of Indian Affairs and Surveyor General of Customs in Florida, appointed as a member of the Council of East Florida on 7 June 1771, in Pensacola, West Florida, husband of Sarah Stuart, died there 1779, pro. July 1783. PCC, [SM#41.341][PC.Col.V.564][PC.Col.1766-1783#564]

STUART, PETER, born 1831, late printer in Peterhead, Aberdeenshire, died in Augusta, Georgia, on 16 June 1862. [AJ#5995]

STUART, SALLY, eldest daughter of John Stuart, Superintendent of Indian Affairs in the Southern Department, married James Graham, late of Savannah, Georgia, a merchant and Indian trader, in July 1767. [SM#29.557]

STUART, WILLIAM, born 1744, his wife born 1760, sons George born 1779, Michael born 1785, David born 1789, and daughters Sally born 1787, Rachel born 1791, and Mary born 1795, arrived in Louisiana 19 April 1797. [NWI.2.230]?

SUTHERLAND, ALEXANDER, born 1711, servant to Mackay of Scourie, emigrated from Inverness on the Prince of Wales, Captain George Dunbar, on 20 October 1735, arrived in Georgia on 10 January 1736. [ESG#98]

SUTHERLAND, ALEXANDER SMITH, formerly of New Orleans late in New York, Admin.October 1828 PCC

SUTHERLAND, ALEXANDER, born in Edinburgh, died in Mobile, Alabama, on 26 January 1857. [EEC#21055]

SUTHERLAND, FRANCIS, born 1756, a weaver in Wick, Caithness, emigrated from Caithness via Kirkwall, Orkney, to Savannah, Georgia, on the Marlborough, Captain Thomas Walker, in

September 1775, settled in Richmond County, Georgia, as an indentured servant of Thomas Brown. [PRO.T47.12][PRO.AO13.34.123-5]

SUTHERLAND, GEORGE G., born in Scotland 1809, a merchant, settled in Vermillion parish, Louisiana, by 1850. [C]

SUTHERLAND, HENRY, born in Scotland during 1830, a Ranger in Gonzales, Texas. [C]

SUTHERLAND, PATRICK, younger son of James Sutherland of Clyne and Jean Gordon, in Sutherland, an officer of Oglethorpe's Regiment in Georgia 1738 -1745, a Hanoverian officer in Scotland 1745-1746, received land grants in Georgia 1748, British army officer in Nova Scotia, died? there in 1766. [SGen.XLI.2][PRO.CO.5.668.130/1; 282/3]

SUTHERLAND, ROBERT, of Leath, Sutherland, born 1700, a laborer, emigrated to Georgia on 20 October 1735, landed on 10 January 1736. [ESG51]

SUTHERLAND, ROBERT, born 1720, a labourer, embarked on the Loyal Judith for Georgia on 21 September 1741, landed on 4 December 1741. [PRO.CO.5.668.45][ESG51] [CRG.30.197/199]

SUTHERLAND, WILLIAM, from Canisbay, Caithness, emigrated from Caithness via Kirkwall to Savannah, Georgia, on the Marlborough, Captain Thomas Walker, in September 1775, an indentured servant of Thomas Brown in Georgia. [PRO.AO13.34.123-5]

SUTHERLAND, WILLIAM, born in Greenock, Renfrewshire, during 1774, a distiller, died on 14 October 1806. [Savannah Death Register]

SWAN, JAMES, born in Dumfriesshire during 1786, [possibly the James Swan baptised on 26 October 1788 in the parish of Lochmaben, son of James Swan and Janet Walls, {Lochmaben OPR}]; died in Savannah, Georgia, on 26 August 1817. [Savannah Republican: 26.8.1817]

SWANN, THOMAS, born in Scotland 1832, settled in Cocke County, Tennessee. [C]

SWINNEY, JEREMY, born in 1819, a 4 year indentured servant, emigrated to Georgia with Captain Thompson 19 November 1737, arrived on 12 January 1738. [ESG51]

SWINTON, WILLIAM, granted 200 acres on 5 April 1763 and 800 acres on 31 October 1765 both in St John's parish, Georgia. [Grant Book D.297 and E.720]

SYME, ANDREW, in New Orleans, brother of Hugh Syme, Admin.January 1821 PCC

SYM, HUGH, land grant in Christ Church parish, Georgia, on 4 December 1770, [Grant book I, #230]?

SYMINGTON, JAMES, born in 1774, a millwright, died on 29 October 1807. [Savannah Death Register]

TAILFER, PATRICK, granted 500 acres in Georgia on 18 October 1733. [PRO.CO.5.668]; a surgeon-physician in Edinburgh, emigrated to Georgia in March 1734, possibly on the snow Hope, Captain Greig, from Leith, arrived on 1 August 1734, [ESG#98][SCGaz,11.5.1734]; settled near River Neuse, Georgia. [PRO.CO5.670.106]; settler in Georgia on 9 December 1738, [AGA#59]; moved to Charleston, South Carolina, in September 1740; Head of the St Andrew's Society of Savannah 1734-1740, [SSS#88]; husband of Mary ....[ESG#98]

TAIS, CHARLES, emigrated to Savannah, Georgia, on the snow Kinnoull, Captain Alexander Alexander, and was granted 100 acres between the Savannah and the Saludy Rivers on 30 May 1768. [Ga.Co.Journal#34.148/151]

TAIT, DAVID, granted 5,000 acres of land in West Florida in 1769. [PC.Col.V.594]

TAIT, ELIZABETH, born 1747, a servant in Bower, Caithness, emigrated from Kirkwall, Orkney, to Savannah, Georgia, on the Marlborough in September 1775. [PRO.T47.12]

TAIT, JAMES, born in Scotland in 1814, a merchant, wife Mary born in New York in 1825, settled in Alabama before 1847, sons James and William H. (both born in Alabama). [C]

TAIT, ROBERT, arrived in West Florida via Grenada, settled on the Escambia River, West Florida, 17... [PRO.CO5.631]

TATE, JOHN, born in Scotland 1749, a carpenter and indentured servant, with his wife and 4 children, emigrated via Whitby, Yorkshire, to Savannah, Georgia, on the Marlborough in August 1774. [PRO.T47.9/11]

TAWSE, THOMAS, Lieutenant of the 71st Regiment of Foot, died in Savannah, Georgia, pro. July 1781 PCC

TAYLOR, ABRAHAM, servant to William Bradley, in Georgia around 1740. [ESG#98]

TAYLOR, ALEXANDER, servant to William and Hugh Stirling, arrived in Georgia on 1 August 1734. [ESG#98]

TAYLOR, ALEXANDER, arrived in Georgia on 31 October 1765. [Ga.Gaz.#130]

TAYLOR, ALEXANDER, born 1804, commander of the ship Magistrate, drowned off Savanna on 15 September 1837. [DPCA#1839]

TAYLOR, Mrs CATHERINE, born 1714, 4 year indentured servant, emigrated from Inverness on the Two Brothers, Captain William Thomson, to Georgia 19 November 1737, wife of Joseph Taylor. [ESG52]

TAYLOR, JAMES, son of William Taylor {1745-1812}, a farmer, and Helen Walker {1759-1847}, merchant in Savannah. [Fordoun g/s]

TAYLOR, JOHN, in Savannah, pro. October 1772 PCC

TAYLOR, JOSEPH, born in 1712, emigrated to Georgia on 19 November 1737 with Captain Thomson, indentured for 4 years, landed on 14 January 1738. [ESG#52]

TAYLOR, WILLIAM, born 1720, a 4 years indentured servant, emigrated from Inverness with Captain Thompson on 19 November 1737, landed in Georgia on 14 January 1738. [ESG52]

TAYLOR, WILLIAM, late a farmer at Thomastown, Drumblade, Aberdeenshire, died on passage from New Orleans to St Louis on 30 March 1842. [AJ#4926]

TELFAIR, EDWARD and WILLIAM, granted 1000 acres in St John's parish, Georgia, on 5 June 1770. [Grant Book I.42]

TELFAIR, EDWARD, born during 1735 in the Stewartry of Kirkcudbright, educated at Kirkcudbright Grammar School, during 1737, emigrated in 1758, arrived in America via Antigua during 1766, settled in Virginia, North Carolina and Georgia, a merchant and politician, father of Thomas, former Governor of Georgia, died on 19 September 1807. [TSA] [Savannah Death Register]; land grants in Christ Church parish, Georgia, on 2 April 1771, and 7 July 1772, [Plat book C, #374; Grant book I, #665]; buried in Bonadventure Cemetery, Savannah.

TELFAIR, W., a settler in Louisiana on 23 February 1764. [GaGaz#47]

THOMSON, ALEXANDER, born 1734, son of James Thomson, Excise accountant, {1714-1770}, and Agnes Smith, {1717-1745}, settled in Savannah, Georgia, married Elisabeth, daughter of William Spencer the Customs Collector of Savannah, in Christ Church, Savannah, on 24 November 1770, HM Customs Collector in Savannah, Georgia, Loyalist, died in Drummond Street, Edinburgh, on 25 September 1798. [EA#3627.315][AJ#2648][Edinburgh Marriage Register][Canongate, Edinburgh, g/s]

THOMSON, ANDREW, baptised on 21 June 1789 in Dunfermline, son of John Thomson of Prior Letham, Fife, and Janet Mercer, apprenticed to John Russell, admitted to the Society of Writers to the Signet in Edinburgh on 23 June 1820, died in Florida on 14 July 1841. [Dunfermline OPR] [WS]

THOMPSON, ARCHIBALD, born in Scotland 1805, a carpenter, settled in Alabama. [C]

THOMSON, DANIEL, servant to Hugh Anderson in Georgia around 1740. [ESG#98]

THOMSON, GEORGE, servant to Thomas Christie, arrived in Georgia on 10 January 1734, settled in Abercorn. [ESG#98]

THOMSON, GEORGE, emigrated to Savannah, Georgia, on the snow Kinnoull, Captain Alexander Alexander, and was granted 100 acres between the Savannah and the Saludy Rivers on 30 May 1768.[Ga.Co.Journal#34.148/151]

THOMSON, JAMES, from Leith, a merchant, died in Washington County, Georgia, in February 1807. [SM.69.798][AJ#3114]

THOMPSON, JOHN, servant to John Baillie, arrived in Georgia on 1 August 1734. [ESG#98]

THOMSON, JOHN, born in Scotland 1811, settled in Alabama. [C]

THOMPSON, PETER, born in Scotland 1808, a engineer, wife Mary born in Scotland 1808, daughter Mary born in England 1838, settled in Coosa District, Coosa County, Alabama. [C]

THOMPSON, THOMAS, born 1746, a laborer, emigrated from Newcastle to Georgia on the Georgia Packet in September 1775. [PRO.T47.9/11]

THOMSON, THOMAS, a merchant in Louisiana, married Isabella, third daughter of Alexander Tweedie a merchant in Edinburgh, in Gayfield Square, Edinburgh, on 20 October 1824. [BM#16.614]

THOMPSON, WALTER, born in Scotland 1821, a tailor, wife Mary born in Ireland, settled in Alabama, father of Jane born in Alabama 1845. [C]

TIMINS, Mrs ELIZABETH, born in Scotland 1825, husband P.H.Timins a bootmaker born in Germany 1810, settled in Alabama before 1843, mother of John, Margaret and Louisa (all born in Alabama). [C]

TINGMAN(?) JOHN, born in Scotland 1811, a merchant, settled in Mobile, Alabama. [C]

TINLEY, JOHN, servant to Patrick Graham and later to William Bradley, before 1746. [ESG#99]

TOD, ALEXANDER, a mariner, born in Scotland 1813, wife Johanna born in Kentucky 1832, son Alexander born in Mississippi 1849, settled in Harrison County, Mississippi. [C]

TODD, ALEXANDER, baptised on 22 October 1819 in Houstoun, Renfrewshire, son of Alexander Todd {1774-1851} and Martha Spiers {1776-1846], settled in New Orleans, Louisiana. [Houstoun OPR] [Houston, Renfrewshire, g/s]

TODD, ANDREW, servant to William and Hugh Stirling, arrived in Georgia on 1 August 1734. [ESG#99]

TOD, LINDSAY, baptised in the parish of Cameron, Fife, on 6 May 1774, son of Andrew Tod and Catherine Adamson in St Andrews, Fife, a cotton planter in Florida, died on 24 February 1820. [Cameron OPR] [BM#7.705] [NAS.SH][S.4.188]

TOLMIE, ALEXANDER, born 1705, a farmer, emigrated from Inverness on the Prince of Wales, Captain George Dunbar, on 20 October 1735, arrived in Georgia on 10 January 1736, died on 16 November 1736. [ESG#99]

TORRY, GEORGE, born in Scotland 1789, a planter, with John L. Torry, born in North Carolina 1814, a planter, and James A. Torry, born in Mississippi in 1827, a planter, settled in Jefferson County, Mississippi. [C]

TRAIL, JANET, from Kirkwall, Orkney, emigrated from Kirkwall to Savannah, Georgia, on the Marlborough, Captain Thomas Walker, in September 1775, an indentured servant of Thomas Brown in Georgia. [PRO.AO13.34.123-5]

TRAIL, Dr ROBERT, died in Augusta, Georgia, on 5 February 1779. [SM.41.286][GaGaz#4/2]

TROUP, GEORGE, a merchant in Savannah, died in Liberty County, Georgia, in March 1789. [GaGaz#3/1]

TULLOCH, JOHN, from Kirkwall, Orkney, his wife Janet Seatter, and children Janet, Samuel, Magnus, Mary and Elizabeth, emigrated from Kirkwall to Savannah, Georgia, on the Marlborough, Captain Thomas Walker, in September 1775, indentured servants to Thomas Brown in Richmond County, Georgia, 1783. [PRO.AO13.34.123-5]

TULLY, JOHN, born in 1791, emigrated to USA in 1807, a merchant's clerk in Augusta 1812. [1812]

TUNNO, THOMAS, a tailor in St Augustine, East Florida, during 1786. [FHR#18]

TURNBULL, ANN, born 1751, a farm servant in Evie, Orkney, emigrated from Kirkwall, Orkney, to Savannah, Georgia, on the Marlborough,Captain George Prissick, in September 1774, settled in Richmond County, Georgia, as an indentured servant of Thomas Brown. [PRO.T47.12][PRO.AO13.34.123-5]

TURNBULL, Dr ANDREW, born in Annan, Dumfries-shire, 1719, a physician educated at Edinburgh University, settled at New Smyrna, East Florida, Secretary and Clerk of the Council of East Florida 1767-; appointed member of the Council of East Florida on

13 May 1767, died in Charleston, South Carolina, on 13 March 1792. [GM#62.673] [PC.Col.V.564][PC.Col.1766-1783#564] [NAS.NRAS#0771

TURNBULL, JAMES, servant to William and Hugh Stirling, arrived in Georgia on 1 August 1734. [ESG#99]; absconded in June 1734. [SCGaz#22]

TURNBULL, JANE, daughter of Dr Andrew Turnbull, granted 5,000 acres in East Florida in 1767. [PC.Col.V.591]

TURNBULL, MARGARET, daughter of Dr Andrew Turnbull, granted 5,000 acres of land in East Florida in 1767. [PC.Col.V.591]

TURNBULL, MARY, daughter of Dr Andrew Turnbull, granted 5,000 acres of land in East Florida in 1767. [PC.Col.V.591]

TURNBULL, NICHOLAS, son of Dr Andrew Turnbull, granted 5,000 acres of land in East Florida in 1767. [PC.Col.V.591]

TURNER, DAVID, born 1780, a cotton machine maker, died on 21 September 1807. [Savannah Death Register]

TURNER, DAVID, a blacksmith, born in Scotland 1814, wife Margaret born in Scotland 1818, son William born in Scotland 1844, son David born in Scotland 1849, settled in Adams County, Mississippi. [C]

TURNER, JOHN, Savannah, Georgia, married Elizabeth Galbraith in Luss, Dunbartonshire, on 17 August 1821. [EA.6025.127]

TURNER, ROBERT, born in Scotland 1815, a laborer, settled in Alabama. [C]

TWEEDIE, ISABELLA, baptised on 14 November 1797 in Edinburgh, third daughter of Alexander Tweedie, a merchant in Edinburgh, and Christian Denhame, married Thomas Thomson, a merchant in Louisiana, at Gayfield Square, Edinburgh, on 20 October 1824. [Edinburgh OPR][BM#16.615]

TWEEDIE, JANET, baptised on 29 August 1794 in Edinburgh, second
daughter of Alexander Tweedie, a merchant in Edinburgh, and
Christian Denhame, married William Finch, a merchant in
Louisiana, at Gayfield Square, Edinburgh, on 20 October 1824.
[Edinburgh OPR] [BM#16.615]

URIE, RACHEL, servant to Patrick Tailfer, arrived in Georgia on 1
August 1734, died 1741. [ESG#100]

URQUHART, GEORGE, Deputy Collector of Customs in Pensacola,
West Florida, 1777. [PRO.CO5.612.70]

URQUHART, THOMAS, born 1773, a merchant, 'one of the first
Scottish settlers on the banks of the Mississippi', died in New
Orleans on 6 April 1841. [GSP#666]

WADE, JOHN, servant to Hugh Fraser, arrived in Georgia on 10 January
1734. [ESG#100]

WALKER, ALEXANDER, a merchant in Glasgow, granted 500 acres in
October 1751. [PRO.CO5/669]

WALKER, ANDREW, a settler in Georgia, on 9 December 1738,
[AGA#59]; land grant in Savannah on 5 March 1756, [Grant book
A, #143]

WALKER, GEORGE C., son of Gabriel Walker, died in New Orleans on
18 August 1851, [W#11260]; cnf 1857. [NAS.SC70.1.95]

WALKER, JAMES, a merchant in Glasgow, granted 500 acres in
Georgia in October 1751. [PRO.CO5/669]

WALKER, ROBERT, in Georgia, on 21 November 1825.
[NAS.RD5.307.20]

WALKER, ROBERT, born in Scotland 1811, a carpenter, wife Ann born
in Scotland 1811, and son William born in Scotland 1832, settled
in Alabama. [C]

WALL, THOMAS, servant to Captain Scott, emigrated on 4 April 1733, arrived in Georgia on 21 July 1733, later servant to Captain MacPherson. [ESG#100]

WALLACE, JAMES, of Ponds, Georgia, pro. August 1798 PCC

WALLACE, JAMES, HM Consul in Savannah, brother of Michael Wallace in Halifax, Nova Scotia, Admin.November 1829 PCC

WALLACE, JOHN, born in 1751, a merchant and British Vice-Consul for Georgia, died in Savannah, Georgia, on 16 September 1804. [SM.67.74][GM.74.1174][AJ#2968][Savannah Death Register]

WALLACE, NORMAN, born in 1784, emigrated to US in 1803, a merchant in Savannah, Georgia, 1812. [1812]

WALLACE, ROBERT, baptised on 17 May 1822, son of Reverend Robert Wallace {1788-1864} and Elizabeth Smith {1796-1873}, died in Mobile, Alabama, on 14 August 1867. [F#2/267] [Dumfries g/s]

WALLACE, ("Wallis"), WILLIAM, servant to Samuel Mercer, arrived in Georgia on 10 January 1733. [ESG#100]

WALTERS, CATHERINE, born in Edinburgh 1764, died on 22 September 1808. [Savannah Death Register]

WALTERWORTH, CHARLES, born in Scotland 1827, an engineer, settled in Alabama. [C]

WARDLAW, Captain RALPH, in Pensacola, 1766. [NLS#MS119]

WARDROP, JOSEPH, born 1706, son of David Wardrope of Easter Quill, a house carpenter in Edinburgh, emigrated to Georgia, arrived on 1 August 1734, [PRO.CO5.670.128]; granted 150 acres in Georgia on 30 January 1734. [PRO.CO.5.668]; reference to on 9 December 1738, [AGA#59]; petitioned for land on Hutchison's Island 1742. [PRO.CO.5.668.107]; moved with his wife Jane and daughter Elinor to Carolina in May 1742. [ESG#100]

WARDROPE, Lieutenant Colonel WILLIAM, late of the 47th Regiment,
married Harriet, daughter of George Baillie, on St Simon's Island,
Georgia, on 8 March 1812. [SM.74.565]; died there in 1812.
[EA.5129.13]

WARE, JONATHAN, born 1775, a seaman, died on 30 August 1805.
[Savannah Death Register]

WARK, JOHN, born 1745, a millwright, emigrated via Newcastle to
Georgia on the Georgia Packet in September 1775, settled in
Friendsborough, Georgia. [PRO.T47.9/11]

WATSON, ANDREW, born 1754, a smith, emigrated from Newcastle to
Georgia on the Georgia Packet in September 1775.
[PRO.T47.9/11]

WATSON, CHARLES, to Georgia on the Success, Captain Thomson, in
September 1746. [PRO.CO.5.668.235]; land grants in Savannah,
on 5 March 1756, 28 March 1758, 7 August 1759, 3 November
1761, 3 August 1762, 7 September 1762, 21 September 1762, 5
December 1769, [Grant book B, #23/26; Grant book C, #258/260;
Grant book D, #175/176/210] Grant book H,
#35];[PRO.CO.5.648.E46] [CRG#28/1.367]

WATSON, HUGH, born 1723, servant to Thomas Baillie, emigrated from
Inverness on the Prince of Wales, Captain George Dunbar, on 20
October 1735, arrived in Georgia on 10 January 1736, murdered at
sea in June 1739. [ESG#101]

WATSON, JAMES, born 1800, son of James Watson {1778-1862} and
Elizabeth Mustard {1806-1870} in Broughty Ferry, Dundee, died
in New Orleans in 1839. [Broughty Ferry, St Aidan's, g/s]

WATSON, WILLIAM, son of James and Jane Watson in Duns,
Berwickshire, a planter in Baton Rouge, West Florida, pro. July
1782 PCC; pro.1781 South Carolina

WATSON, WILLIAM, son of Thomas Watson, a writer in Hawick, Roxburghshire, and Margaret Charteris, in St Augustine before 1818, later a merchant in Bristol. [NAS.SH]

WATT, ALEXANDER, a merchant in Kinross, now in West Florida, 1785. [NAS.CS17.1.4/49]

WATT, JAMES, born in Scotland 1805, a laborer, settled in Alabama. [C]

WATT, Mrs MARY, born 1771, wife of Alexander Watt, died on 7 December 1804. [Savannah Death Register]

WATT, WILLIAM, land grant in Christ Church parish, Georgia, on 3 October 1765, [Grant book G, #449]?

WAUGH, EDWARD, born in Scotland 1822, a laborer, settled in Alabama. [C]

WEATHERSPOON, DAVID, born 1752, a weaver, emigrated via Newcastle to Georgia on the Georgia Packet, Captain Thomas Walker, in September 1775, settled in Friendsborough; land grant in St Andrew's parish, Georgia, on 21 May 1762. [PRO.T47.9/11][CRG#28/1.424]

WEBSTER, Mrs AGNES, born in Scotland, settled in Mobile, Alabama. [C]

WEBSTER, WILLIAM, servant to Hugh Anderson in Georgia around 1740. [ESG#101]

WEDDERBURN, ALEXANDER, granted 20,000 acres of land in East Florida on 9 March 1774. [PC.Col.V.593]

WEDDERBURN, Lieutenant Colonel DAVID, granted 20,000 acres in East Florida 1767; regranted to his brother Alexander Wedderburn on 9 March 1774. [PC.Col.V.591/593]

WEID, CHARLES, born 1775 a mariner, died on 14 February 1808.
[Savannah Death Register]

WEIR, WILLIAM, emigrated to Savannah, Georgia, on the snow
Kinnoull, Captain Alexander Alexander, and was granted 100
acres between the Savannah and the Saludy Rivers on 30 May
1768.[Ga.Co.Journal#34.148/151]

WELCH, J., born in Scotland 1812, a gardener, settled in Autauga
County, Alabama. [C]

WELLS, JOHN, baptised on 30 April 1821 in the parish of Mousewald,
Dumfries-shire, son of John Wells, a merchant, and Janet Wilson,
in Collin, Dumfries-shire, settled in Nashville, Tennessee, died on
4 September 1845. [Mousewald OPR] [Torthorwald g/s]

WEMYSS, WALTER, born in 1764, an auctioneer and merchant in
Savannah, Pro.5 November 1804, Chatham County, Georgia. [Will
book D] (refers to wife Mary, executors George Buchanan and
Company, William and James Dixon, subscribed on 17 September
1804) [Savannah Death Register]

WHAIR, WILLIAM, born in 1755, a farm servant in Wick, Caithness,
emigrated from Caithness via Kirkwall, Orkney, to Savannah,
Georgia, on the Marlborough, Captain Thomas Walker, in
September 1775, settled in Richmond County, Georgia, as an
indentured servant to Thomas Brown.
[PRO.T47.12][PRO.AO13.34.123-5]

WHEY, HENRY, (?), servant to Donald Stewart in Georgia around 1740.
[ESG#101]

WHITAKER, Mrs FRANCES, born 1782, wife of Richard Whitaker,
died on 28 September 1812. [SR: 6.10.1812]

WHITE, Mrs A., born in Scotland 1805, settled in Alabama. [C]

WHITE, WILLIAM R., born in Scotland 1806, a farmer in Autaugo
County, Alabama. [C]

WHYTE, AGNES BRYSON, baptised on 6 May 1822 in Edinburgh, third daughter of Robert Whyte, merchant in Edinburgh, {1778-1851}, and Agnes Bryson, {1787-1847}, married James Sneddon, a civil engineer in Savannah, Georgia, in New York on 14 December 1851, died on 2 December 1854. [Edinburgh OPR][W#1279][Greyfriars, Edinburgh, g/s]

WICKS, Mrs MARGARET, born in Scotland 1825, emigrated to America, husband Charles Wicks a clerk born in Maryland 1815, daughter Emma born in Alabama 1847. [C]

WIGHTON, GEORGE, son of James Wighton {1767-1843} and Jean Watson {1768-1815}, an engineer in New Orleans, [Dundee, Old Mains, g/s]

WILDRIGE, JAMES, born 1757, a farm servant in Holm, Orkney, emigrated from Kirkwall, Orkney, to Savannah, Georgia, on the Marlborough, Captain George Prissick, in September 1774, settled in Richmond County, Georgia. [PRO.T47.12]

WILKIE, JAMES, born 1799, third son of George Wilkie of Auchlishie, a merchant in New Orleans, died on 18 August 1834. [Dundee g/s]

WILKIE, THOMAS, servant to Patrick Tailfer, arrived in Georgia on 1 August 1734. [ESG#103]

WILKINS, W., in Fredericia, Georgia, 1756. [NAS.NRAS#0631/39]

WILLIAMS, Mrs BARBARA, born in Scotland 1814, husband Charles a merchant born in Wales 1812, children George (born in England), Ellen, John, Charles, Barbara, and William (all born in Alabama), settled in Alabama. [C]

WILLIAMSON, ALEXANDER, from Northfield, Edinburgh, died in New Orleans on 3 October 1838, cnf 1852. [NAS.SC70.1.75]

WILLIAMSON, BENJAMIN, eldest son of Captain Williamson of 5 Raeburn Place, Edinburgh, died in New Orleans during April 1841. [EEC#20224]

WILLIAMSON, CHARLES, born in Edinburgh 1757, an army officer, settled in America 1790, estate agent for Pultenet, western New York State, 1790-1800, died in New Orleans during September 1808. [TSA]

WILSON, ALEXANDER, a carpenter, died on 2 October 1812. [Colonial Museum and Savannah Advertiser: 5.10.1812]

WILSON, ALLAN, a mason in Florida around 1820. [NAS.CS17.1.39/633]

WILSON, DAVID, born in Scotland 1800, a baker settled in Coosa District, Coosa County, Alabama. [C]

WILSON, DAVID L., born in Scotland during 1807, son of James and Susanna Wesley Wilson, settled in Nacogdoches, Texas, died at the Alamo 6 March 1836. [DRTL]

WILSON, J., born in Scotland 1804, a machinist, wife Ruth born in England 1804, settled in Mobile, Alabama. [C]

WILSON, JAMES F., born 1789, eldest son of Alexander Wilson a merchant in Inverness, settled in New Orleans, died in Virginia on 5 October 1821. [BM#40.263][DPCA][SM]

WILSON, JANE, born in Scotland 1752, a spinner and indentured servant, emigrated via Whitby to Savannah, Georgia, on the Marlborough, Captain George Prissick, in August 1774. [PRO.T47.9/11]

WILSON, PHILIP, born 1775, a merchant, died on 6 September 1804. [Savannah Death Register][CM: 12.9.1804]

WINTER, Mrs Elizabeth, born in Scotland 1820, husband F. Winter a cabinet maker born in Belgium 1821, settled in Alabama. [C]

WITHERSPOON, J., land grant in St Andrew's parish, Georgia, on 11 September 1764. [Ga.Gaz.#78]

WOOD, JAMES, born in Scotland 1776, a merchant, arrived in Savannah late 1821 on the ship Pallas, Captain Land. [USNA/par]

WOODHOUSE, ROBERT, merchant in Savannah, Georgia, pro. 10 July 1800, Chatham County, Georgia.[Will Book A] (refers to brothers William, Archibald and George; parents Thomas and Elizabeth Woodhouse; children of Agnes, wife of James Shaw, blacksmith in Dalbeath, Galloway; Mary, daughter of John Cusack tailor, executors Daniel Johnston, Daniel Johnston his nephew, Cunningham Newall a merchant, and Ulrick Tobler a merchant, subscribed 19 March 1800)

WRIGHT, LEVI, born 1782, a mariner, died on 11 September 1810. [Savannah Death Register]

WRIGHT, ..., an Indian trader in Mobile in 1764. [NLS#MS119]

WYLLY, ALEXANDER, land grants in Savannah on 16 December 1756, in Hardwick on 7 August 1759, land grant in Savannah on 1 July 1760, land grant in St Phillip's on 1 July 1760, land grant in Savannah 13 April 1761, land grants in Christ Church parish on 29 October 1765 [CRG#28/1.59, 365, 420] [PRO.CO5.648.E46] [Grant book A, #53/387; Grant book E, #290/291/292; Grant book F, #433]; co-owner of the brigantine Lileah and Susannah, built in New England during 1762, registered in Savannah on 12 April 1763, arrived in Savannah from St Kitts on 20 August 1763 with a cargo of 60 negroes. [PRO.CO5.709]; later settled in Antigua. [Caribbeana.4.31];1767, [NLS#MS119]

WYLLIE, ALEXANDER, baptised on 2 December 1824 in the parish of Borgue, Kirkcudbrightshire, son of John Wyllie and Margaret Conning, died in Savannah on 7 January 1852. [Borgue OPR] [Borgue g/s]

WYLIE, ANN, born in Scotland 1798, settled in Mobile, Alabama. [C]

WYLLY, ANTONY, an Indian trader, shot himself in 1742. [ESG#102]

WYLLY, CAMPBELL, land grant in Christ Church parish, Georgia, on 6 September 1774, [Grant book M, #387]

WYLLY, MARGARET, a widow in St Simon's Island, Georgia, mother of Alexander William Wylly, Admin. October 1852 PCC

WYLLY, RICHARD, land grant in Christ Church parish, Georgia, on 2 February 1768, and on 7 February 1775, [Grant book G, #30, Grant book M, #1057]

WYLLY, WILLIAM, co-owner of the sloop Charming Kitty, registered in Savannah on 19 June 1764, arrived in Savannah from Tortula on 19 September 1764 with a cargo of 29 negroes. [PRO.CO5.709]

WYLLY, WILLIAM, granted 800 acres in St John's parish, Georgia, on 5 September 1769. [Grant Book G.419] ? ; land grant in Christ Church parish on 6 September 1774, [Grant book M, #386]

WYLLY, ..., a Ranger captain, during 1738. [CRG, 10.5.1738]

WYLLIE, ..., a merchant in Mobile 1764. [NLS#MS119]

YOUNG, ANDREW, a raftman, born in Scotland 1818, settled in Warren County, Mississippi. [C]

YOUNG, DAVID, born 1800, died in Augusta on 21 January 1829. [Augusta Herald: 10.2.1829]

YOUNG ELIZABETH, land grant in Savannah on 2 October 1759, [CRG#28/1.328][Grant book B, #465]

YOUNG, GEORGE, born in Cortachy, Angus, 1789, a merchant, emigrated via London to America, settled in Alabama, naturalised in New York on 10 November 1817. [NYNats.][possibly baptised on 2 October 1789 in the parish of Kinnettles, Angus, son of George Young, {Kinnettles OPR}]

YOUNG, HUGH, a merchant, second son of James Young the sheriff substitute of Kincardineshire, died in New Orleans 5 February 1833. [AJ#4449]

YOUNG, JOHN, a settler in Georgia on 9 December 1738, [AGA#59]; land grant in Christ Church parish on 3 August 1762, [CRG#28/1.433][Grant book D, #162]

YOUNG, JOHN G., born 1787, emigrated to USA 1808, a housecarpenter in Savannah 1812. [1812]

YOUNG, Mrs MARGARET, wife of Thomas Young, land grant in Abercorn, St Matthew's parish, Georgia, on 3 August 1762, [CRG#28/1.433]

YOUNG, PETER, land grant in Vernonburgh, Georgia, on 4 December 1759, [CRG#28/1.420][Grant book D, #70]?

YOUNG, THOMAS, a settler in Georgia on 9 December 1738. [AGA#59]

YOUNG, THOMAS, granted 300 acres in Midway, Georgia, on 5 April 1757, 300 acres in St John's parish, Georgia, on 6 January 1767, 57 acres there on 5 July 1774, 90 acres there on 5 July 1774, 100 acres on Bermuda Island, St John's, on 1 November 1774, 141 acres in St John's on 1 November 1774 and 311 acres there on 6 December 1774. [Grant Books A.360; F.45; H.109/110; M.768/769/837]; land grants in Savannah and in Christ Church parish, Georgia, on 4 July 1758 and on 1 November 1774, [Grant book A, #669, Grant book M, #764]

YOUNG, THOMAS, President of the St Andrew's Society of Savannah 1797-1798. [SSS#88]

YOUNG, THOMAS, sr., born 1734 in Dalmany, Queensferry, West Lothian, a planter in Savannah, Georgia, died on 7 November 1808, pro. 14 November 1808, Chatham County, Georgia, [Will Book E]; land grant in Savannah on 4 July 1758, [CRG#28/1.245];

in Chatham, Georgia, on 2 April 1811, [deed refers to Alexander
Kettle WS; mother Mrs Sarah Young; Reverend Thomas Kettle]
[NAS.RD4.294.609]; there 1812.; deed for the sale of lands on St
Simon's Island, Glyn County, Georgia, on 6 June 1812 [refers to
Colonel William Wardrobe; John Graham; Charles Harris; Joseph
S. Pilot, NP] [NAS.RD5.87.15] [Savannah Death Register] [CM:
11.11.1808][Georgia g/s] [will refers to Ann Nasmith and Sarah
Patton daughters of his uncle Reverend James Nasmith dec., and
Margaret, daughter of Margaret Parlane, James Kettle writer in
Edinburgh, Helen Fleming in Savannah, nephew Thomas Young
Kettle, eldest son of Thomas Kettle and wife Sarah, subscribed 3
September 1804]

YOUNG, THOMAS, a brickmaker, born in Scotland 1826, settled in
Harrison County, Mississippi. [C]

YOUNGHUSBAND, JOHN, emigrated from Inverness to Georgia on the
Two Brothers in 1737. [SPC.3.161]

YUILLE, ANN, born in Scotland 1790, settled in Alabama. [C]

YUILLE, CATHERINE, born in Scotland 1819, settled in Alabama. [C]

YUILLE, GAVIN B., born in Scotland 1825, an engineer, settled in
Alabama. [C]; an Alderman of Mobile, died there 17 September
1849. [SG#1867]

YUILLE, JOHN, born in Scotland 1821, a baker, settled in Alabama. [C]

YUILLE, Mr R.L., born in Scotland 1823, a baker, settled in Alabama.
[C]

YUILLE, WILLIAM S., born in Scotland 1826, a physician, settled in
Alabama. [C]